Origins of the
Chinese Revolution
1915–1949

Origins of the
Chinese Revolution
1915-1949

Lucien Bianco

Translated from the French by Muriel Bell

Stanford University Press, Stanford, California

To the memory of Graham Peck

Origins of the Chinese Revolution, 1915–1949 was originally published in French in 1967 under the title *Les Origines de la révolution chinoise, 1915–1949*, © 1967 by Editions Gallimard. The present edition has been revised by the author in a number of matters of detail and presentation.

Stanford University Press, Stanford, California
London: Oxford University Press
© 1971 by the Board of Trustees of the Leland Stanford Junior University
Printed in the United States of America
Cloth ISBN 0-8047-0746-4
Paper ISBN 0-8047-0827-4
This translation first published in 1971
Last figure below indicates year of this printing:
93   92   91   90   89

Contents

Foreword

Lucien Bianco's *Origins of the Chinese Revolution* is a tour de force, at once a seminal interpretation and a lucid introduction to China's passage to revolution. Its central theme is the relationship between China's social crisis and the revolutionary movement that it bred. In tracing the revolution to its rural roots and analyzing the response of Chinese political forces to the growing rural crisis, this work clearly relates China's twentieth-century history to the tide of revolution that began in France in 1789 and has swept the Third World in our time.

Though the author's most original contributions come from his research on Chinese rural society, he generously acknowledges a heavy debt to the work of a generation of Asian scholars in the United States. Like American scholars before him, for example, he analyzes the Chinese Communists' early years in terms of their fidelity to Marxism-Leninism, and their rise to power after 1937 in terms of Chalmers Johnson's thesis of peasant nationalism. Yet when all is said and done, Bianco's emphasis on social crisis presents not only a bold new interpretation but a powerful critique of the major approaches and assumptions of American scholarship, a critique all the more powerful because it is for the most part implicit.

Clear though it is to all that the roots of China's revolution lay in the countryside, American scholarship has virtually ignored the relationship between rural discontent and the rise of the Communist movement. Among American China specialists, only Franz Schurmann has joined with such students of global revolution as Barrington Moore and Eric Wolf in insisting that the seminal issues of social revolution are all-important in understanding what happened in China. Bianco agrees. If I read him correctly, he is saying that whatever the inherent fascination of theoretical problems of Marxism and nationalism, without a firm grasp of the contemporary social crisis we cannot begin to make sense of twentieth-century Chinese history.

With a sure hand Bianco sketches the dimensions of a crisis compounded of dynastic collapse, imperialist incursions, the natural and man-made ravages of the warlord era, the oppression of the landlord class, and a dramatic increase in population. Drawing on contemporary descriptions of peasant life, he shows us a society in which people were forced to sell their children, to eat grass and bark in bad times, to pay rent and taxes beyond all reason—a society in which tens of millions literally starved to death while a tiny elite looked on indifferently. To the empathy and perception of such extraordinary American observers as Edgar Snow, Graham Peck, William Hinton, and Jack Belden, whose works a generation of China specialists have praised as classics while ignoring their fundamental insights into the revolutionary process, Bianco adds telling details from Chinese writers like Lu Hsün and Han Suyin. The combination of this rich descriptive material with a broad analytical grasp of the socioeconomic roots of revolution produces a humanist scholarship that is all too rare among China specialists, an approach at once sensitive to the plight of human beings ravaged by poverty, oppression, and war, and committed to a search for truth that transcends the limitations of prevailing orthodoxy.

The conclusion of this search is inescapable: revolution, however painful and fraught with individual tragedy, was the natural way—indeed the only way—of resolving China's rural crisis. In this book revolution is seen neither as an alien imposition, nor as a threat, nor as irrelevant to the "modernization" process —the chief alternatives perceived by a generation of American scholars wedded to a Cold War vision of revolutionary China and to an elite-reformist view of modernization. Rather, Bianco finds with Graham Peck that "in a society like China's, revolution can be a fundamental and entirely natural fact of life." Alone among the political forces of twentieth-century China to grapple seriously with the problems of a disaffected peasantry, the Communist Party was propelled to power by that peasantry's fundamental and entirely natural desire for radical change. For Bianco, revolution in China was necessary, perhaps inevitable. Yet ultimately he remains almost as pessimistic about the revolutionary process as he is critical of the appalling human costs of the Kuomintang era.

If Bianco takes us far down the path toward an understanding of China's revolutionary origins, his study also poses a number of basic problems that will long preoccupy historians of the Chinese Revolution. One such problem is to refine his analysis in such a way as to distinguish the contributions to the revolution of the peasantry's many components: poor and middle peasants, the rural proletariat, the totally disenfranchised (*éléments déclassés*), and others. Another is to assess the revolutionary impact of several trends barely touched on here, notably the rapid commercialization of parts of rural China and the inexorable monetization of a rural economy increasingly integrated in a world capitalist market system. A third, and perhaps the ultimate problem for historians of revolutionary China, is to assign convincing relative weights to domestic and foreign pressures—to internal conflict and imperialist exploitation—in precipitating the rural crisis and shaping the course of the Chinese Revolution. That these questions remain open is a measure of how far we have to go. Bianco's analysis of internal events advances us toward a final synthesis and challenges us anew to focus on the profound consequences of imperialism in China. In the tradition of the great French social historians Marc Bloch and Georges Lefebvre, it is an important contribution to our understanding of social revolution.

MARK SELDEN

Author's Preface

Any book that aims to offer a preliminary synthesis of our knowledge is inevitably much indebted to its predecessors. Indeed, the present undertaking would have been altogether out of the question had I not been able to draw on the work of American China specialists, work with which the European student may not always entirely agree but on which he must rely. The books of such men as John King Fairbank, Benjamin I. Schwartz, Chalmers Johnson, Chow Tse-tsung, and the late Joseph R. Levenson represent the necessary points of departure in their respective fields. Even outside the realm of strictly "scholarly" literature, the first-rate works of such journalists as Jack Belden, Theodore H. White and Annalee Jacoby, and above all Graham Peck are indispensable sources—not always objective, but always to the point.

In addition to these writers and the others cited in the text and the Suggested Readings, a great many scholars have written articles or studies too specialized for inclusion in a brief bibliography meant to guide the reader, not frighten him away. Two American colleagues, James C. Thomson, Jr., of Harvard and James P. Harrison of Columbia, kindly allowed me to read their then unpublished dissertations while I was writing the French edition of this work. I have also drawn on archives and source materials both in Europe and in the United States. Except in special cases, however (e.g., of specific facts whose source the specialist would want to know), I have omitted references to such sources, so as not to burden with critical apparatus a book whose primary aim is not original scholarship.

Finally, I am greatly indebted to Mme. Marie-Claire Bergère of the Centre National de la Recherche Scientifique, Paris, to John Schrecker of Princeton University, and to Mark Selden of Washington University, St. Louis, who has written the Foreword. The present work owes much to the many comments, suggestions, and criticisms that emerged from their attentive reading of earlier versions. The book has also profited from the sympathetic attentions of Muriel Bell, whose competence goes well beyond the mastery of a foreign language.

The French edition of this work was written in 1966. As a result of subsequent studies by other scholars and further reading of my own, I have corrected a number of factual errors for the present edition; I have also made changes in various matters of detail and presentation. In general, however, though there are things I would treat differently if I were writing the book today (notably in my introductory account of the late Ch'ing and the first years of the Republic, a period about which our knowledge and understanding have grown tremendously in the last few years), I have made no major changes in interpretation. Rightly or wrongly, I have thought it best to allow American and English readers to read the book, the product of a different historical tradition, substantially as it first appeared. One fairly substantial change must be mentioned here, however: I have eliminated a sizable section of the original Conclusion, whose main thrust was to refute or qualify certain ideas then current in France. In particular I stressed certain fundamental differences between the Russian and Chinese Revolutions, and warned on the one hand against what seemed to me an exaggerated emphasis on the Chineseness of the Chinese Revolution, and on the other a tendency to confer universal status on the "Chinese model" for revolution.

L.B.

Origins of the
Chinese Revolution
1915–1949

1. The End of a World

1789, 1917, 1949: of these three dates, the last is by no means the least important. Since the Chinese Revolution is also the one most directly relevant to human concerns in the second half of the twentieth century, we cannot avoid coming to grips in some sense with both its wider meaning and its practical bearing on today's problems. Yet at the same time the Chinese Revolution represents the culmination of a history unique to China. To study it directly as the prototype of contemporary revolution— i.e., revolution in an underdeveloped or semicolonial country —is to risk serious misunderstandings.

To assess the significance of the Chinese Revolution we need the historical background, but if we are to stick to essentials, the background must be kept simple. That is the compromise adopted here. Only the first chapter is pure narrative; it concerns the China of yesteryear (1839–1916). In this three-quarters of a century between traditional and contemporary China is compressed all of China's modern history. The men who lived through this period witnessed something like the crumbling of a world, a civilization, a *Weltanschauung*; the death of the Confucian world view, which had been accepted by virtually every Chinese whose income, upbringing, and leisure allowed him to look beyond the narrow confines of his village.[1]

[1] To begin this brief historical survey in 1839 (and not, for example, at the end of the eighteenth century) is inevitably to emphasize the role of imperialism. But the forcible opening of China to the West was not the sole cause, or even the starting point, of the disintegration of an Empire that, from afar, appeared immutable. On this point see Ho Ping-ti's classic work, *Studies on the Population of China, 1368–1953*

By 1916 the revolution was under way, but it would take another third of a century to finish off the old China. This period, from 1916 to 1949, is the real subject of the present work, and of every chapter except the first.[2] In each of the subsequent chapters an effort is made to apply a general theme to a different historical topic—e.g., a particular series of events or a socioeconomic analysis. The present chapter closes with a brief summary of the events of 1916–49. Designed to facilitate the reading of later chapters, it necessarily includes only the bare essentials needed for an understanding of the general analysis.

The Crumbling Empire

Before recent changes in the school curriculum, the Opium Wars were the gong that announced China's entrance on the stage of world history, i.e., the first mention of China in the pages of high school textbooks. In 1842, after three years of unequal combat, the Treaty of Nanking opened five Chinese ports to British trading vessels and gave Great Britain possession of Hong Kong. Eighteen years later, another war—actually a series of Anglo-French expeditions—completed the "opening of China." The Treaty of Peking of 1860 provided, among other things, for representation of the Powers at Peking.

For the rulers of the Empire and the Chinese literati, these events were tragic beyond measure. For these men China's geographical centrality and its corollary, China's moral and cultural superiority over the rest of the world, were self-evident. In Chinese the word for China is *Chung-kuo*, the Middle Kingdom, the realm closest to the beneficent influence radiating from Heaven. Since Heaven was round and the earth was square, obviously the peoples consigned to the corners could not be as civilized and well governed as the inhabitants of the Celestial

(Cambridge, Mass.: Harvard University Press, 1959), and Philip A. Kuhn's recent study, *Rebellion and Its Enemies in Late Imperial China: Militarization and Social Structure, 1796–1864* (Cambridge, Mass.: Harvard University Press, 1970), pp. 1–10.

[2] Or more precisely, as the title of this book indicates, the period *1915* to 1949, for my real point of departure is not the political developments of 1916, but the appearance in September 1915 of the journal later known as *Hsin ch'ing-nien*, which played an important role in the intellectual history of the revolution.

Empire. (In the corners also were the four seas, which carried Western sailors to China in the nineteenth century.) A unique system governed the relations between China and the rest of the world—the tributary system. Since the radiance of China's civilization, the merit and prestige of her sovereign, were irresistibly attractive to uncivilized peoples, delegates from these peoples had to be received in Peking. These delegates respectfully presented a tribute to the Son of Heaven, who had no need whatever for it, as a sign of submission. To these subservient envoys of tributary peoples, the Emperor in return gave gifts that reflected China's greatness and wealth. This was the established mode of international trade.

No irony is intended in this description. It is no more outrageous to regard as uncivilized all those who do not live under a Confucian monarchy than it is to regard as barbarians all those who do not speak Greek. In the course of China's long history, nearly all her sustained contacts had been with less important peoples, of whom a fair number had been strongly influenced by Chinese civilization, some even to the point of adopting Chinese writing. The Empire was bounded largely by almost impassable mountains and by deserts inhabited only by nomadic tribesmen. Sinocentrism was deeply rooted in geography as well as culture.

Still reeling from the Western barbarian invasion, the Empire was almost brought down by revolutionary disturbances in the third quarter of the nineteenth century, which spread throughout the country. In 1854–55 at least sixteen of the eighteen provinces (there is some question about two provinces in the extreme Northwest) threw off Imperial rule.[3] Rebellion and suppression resulted in tens of millions of deaths and left a number of provinces in ruins.[4] Of all the insurrectionary movements,

[3] That is, the provinces comprising China proper, excluding the peripheral regions of Tibet, Mongolia, and Manchuria.

[4] There are few more striking illustrations of how narrowly focused on Europe our study and teaching of history is: most French textbooks on this period devote several chapters to the European revolutions of 1848, but only a few lines to these twenty-five years of revolution in China.

the most important was unquestionably the Taiping Rebellion (1851–64), which set up a rival dynasty with a capital at Nanking. The "Heavenly Kingdom of Great Peace" (T'ai-p'ing T'ien-kuo) controlled much of South and Central China, and for a time threatened Peking and Tientsin. The extraordinary importance of the Taiping Rebellion, however, lies not only in the amount of territory it controlled and in the seriousness of its challenge to the Manchu dynasty, but also in two features that were later echoed, at least in part, by the Communist Revolution. They were the rejection of Confucianism in favor of an eclectic religion that included poorly assimilated or deliberately distorted Christian influences; and a program of agrarian communism (notably collective cultivation of the land), together with such resolutely modern social doctrines as equality of the sexes and the prohibition of concubinage, arranged marriages, foot-binding, opium-smoking, and gambling.

But apart from the fact that most of these reforms never got past the planning stage, they did not keep the Taipings from preserving and even perfecting certain features of the order they claimed to have destroyed: corruption, nepotism, faction-ridden and indecisive leadership. These characteristics both explain the ultimate failure of the rebellion and deprive it of any claim to being a modern revolution, for all that it was more than a simple jacquerie. To use a definition proposed elsewhere, let us call the rebellion a millenarian movement; in the modern era, such movements are fairly common in traditional societies that are beginning to change under the impact of such external forces as imperialism.[5] The Taiping Rebellion had several characteristics typical of millenarian movements: a heightened consciousness of genuine ills, but only a confused notion of how to remedy them; eschatological expectations that encouraged heroism

[5] Although it was far from the most important cause of the rebellion, the intrusion of Westerners contributed to its outbreak. Not only did the dynasty's inability to repel the barbarians undermine its prestige and show up its weaknesses; but in the South, the birthplace of the Taiping movement, a great many boatmen and dockhands were thrown out of work by the Treaty of Nanking, which diverted much of China's trade with the West from Canton to other cities.

and ruthless fanaticism (the movement had its messiah, a Heavenly King who was allegedly the younger brother of Jesus Christ); and the heralding of more fundamental changes, of better-run revolutions. The Taipings were in a sense the precursors of the Communists.

The Taipings' defeat cannot be explained simply in terms of their weaknesses. Threatened with extinction, the Empire pulled itself together. Between 1860 and 1870–75 a handful of energetic statesmen—literati and government officials by vocation, military leaders by necessity—systematically put down the rebel forces. To this end they organized new armies, which were better equipped to fight the rebels than the old Imperial armies. They also tried to consolidate their gains by reorganizing the country's civil administration. In this effort, the so-called T'ung-chih Restoration (1862–74), they took the Confucian ideal of good government as their model and tried to give new life to Confucianism, which had been implicitly challenged by the values of the Western barbarians and explicitly repudiated by the Taipings. This pathetic attempt to bring back the past and preserve obsolescent values was predestined to failure. In the short run, however, the conservative policy succeeded, thanks to the perseverance of the men behind it: order was reestablished, corruption was effectively controlled, the ruins of war were rebuilt. But the very dynamism and apparent success of this vigorous attempt at restoration may have impeded efforts to work out a more appropriate response to the challenge of the West.

This is not to say that China made no effort in this period to master some of the secrets of the new barbarians' strength. The Restorationists themselves supplemented their policy of reviving Confucianism and restoring the old order with certain Westernizing measures: building arsenals and steamships, translating European scientific and technical manuals, establishing an interpreters' school at Peking. These measures show a predilection for Western technology, and more specifically for Western armament, which had proved its importance in the Opium Wars. Imitation of the West continued long after the relatively short-lived Restoration, but remained within the same limits, limits that were neatly spelled out toward the end of the century in the famous formula of the provincial governor Chang Chih-tung, whose enlightened conservatism made him a worthy heir to the Restorationists of the preceding generation: "Chinese learning as the basis; Western learning for practical use."[6] Inevitably, however, the innovations introduced in one field after another tended to undermine still further the traditional values they had been intended to protect, while at the same time they were not introduced systematically enough or carried far enough to strengthen China sufficiently to withstand the threat she faced.[7] All in all, progress was slow, results were meager, and conservative obstinacy was pervasive at the top: the Middle Kingdom's response to imperialist expansionism was utterly inadequate to the seriousness of the challenge.

A move by China's increasingly powerful rival Japan, which twice in modern times has served as midwife to its neighbor, saved China from stagnation.[8] The Sino-Japanese War of 1894–95, which ended with Japan's easy but unexpected victory, forced Chinese history into a distinct new phase with a new, accelerated rhythm. Henceforth everything moved fast, very fast. There are few examples in human history of upheavals as frequent and far-reaching as those China has undergone since 1894—that is, within the span of a human life. Consider Mao Tse-tung, for example, who was born in 1893.

The rapid course of events in the seventeen years from 1894 to 1911 clearly shows the new rhythm of Chinese history. Imperialism flung itself into the assault on China; or rather, rival

---

[6] In 1872, the first group of Chinese sent to study at an American university were accompanied by teachers assigned to instruct them in the Confucian classics.

[7] Modern industry made its timid debut toward the end of the nineteenth century. The main projects were sponsored by high government officials, in accordance with the formula "Direction by officials, management by merchants" (*kuan-tu shang-pan*). The semiprivate, semipublic nature of these new businesses inhibited their development, the more so since merchants and bureaucrats were in complete accord on the desirability of periodically siphoning off profits rather than reinvesting them.

[8] The second time (the Japanese invasion beginning in 1931 and culminating in the Sino-Japanese War of 1937–45), the role of midwife would be even more decisive in the birth of the Chinese Revolution.

imperialists swarmed over China's enormous, decaying corpse. Within a few years this rush for spoils led to a daring but belated and quickly squelched effort to save the dying Empire; to a terrible upheaval, much more violent but even more out of touch with reality; and finally, after last-ditch attempts at reform, to revolution—the sudden collapse, in a matter of weeks, of the world's oldest Empire.

These celebrated events can be grouped in three phases: crisis (1894–1901), respite (1901–11), and revolution (1911–12).

We will not pause to consider in detail the concessions wrested from China by every imperialist power except the United States in the closing years of the nineteenth century. Suffice it to say that the Powers either appropriated or laid claim to much of the area along the coast, which was more accessible and more easily exploited than the interior, from the Southwest (France), through the Yangtze Valley (England) and the Shantung peninsula (England and Germany), to the Northeast (Russia and Japan). The economic grip of the contending imperialists tightened rapidly, especially in the "modern" sectors of the economy. Great Britain controlled the Kaiping coalfields, Japan the Fushun coal mines and the Anshan iron mines. Nearly every new railroad brought European and Japanese capitalists an opportunity for direct investments or lucrative loans. Whereas imports of petroleum and goods manufactured in the West (e.g., tobacco and cotton fabrics) rose steadily, tea exports fell 30 per cent between 1886 and 1905. The fears of the Chinese, whether radical reformers or tradition-bound xenophobes, proved only too justified.

"Radical reformers" perhaps best describes the unfortunate heroes of the episode in the summer of 1898 known as the Hundred Days' Reform: radical by virtue of their passionate anti-traditionalism but above all by contrast with the moderate Restorationists of the preceding generation; reformers, not revolutionaries, because they still hoped to adapt the old Imperial order, to restore its vitality without calling its existence into question, to assure its survival as an inseparable aspect of the nation. Thus it was naturally by winning over the young Man-chu Emperor Kuang Hsü that the Reformers' leader, K'ang Yu-wei, undertook to get his program adopted in June 1898. He suc-ceeded, but only on paper, for the crude and disorganized series of decrees reforming the educational system, the economy, the administration, and the army at one stroke provoked amaze-ment, indignation, and finally revolt among conservative scholar-officials—and a large majority were conservative. The coup that put a premature end to the experiment on September 21, 1898, did more than reassert the prerogatives of the sacred Imperial Household's two leading members, the young Emperor and his "adoptive mother," the Empress Dowager Tz'u-hsi; it tempo-rarily halted the inevitable conflict between the radical minor-ity and the body of the Establishment. The Emperor was in-terned and his edicts withdrawn; he never again exercised any power. K'ang Yu-wei and his leading disciple and collaborator, Liang Ch'i-ch'ao, fled to Japan. Six Reformers, including the young philosopher T'an Ssu-t'ung, were executed. The failure of the Reformers, who worked from within the system, was the failure of "revolution from above," the failure of a literati clique in conflict with its own class and lacking support from any other class. China would have no Meiji Restoration; the necessary changes would have to be made in some other, more costly way. Was the Reformers' failure due to the obduracy of a ruling elite bent on preserving its sinecures along with the Confucian clas-sics? Certainly. But it was due above all to the resilience, strength, and internal cohesiveness of traditional China.

The Hundred Days' Reform had barely ended when another crisis shook traditional China, the notorious Boxer Rebellion.[9] But in this case traditional China rose against the scourge of the modern world—imperialism. The attack was directed first against foreign missionaries and Chinese Christians, and then against the Western diplomats themselves. The murder of the

9 Although the first manifestations of the Boxer movement antedate the Hundred Days' Reform, the movement reached its peak only in 1899–1900, and the diplomatic settlement that ended it was not signed until September 1901. The Boxer episode is famous in the West because of the ordeal to which Western residents of China were subjected.

German minister, Baron Klemens von Ketteler, and the siege of the diplomatic quarter of Peking in June–August 1900 are still featured in popular Western histories and films of the Yellow Peril school.

The sympathy with which Chinese Communist historians view the Boxer Rebellion can be explained largely by the Boxers' assault on foreigners and foreign influence. Moreover, unlike the Hundred Days' Reform, the movement had a popular base. The great majority of Boxers were either poor peasants, forced by two consecutive bad harvests in northern Kiangsu, the flooding of the Yellow River in Shantung, and drought in other provinces of North China to leave the land or starve, or marginal social groups (boatmen, cart drivers, and artisans, for example) whose livelihood was threatened by modern transportation and industry (e.g., the importing of cotton cloth).

For my part, I think the characterization of the Boxer movement by present-day Chinese revolutionaries as progressive, even as a forerunner of their own revolution, needs serious qualification. The movement's archaic features seem to me more striking than its modern ones. Superstitions, magic spells, trances, séances, sacred boxing (to which the movement owes its name), rituals that imparted invulnerability to the participants—all these features are reminiscent of traditional Chinese secret societies, from which the Boxers were directly descended.[10] But above all, the Boxers' "anti-imperialism" was very close to traditional xenophobia, and even their popular support had serious limitations. The Boxers were frequently supported, encouraged, and even led by the most stubbornly conservative literati and government officials.[11] At first hostile to the dynasty like other

[10] See the chapter on the Boxers in Jean Chesneaux, *Secret Societies in China: In the Nineteenth and Twentieth Centuries* (Ann Arbor: University of Michigan Press, 1971).

[11] The massacres of missionaries in Shansi province in 1900 seem to have been largely the responsibility of the governor, Yü Hsien, who had been transferred from Shantung for showing excessive indulgence toward the Boxers. At first, the Shansi peasants responded to his incitements to murder with indifference or hostility, even when he blamed the missionaries for causing drought by offending the fertility gods. See Ng Kee-lian, "Peasants, Boxers, and Missionaries in Shansi," an unpublished paper written at Harvard University.

secret societies, the movement became openly pro-dynasty in the fall of 1899, when it formed an alliance with anti-foreign officials.[12] Thus the new slogan "Support the Ch'ing! Kill the Foreigners!"

Indeed, the Court's collusion with the so-called rebellion did not end there. Hardly had the Boxer bands entered Peking when they were ordered by an Imperial edict to resist the international rescue column approaching the capital from Tientsin, and on June 21, 1901, the day after von Ketteler's death, the dynasty declared war on the Powers. Thus, at this point at least, there was no question of rebellion, as the usual name for the movement misleadingly suggests; what was involved was out-and-out war between the imperialists and the government of China, a war sought by the most tradition-bound and ignorant of the men and clans in power, i.e., the opponents of the Reformers of 1898. Happily for the dynasty, the prudent independence of the most influential provincial governors, who managed to confine the hostilities to North China, and the imperialists' patent interest in accepting the fiction of a pure and simple rebellion, gave the Imperial regime, in return for a huge indemnity, one last decade of reprieve.

The Hundred Days' Reform and the Boxer Rebellion, along with the "Battle of the Concessions"[13] that preceded and provoked them, are the classic landmarks of the crisis of the Chinese Empire. The following decade, the 213th and last of the Celestial Empire, was much less colorful, and hence is less well known. Still, the events of this period proved very different from the expected inexorable decline, the gradual crumbling of the regime; never, in fact, had reforms been so numerous. They seemed to augur a renaissance, a start toward genuine transformation of the Empire, not the end of an era but the beginning.

In a few years, the Ch'ing dynasty moved (timidly, to be sure) toward the establishment of a constitutional monarchy,

[12] At least so far as a majority of the Boxers were concerned; a minority remained steadfastly hostile to the Manchus and even fought with those who had gone over to the dynasty.

[13] This is the title of a 1957 Cambridge University thesis by Lo Hui-min.

undertook essential and far-reaching administrative, judicial, and fiscal reforms, created a modern army, lent its support to Chinese efforts at industrial development (notably in textiles and railroad building), and last and most important, abolished the traditional civil service examinations and laid the basis for a new educational system, one that drew more heavily on the Western barbarians than on the Chinese classics.

But these efforts came too late, much too late. Introduced under the aegis of the traditionalists (including the Empress Dowager herself), who had fought the Reformers of 1898 and then espoused, often grudgingly, the essence of their program, the reforms could all too easily be seen as further evidence of weakness, concessions forced on the regime by the pressure of public opinion. In fact this was not the case, at least not until the very end of the decade, when the revolutionaries first became a serious threat. On the contrary, it was the reforms that gave the revolutionaries their chance. The long-deferred changes that were at last introduced, or at least adumbrated, could not help but undermine the established order. Institutions of higher education that once had turned out Confucian scholar-officials now began to graduate revolutionaries. In the new army as well as the new military schools, activist groups of patriotic young officers were organized; modernizers at first, these men were soon driven by nationalism to espouse revolution.[14] Chinese investment in business and industry and the particular timid pattern that Chinese capitalist ventures developed gave rise to a new class, of merchants as well as scholar-officials, whose needs and values differed from those of the old ruling class. Administrative reorganization made it possible for representatives of this emerging class, as well as the traditional gentry, to make their complaints heard. This was especially true after 1909, when the newly created provincial assemblies became natural centers of political agitation.

[14] The young Chiang Kai-shek, after studying at the Paoting Military Academy near Peking, continued his military studies in Japan. At the other end of China, in Yunnan, a young man from Szechwan was also preparing himself for a military career—Chu Teh, the future commander-in-chief of the Red Army.

The assemblies called for liberalization of the regime and pro-
tested against its attempts at centralization. These attempts were
essentially efforts to recapture authority that had been gradually
lost to the provincial governors in the preceding decades;[15] and
yet centralization was indispensable to any effective reform.
Soon an issue was made of the foreign origin of the dynasty,
which became the target of Chinese nationalism just when its
struggle to prolong its own existence had finally brought it
around to working for the salvation of China herself.[16]

By 1910 the new voice of parliamentary agitation was merely
the most obvious and in a sense official expression of opposition
to the regime. Nor did the revolutionary diatribes and professions of faith appearing in Chinese newspapers published in the
foreign concessions of big cities like Shanghai represent the real
underground opposition. Plots were being hatched in the army
and among students exiled in Tokyo; attempted uprisings were
followed by attempted assassinations.[17] Revolution, which no
one had spoken of ten years before, was the next item on the
agenda.

Revolution and the End of the Empire

No one? Not quite. Certain isolated individuals had been
preaching in this wilderness of half a billion souls—first of all, of
course, the man who long stood for the Chinese Revolution in
Western schoolbooks, Sun Yat-sen. Small matter that the man
himself, opportunistic and changeable, superficial and vague,
did not exactly fit today's traditional picture of China's "Father

[15] A development traceable to the Taiping Rebellion: to fight the rebels, it was necessary to organize provincial armies, which became the main support of partially autonomous regional leaders.

[16] To be sure, the persistent maladroitness of the Manchu princes left them open to
denunciations as foreign "usurpers" by Han, i.e. Chinese, nationalists. In April 1911,
when the Prince Regent (the father of the young Emperor, who had succeeded Kuang
Hsü two and a half years earlier) finally agreed to appoint a genuine cabinet, he
named four Chinese ministers and eight Manchus!

[17] Wang Ching-wei tried to kill the Prince Regent in 1910, escaping execution despite or perhaps because of his defiance of the judges who tried him. He thus began
as a national hero the career he would end as a traitor. See below, pp. 25 and 167.

of the Republic." The important thing is that circumstances,[18] along with his talents as a visionary and organizer and his revolutionary seniority, made him at once the indispensable leader and a sufficiently elusive and moving symbol to rally the majority of impatient men of good will to his standard.

These new revolutionaries came almost exclusively from China's narrow modern sector. To this social and geographic fringe belonged the potential rebels—students, officers, and merchants from the treaty ports—together with the Chinese overseas, notably the students in Japan and the Chinese emigrants scattered along the shores of the Indian and Pacific oceans. It was in Tokyo in 1905 that a group directed by Sun Yat-sen and other revolutionary organizations[19] merged to form the T'ung Meng Hui (Revolutionary Alliance), the predecessor of the Kuomintang. In Tokyo, too, the journal *Min-pao* (The People), the organ of the T'ung Meng Hui, defended republican ideology and the revolutionary road against the partisans of constitutional monarchy. Japan served not only as the common refuge for opponents of Manchu absolutism and as the go-between for rival groups of revolutionaries (it was a Japanese who introduced Sun Yat-sen to Huang Hsing), but also as a model of government that impressed even the Republicans.[20] Finally, and more prosaically, Japanese money, arms, and advice were con-

[18] He was born in a region—the delta of the Sikiang (West River), the great river of South China, close to Macao and the "South Seas"—that was more open to the world than most, to the world of the overseas Chinese and through them the Western world. At fourteen Sun was learning English and mathematics in Honolulu, at nineteen medicine in Hong Kong. After the failure of his first plot, against the provincial government of Kwangtung (1895), several of his co-conspirators were executed, but he managed to escape. A year later he was caught—in London, where he was kidnapped by the Chinese embassy. Saved by the publicity given the case by an English newspaper that had been tipped off, he became at thirty a leading figure in world politics. From then on, he roamed the world as the traveling salesman of the Chinese Revolution, seeking ideas and funds for his cause.

[19] Notably the Society for China's Revival (Hua Hsing Hui), founded in Hunan province in 1903 by Huang Hsing, who became Sun's deputy in the new organization and later played a leading role in preparations for the Revolution of 1911.

[20] The impact of Japan's defeat of Russia in 1905 on nationalists throughout East Asia is well known. Nationalism was the chief factor in the revolutionary sentiments of most of Sun's followers.

tributed to the revolutionary cause by diverse groups of patriotic Japanese, who were interested for reasons of varying degrees of purity in weakening or bringing down the Manchu dynasty.[21]

Most of the revolutionaries' financial support, however, came from the overseas Chinese and in particular from successful businessmen. For these men it had become more and more difficult to reconcile, much less equate, nationalism with loyalty to the Manchu regime. Their profession, their dynamism, the capitalist values they had adopted, all made them regard mainland China much as the colonizers of Magna Graecia must have regarded their native cities. Detached but pitying, they were by no means resigned to letting their native land sleep, a land that exile had made all the dearer to them. Hence their generous contributions to a revolutionary movement they correctly regarded as essentially a nationalist and modernizing movement.

By 1909, however, the revolutionaries' repeated failures (including, in the southern provinces alone, six poorly planned military ventures between May 1907 and May 1908) had discouraged the flow of overseas support, and Sun left to raise funds in the West. He was there when the revolution broke out. Tradition, or legend, counts the unhappy outcome of a mutiny incited by Huang Hsing in Canton in April 1911 as the tenth failure of Sun's followers. The eleventh attempt came six months later, at Wuchang, on the middle Yangtze.[22] The plot was quickly uncovered. An eleventh failure? No, because the discovery of the plot (on October 9) precipitated the revolution; in trying to save themselves, the Wuchang conspirators brought down an Empire. "Double ten" (tenth month, tenth day: October 10, 1911) has been celebrated ever since as the day the Republic was born.

The rebels quickly took control of Wuchang, following the flight of the governor-general and the commandant of the gar-

---

[21] They ranged from chauvinism to idealism, from the crudest expansionism to awareness of Japan's cultural debt to Chinese civilization.

[22] In fact it was the doing of two revolutionary groups, one of which had very loose ties with the T'ung Meng Hui, the other none at all.

rison. Less than two months later all the provinces of Central and South China, along with the Northwest, had proclaimed their independence. Sun Yat-sen, who learned in Denver, Colorado, both that the revolt had broken out and that it had succeeded, took his time returning home. He stopped in London to try to arrange a loan (he failed) and persuade the Foreign Office to exert pressure on the Japanese not to support the Manchus, and made another stop in Paris.[23] He finally arrived in Shanghai on December 24, 1911, just in time to become Provisional President of the Republic of China, taking office on January 1, 1912, at Nanking.

What an astonishingly easy victory for the revolution—a spur-of-the-moment coup, to which everyone immediately rallied. Was the collapse of the Empire an accident, like the initial spark —the revolt at Wuchang—that set off the movement?

That so many provinces seized on the Wuchang uprising as a pretext for declaring their independence, that the revolution carried the day in so many places without a shot being fired, was certainly not a matter of chance. At the least, these developments suggest a fairly widespread hostility to the Ch'ing. In fact, hostility to the dynasty extended far beyond the small circle of revolutionaries and the handful of Republicans who followed Sun Yat-sen and others. Discontent was rife among the privileged. For the modern men (capitalists, students, officers) from which the T'ung Meng Hui and other revolutionary organizations drew much of their membership belonged to the privileged classes. Even more patently among the privileged were those who swelled the revolutionaries' ranks at the last minute. These were the traditional privileged classes: landowners, scholars and bureaucrats, civil and military officials—in short, the pillars of the Imperial regime.[24] To be sure, not all members of the

---

[23] Needless to say, the policy of the Japanese government would not necessarily coincide with that of the various groups of Japanese patriots mentioned earlier.

[24] This is not to suggest that the lower classes played no role in the revolution; in some areas lower-class uprisings made it possible for the revolutionaries to seize power. The lower classes were even more important in the prerevolutionary years: witness, for example, the endemic peasant agitation in the middle and lower Yangtze basin from

traditional ruling class suddenly turned against the order that had sustained them, but a far from negligible number of them did. The anti-regime agitation of these men, and the resulting tumult and disorder—particularly in Central China, where the Wuchang uprising broke out—paved the way for the revolutionaries, much as the revolt of the French aristocracy led to the events of 1789. Many a d'Eprémesnil and Montsabert could be found among the vociferous members of the provincial assemblies, and many more among the delegates of the sixteen provincial assemblies who met in Peking in February 1910 and demanded a national parliament.[25]

But far more was involved than simple parliamentary agitation. We go on saying that the revolution broke out on October 10, 1911, at Wuchang, but did it not in fact begin the previous summer in the neighboring province of Szechwan? From the extremely serious disturbances in Szechwan (riots, then rebellion and a tax strike, and finally the "liberation" of a district), we can see what led the ruling class to oppose the Manchus. Whatever their announced purposes may have been, the Szechwanese were basically motivated by a desire to preserve or extend Szechwan's provincial autonomy and to defend local special interests. The agitation began as a "Movement for the Protection of the Railroad," i.e., the projected railroad from Hankow to Szechwan, which had been underwritten largely by local landlords and merchants. The nationalization of the provincial

---

1906 on; the food riots in Changsha, the capital of Hunan province, in 1910; and the tax riots in Shantung province. There was even at least one case of cooperation between workers and peasants: in 1906 the miners at Pingsiang, in Kiangsi province, joined a revolt fomented by a secret society in neighboring Hunan province whose members were mostly peasants. But almost all these disturbances were simply local or provincial responses to deteriorating economic conditions—and in many ways traditional, not to say archaic, responses. The about-face of part of the ruling class was the new and decisive fact.

25 The provincial assemblies, it will be recalled, were created in 1909. [Duval d'Eprémesnil and Goislard de Montsabert led the opposition of the Parlement of Paris to Louis XVI's attempt in 1788 to impose taxes on the nobility without convoking the Estates General. As a delegate to the Constituent Assembly, d'Eprémesnil defended the nobility's privileges against encroachment from below as vociferously as he had championed them against the King; he was executed by the Convention in 1794.—Trans.]

railroads decreed in May 1911 touched a sensitive nerve in Szechwan and several central provinces; it was this move that set off the explosion. Yet this conservative and particularist movement ("Szechwan for the Szechwanese" was the rioters' slogan)—this effort to preserve a railroad company crippled by speculation, corruption, and managerial incompetence, and at bottom by the insufficiency of provincial capital—was also in its way a profoundly nationalist movement.[26] Private interests were being defended, but at the same time a conscious stand was being taken against imperialist expansion and a government that was "selling out the country" to foreign interests; nationalization meant the intrusion of Western capital in a business matter that should have been purely Chinese and provincial.[27] A stand against corruption, too, the well-known corruption of the chief advocate and architect of railroad centralization, Sheng Hsüan-huai. And soon a stand against terrorism as well, for what began as the suppression of rioting turned into out-and-out massacre. In the end, Szechwanese of different classes were united by a nationalist movement that was anti-Western in intent, anti-Manchu in fact, opposed to absolutism, and already revolutionary.

Nevertheless, the revolution was brought about by the convergence of two fundamentally different oppositions, which had little more in common than opposition to the dynasty. In short, an entirely negative goal was the chief point of agreement between the first wave of revolutionaries and those who joined the revolution on its eve.[28] On all other points, the insurgent officers and men at Wuchang (whose brothers had revolted and been killed in earlier, ill-fated uprisings) had nothing in common with the gentry who unleashed the agitation in Hunan. The lat-

---

[26] Han Suyin's book *The Crippled Tree* (New York: Putnam, 1965), pp. 116–41, makes clear both how complex and how extensive the movement was. The book also describes how Chinese engineers were treated, and paid, by European railroad companies.

[27] In that same month, May 1911, the Chinese government signed a contract with a foreign financial consortium (American, English, French, and German) formed the year before.

[28] Not to mention the many others, notably high officials of the Imperial regime, who joined the movement after the insurrection was over.

ter were representatives of the traditional aristocracy; the former were spokesmen for a new world. And the creatures of a new world as well, for these officers of the new army, these students returned from abroad, these businessmen from the treaty ports and overseas Chinese communities who supported the T'ung Meng Hui, were not only modern, they were new: their very existence, and not just their mentality or outlook, was a new fact. They did not yet constitute a class that could challenge the old ruling class, but were at most social groups in the process of formation, groups beginning to define their identity in response to stimuli introduced into the Middle Kingdom by recent history. One such stimulus, national (as opposed to foreign) industry, had been operating in a modest way for a generation; others (the reforms effected by the dynasty itself) were younger than the century. It is not surprising that the new forces produced by these stimuli, weak and badly outnumbered as they were, could not by themselves make a revolution,[29] and that only the broad support of part of the traditional ruling class made victory possible. Yet that support immediately compromised the victory it had helped to win; its claims weighed heavily on the young Republic.

What were the net results of the Revolution of 1911? In the first place, there are no grounds for surprise. That the earliest and most committed servants of the revolution, like the adventitious revolutionaries who came to their support, belonged to the privileged classes—this key fact, which helped set *a priori* limits to the revolution, is in no way surprising. The Revolution of 1911 brought down the Empire, a result completely in line with the negative ends that had united the opposition. It brought no fundamental changes in Chinese society, but it paid off a mortgage. Sun Yat-sen, who ten years earlier had been regarded as an extravagant dreamer, became a great man overnight.

[29] The more so since one of these groups, the commercial bourgeoisie, was revolutionary only up to a certain point, as its attitude during the revolution would prove. On this point see Marie-Claire Bergère, "The Role of the Bourgeoisie," in Mary C. Wright, ed., *China in Revolution: The First Phase, 1900–1913* (New Haven, Conn.: Yale University Press, 1968), pp. 229–95.

Finally, the revolution compelled its makers to go further. For much of what it had swept away had been superficial, such as the "Manchu oppression" denounced by the revolutionaries. Some of them, following Sun Yat-sen's example, couched their nationalism in terms of opposition to a foreign dynasty as a way of playing up to the imperialist powers, whose support or at least neutrality could prove decisive. For others, no doubt the majority, anti-Manchu nationalism represented the first stage of an awakening; by distracting attention from more fundamental difficulties, it served all the better as a spur to action. When the difficulties persisted, it would be necessary to go deeper and seek the truly national causes of a national crisis, without, however, losing sight of the real enemy—imperialism. Whatever the revolutionaries may have said, imperialism lay at the heart of the first revolution, a *nationalist* revolution. Nationalism was the force that created the paradoxical unity of all participants.[30] If protest over the railroads has a symbolic significance, it is because railroads were the most obvious sign of the imperialist penetration of China.

Within a few brief years, a high official of the old regime first took over the revolution and then tried to restore the Empire for his own ends. This "usurper," the indispensable man behind whom the revolutionaries themselves were willy-nilly forced to rally—"the strong man of China," as the Western newspapers called him with mingled condescension and respect—was Yuan Shih-k'ai.

He was hardly a revolutionary. Indeed, he had contributed more than anyone else to the defeat and destruction of the reform movement of 1898, by putting his army at the service of the Empress Dowager against the young Emperor and the forces of reform. But he had been lucky enough to spend the last two years of the Empire in semi-disgrace. What was he, then, and what was the source of his influence? In a word, he was a man-

---

[30] The traditional privileged classes were Chinese, after all, and thus humiliated and frustrated. And for much more profound reasons than men like d'Eprémesnil and Montsabert.

darin, a career official who in the last decade of the Empire had worked with some success to build a modern army. This accomplishment gave him a reputation as a modernist, as a man receptive to the new ideas, and its most important result was to enable him to establish a kind of personal empire. The Northern (Peiyang) Army that he had created became China's most powerful organized military force. The praetorian outlook of its generals and other high-ranking officers assured Yuan a devoted following.

The man was an opportunist. Self-interest explains the choice he made in 1898, and his conduct in the 1911–12 crisis can be accounted for in the same way. After being called on for help by the Manchus and invested with the Empire's highest military command, Yuan managed to arrange both the abdication of the dynasty and his own elevation to the presidency of the Republic. His success in these maneuvers, however, is attributable mainly to the fact that many Chinese were drawn to him as the only man who was capable of preserving a unified and independent China.

The revolutionaries were soon converted to cooperation with Yuan; they were aware they represented but a tiny minority, unknown to the peasant masses and unacquainted with their aspirations. They lacked not only mass support but financial resources: the imperialists who turned down Sun Yat-sen lent money to Yuan Shih-k'ai. Sun accordingly stepped aside in Yuan's favor on February 13, 1912, the day after the Emperor's abdication, and soon was devoting his energies to an ambitious railroad development scheme—the ideal refuge for a repentant Saint-Simonian.[31]

The Republicans nonetheless ended up in open opposition to Yuan, though only after he had consolidated his power. What is known as the Second Revolution broke out in mid-1913, following the assassination (in all probability ordered by Yuan) of

[31] All such comparisons are made for didactic purposes only. Sun Yat-sen, for example, was not literally a Saint-Simonian, but the term economically evokes what I consider an important facet of his personality.

an important Kuomintang leader. The revolt was crushed in a matter of months. This military victory paved the way for Yuan's coup d'état of November 1913, which eliminated the Kuomintang's parliamentary opposition and such other constraints as the constitutional regime theoretically imposed. Yuan's dictatorship might have lasted longer if he had not tried to found a new dynasty in 1915. His Imperial pretensions precipitated a new insurrection, one more widespread and better organized than that of 1913. Eight provinces in the South and West had announced their opposition when he suddenly died, on June 6, 1916.

The Yuan Shih-k'ai episode was accordingly a classic effort to establish a regime identical except in personnel to the one just overthrown.[32] That Yuan saw his own future and his country's in terms of the precedents of Chinese history clearly shows the limited nature of the "modernism" that so upset his conservative peers. His strength lay above all in being an energetic administrator. In this he represented a class of men (the traditional aristocracy of landlords and literati) who, like him, abandoned the crumbling Empire only to seek an immediate return to order. Yuan's success had signaled the failure of 1911. His ultimate failure confirmed the small but real extent of the revolution's success: henceforth certain traditional roads to power could not be taken.

China from 1916 to 1949: A Rapid Survey

Instead of giving the Republic a new lease on life, the failure of the "usurper" hastened its decline. With Yuan gone, there was no political figure with sufficient prestige or following, particularly among the military, to impose his authority. Nominally, the Republican regime survived; there was still a President of the Republic, whose election sometimes depended on buying the necessary votes in parliament (described by a contemporary as "a herd of pigs at the trough"), more often on the support of the political-military clique that temporarily con-

[32] Despite some efforts at reform; a new dynasty would have done no less.

trolled Peking, the seat of the central government. But real power did not rest with this "government"; like its many rivals, it was in fact a regional power whose authority extended little farther than the two or three provinces around the capital.[33] As might be expected, the potentates who had divided up China were constantly at war with one another. As their fortunes waxed and waned, alliances and coalitions were made and broken. Feudal wars? Perhaps. But these great vassals recognized no suzerain and claimed no aristocratic heritage. The term used to describe them, warlords, suggests the origin of their power; they were preeminently men who owed their fortune to war.

It took less than ten years to seal the doom of the Republic; its end was clearly in sight by 1920. One of the main differences between the Republic and the Empire seems to have been precisely this regionalization of politics,[34] this increasing weakness not only of the central government but of the country as a whole. Some of China's well-wishers, recognizing the de facto division of the country and despairing of reunification, were driven to proposing a federalist system; provincial autonomy should be reinforced, they argued, so that it would be possible to do at the provincial level what could no longer be done nationally.[35] The federalist movement, though extremely fashionable at the time, had little lasting significance. But it points to a fundamental factor in the development of modern China: the importance of regionalism and centrifugal tendencies in a country as large as Europe and as imperfectly unified as France under the Old Regime.

Nevertheless, the significance of the period lies elsewhere. The much vilified warlord period, which brought the country to the brink of disaster, was also the period that gave birth to

---

[33] It had, however, one sizable advantage: its official standing enabled it to contract foreign loans.

[34] A process that began, to be sure, in the last half-century of the Manchu dynasty.

[35] On this point, see Jean Chesneaux, "Le Mouvement fédéraliste en Chine, 1920–1923," *Revue Historique*, No. 480 (Oct.–Dec. 1966), pp. 347–84. On the general significance of provincialism in the last years of the Empire and at the beginning of the Republic, see the conclusion (p. 382) of Yoshihiro Hatano's article "The New Armies" in Mary C. Wright, ed., *China in Revolution*.

modern China—to a new world arising from the remains of the old Confucian Empire. Two highly effective revolutionary currents emerged in the decade following Yuan's death. The first was a genuine cultural revolution before that term was invented—the May Fourth Movement, named for a student demonstration in Peking on May 4, 1919.[36] The second, in part an offshoot of the first, was an extreme radicalization of political life, the chief sign of which was the creation and rapid growth of revolutionary movements that planned not another 1911, not just a nationalist political revolution, but a social revolution as well. One sign of the times was that the Kuomintang, drawing a lesson from its defeat, adopted a new line.[37] On Sun Yat-sen's initiative, it made overtures to the new Russian revolutionary regime (Chiang Kai-shek was sent on a mission to Moscow in 1923) and adopted the Bolsheviks' organization and techniques. Before Sun's death in 1925 the old leader, as faithful to his revolutionary ideal as he was changeable in his ways of serving it, effected one last transformation of the instrument he had created; in 1924, he had the Kuomintang's Reorganization Conference[38] adopt the so-called Three New Policies: alliance with the Soviet Union, support for workers' and peasants' movements, and collaboration with the Chinese Communist Party, then barely three years old. Not just united but merged in a single organization, the two parties, the Communist Party and the Kuomintang (Nationalist Party) that same year established a military academy at Whampoa, near Canton, to train cadres for the revolutionary army. Two years later, in July 1926, that army set out to conquer China. In this campaign, the so-called Northern Expedition, the revolutionary army scored easy victories over its disunited and hopelessly old-fashioned adversaries,

---

[36] See Chapter Two.

[37] The decade following the failure of 1912–13 brought the Kuomintang many disappointments, particularly from the Westerners, who continued to refuse financial aid. There were other setbacks. Sun Yat-sen established a revolutionary base in Canton and was soon involved despite himself in the local complications of warlord politics. A period of awkward collaboration with a local general (Ch'en Chiung-ming) ended when the general drove Sun out of Canton.

[38] See p. 55 below.

the warlord armies; and its successes strengthened the revolutionary movement that had helped to clear its path.

The Northern Expedition did not just win victories, it won *the* victory.[39] It put an end to one era, the warlord period, and inaugurated another, the Kuomintang period or "Nationalist interregnum."[40] It was the revenge for 1912, the posthumous revenge of Sun Yat-sen, who in his lifetime had worked untiringly for just such a Northern Expedition, a campaign to extend Canton's revolutionary regime to the rest of the country. In 1927 Sun's heir, General Chiang Kai-shek, who became commander-in-chief of the Northern Expedition after serving as commandant of the military academy at Whampoa, married Sun's sister-in-law, Soong Mei-ling, as if to bolster his claim to revolutionary legitimacy.

By this time the revolution had been shorn of its most revolutionary members, the Communists, whom Chiang attacked as soon as their joint victory was certain. The government he headed at Nanking from 1928 on was distinguished as much by its hostility to the Communists (and to workers' and peasants' movements) as by its triumph over the "old China" of the warlords. So much for the Three New Policies. I have called the Northern Expedition the posthumous revenge of Sun Yat-sen, but in fact Chiang betrayed Sun's aims in the very course of achieving them. If we wished to credit the new master of China with political views as grandiose as his ambition, we might say that if the first revolution (1911–12) was a failure, Chiang's accomplishment in the second (1926–27) amounted to an attempt to stabilize the revolution at a certain point.

Stabilization implied unification of the country, and political unification was in fact the leading concern of the regime throughout the two decades of its existence (1928–49). The Kuo-

---

[39] The Northern Expedition was essentially completed in the spring of 1927, when the revolutionary army took control of the Yangtze basin. North China would not be conquered or won over until the following year, but by 1927 the outcome was clear.

[40] This is the term used by O. Edmund Clubb in *Twentieth Century China* (New York: Columbia University Press, 1964). Here and elsewhere in this book, Nationalist with a capital N refers simply to the Nationalist Party (Kuomintang).

mintang's primary objectives can be described as first to achieve unification (1928-37), then to defend it (1937-49).

The years 1928-37 were almost the only "normal years," the only years of peace and order, that China experienced between 1911 and 1949. The peace and order were relative, just as the unification achieved in this decade was more apparent than real; yet this was the most evident change of all from the preceding warlord era.

The warlords, of course, continued to challenge the regime and to fight among themselves. Patiently Chiang set about eliminating them from contention, one after the other, by war or negotiation. He had more difficulty disposing of the second internal threat, the one posed by the Communists, which is to say the Chinese Revolution. He did, however, contain this threat and even force it to recede; and for a time he seemed on the point of destroying it. But at this juncture a foreign enemy entered the picture and wiped out all Chiang's hard-won advantages over his domestic opponents. Japan had occupied Manchuria in 1931 and had already weakened the regime by nibbling away at North China. The deathblow came in 1937 with the Sino-Japanese War.

That this was the end was not immediately apparent; on the contrary, the regime had never been more widely accepted, its leader never more popular, than in the years of ordeal (1937-38) when the enemy seized everything in China that counted. The national government withdrew to Hankow, then to Chungking in remote Szechwan. The flight of Wang Ching-wei, who left to play quisling in the occupied zone, further enhanced the stature of the Generalissimo, Chiang Kai-shek, whose stubborn perseverance came to symbolize the indomitable resistance of the Chinese people. In these first years of the war, a nation was forged and shaped; and the "Dwarfs," as the Chinese derisively called the Japanese, were largely responsible.

Reassured of ultimate victory by the attack on Pearl Harbor in December 1941, the Kuomintang allowed its resistance to Japan to slacken; better to leave to the Americans a task that was seemingly as easy for them as it would have been exhausting for China. And better to husband the Kuomintang's strength for the great postwar confrontation already on the horizon—the settling of accounts with the Communists.

In the course of the war, the Communists had in fact grown sufficiently in strength and numbers to become serious contenders for national power. Hiroshima left the two Chinese camps face to face, but open warfare between them did not break out until 1946. Although the legal government at first had the upper hand, the advantage gradually passed to the revolutionaries; American aid and Nationalist superiority in numbers and armament did not prove decisive in a war that called into play less classic sources of strength. The Red Army paraded triumphantly through the streets of Peking in January 1949 and crossed the Yangtze in April; six months later the People's Republic of China was proclaimed.

The Nationalist regime had been founded by military conquest, and by military conquest it was overthrown. In retrospect, it seems to have been little more than a brief transition between the old Confucian order and the new order of Communist China.

2. Intellectual Origins of the Chinese Revolution

In summarizing the major episodes of a little-known history, the preceding chapter somewhat arbitrarily divided into discrete periods what in reality was an uninterrupted flow of events. In general the dividing lines were determined by political developments, that is, by surface events. At most they created a convenient framework, within which we can now get down to essentials. In the most flagrant case, we chose an insignificant event—the death of Yuan Shih-k'ai—to bring the narrative to a close (before the rapid survey of the subsequent decades), rather than the May Fourth Movement of 1919, a movement so important that Chinese Communist historians take it as the starting point of the contemporary era. In their eyes, between 1839, the beginning of China's modern era, and 1949, the year the China of the future came into being, the key date is 1919, not 1911. If only to understand their point of view, it would be worthwhile to devote the major portion of this chapter to the significance of May 4, 1919.

What was the May Fourth Movement? In part it was an intellectual reawakening, sometimes called the Chinese Renaissance but in fact, if a comparison with European intellectual history must be made, closer in spirit to the eighteenth century. The May Fourth Movement was a kind of Chinese Enlightenment, a movement that advanced such eminently reasonable ideals as science and democracy. More important, it was a ground-clearing enterprise; it foreshadowed and paved the way for 1949 just as Voltaire had for 1789. The established order to be crushed in the Chinese case was also the Church, or at least that religion without dogma, clergy, or prescribed form of worship known as Confucianism. In this sense 1919 was more important than 1911: the second attack went beyond the tottering Empire, beyond a particular dynasty, to the ideological underpinnings of the Imperial regime, to a system of thought and social organization that had been accepted for centuries and had survived every change in dynasty. The May Fourth Movement called into question the very basis of Chinese society. The young students who wished to be rid once and for all of the evils they denounced were not wrong to hurl themselves against the Confucian citadel crying "Overthrow Confucius & Sons!" (*Ta-tao K'ung-chia-tien*).

The importance of the May Fourth Movement should by now be apparent. Intellectually, the Chinese Revolution originated in the challenging of China's cultural heritage by Western civilization. May Fourth was the culmination of that challenge: the brutal, wholesale repudiation of Confucianism, the symbol of Chinese culture and Chinese history.

Confucianism Under Attack

The repudiation of Confucianism was brutal in the sense of being violent, impassioned, and destructive, not in the sense of being sudden or unpredictable. On the contrary, the May Fourth Movement was the climax of a long development. Its antecedents were all those assaults that had shaken Confucianism since 1840, all those timid, reluctant, but inevitable changes that could not help but take hold once the lesson of the European intrusion was learned: to wit, that Confucianism, contrary to what the Chinese had believed, could not be equated with civilization, but only with one civilization, a civilization, moreover, that was ill-suited to assuring China's survival in a world of technological progress and ruthless competition.

Chinese officials actually sought to strengthen the position of Confucianism with borrowings from the West during the early stages of intellectual competition; indeed, their great respect for

Confucian wisdom is clear from what they elected to borrow and what they chose to ignore. Deliberately limited first to the art of war, which brought power, then to industry, which brought wealth, and finally to applied science, which brought both, China's borrowings from the West carefully left untouched the essential, the unalterable, what was proper to China herself, or more precisely what for centuries had made China China—the teachings of the Master, which were not, like foreign formulas, merely utilitarian and transitory.[1] But whatever the spirit in which innovations were accepted, their effects were unalterable. Soon, through translations and teaching, the whole structure of Western thought crept in and then began to dominate; it ended up destroying the order that modern arms and railroads first had shaken. By the end of the century, men like Yen Fu and Lin Shu were publishing new translations of Western works almost every year. These now included philosophical works as well as the usual engineering manuals. New schools offering a modern, i.e. Western, education sprang up everywhere. At the same time the number of young Chinese who left to study in European and American universities continued to increase, and so did the number of Chinese attending Japanese universities, which had long dispensed an imported Confucianism but would henceforth administer an imported antidote, the spirit of the West.[2] In 1906 there were 13,000 Chinese students in Japan. In the same year, China's traditional triennial examinations were for the first time not held, having been abolished by the Impe-

[1] "I know that within a hundred years China will adopt all Western methods and will excel in them.... However, they are all instruments; they are not the Way, and they cannot be called the basis for governing the state and pacifying the world. The Way of Confucius is the Way of Man. As long as humankind exists, the Way will remain unchanged." Quoted in Wm. Theodore de Bary, Wing-tsit Chan, and Burton Watson, eds., *Sources of Chinese Tradition*, I (New York: Columbia University Press, 1960), 718. The same assurance underlies these remarks by Wang T'ao, the founder of modern journalism in China, and the famous formula of Governor Chang Chih-tung cited in Chapter One.

[2] At the turn of the century, most Chinese literati discovering Western thought assumed that there was a single spirit of the West, a spirit that could be summed up as the cult of material progress. Imagine their confusion when they discovered the chaotic and contradictory pluralism of Western values, from Darwinism, then in its heyday, to Christianity. "Where is the essence of the West, and how shall I ever understand it?" the father of the novelist Han Suyin exclaimed in anguished bewilderment. *The Crippled Tree*, p. 164.

rial government the year before. This was a key measure in the destruction of the old order, for the examination system, which had kept all government posts in the hands of traditionally educated literati, was one of Confucianism's main institutional strongholds.

Once Confucianism had been stripped of its ideological underpinnings, it was openly challenged intellectually. Of course it had been challenged earlier by the Taipings, who had been put down in its name; indeed, the Taiping Rebellion, which began just ten years after the intrusion of the West, was the first Chinese rebellion not to invoke the eminently Confucian argument that the ruling dynasty had lost the Mandate of Heaven. By the end of the nineteenth century, however, the men storming the Confucian stronghold were not just insurgent bands, but eminent literati and government officials. In traditional memorials to the Emperor they submitted all sorts of heterodox proposals. And they succeeded, for a while, in getting them adopted. The reader will have recognized these men as the Reformers of the Hundred Days. But even for them the prestige of Confucian culture was so overwhelming that they felt compelled to discover a "real" Confucius, concealed by the orthodox and oppressive Confucius of tradition, who understood, accepted, and encouraged everything they were fighting for: reforms, enlightened evolution, concern for the greatest number. Needless to say, this Confucius, this champion of the masses and of progress, existed mainly in their pious imagination. The Confucius important to history, the one attacked by the iconoclasts of the May Fourth Movement, was the ideological mainstay of a conservative and authoritarian order, the order of orthodoxy, of those who opposed the Hundred Days' Reform. And powerful opponents they were still, as is clear from the quick end they put to the Hundred Days' experiment with nonrevolutionary adaptation to the modern world.[3]

The millenarian Christianity of the Taipings and the Reformers' call to support the spirit of the Sage against the letter

---

[3] Joseph Levenson, from whom I have borrowed this analysis, writes very justly of K'ang Yu-wei and his reformer disciples: "Their Confucian-Western syncretism was

of established dogma was followed by a third thrust against Confucian orthodoxy: the spread of anarchist ideas in the last years of the Empire. The anarchists were just as revolutionary as the Taipings, and just as opposed to Confucian doctrine, but like the Reformers they were ruling-class intellectuals. Indeed, many of them were the most favored members of the privileged classes, the *liu hsüeh-sheng*, or returned students. In France and Japan they had discovered Bakunin and Kropotkin; it was in France that they published their main journal, *Le Nouveau Siècle*. It was not long before they tried to put the ideas of their Western mentors into effect in China. They founded groups like the Heart Society, whose members undertook to obey twelve commandments, all of them prohibitions: against sensual indulgence (commandments 1–3), social exploitation (4–5), traditional customs (6–7), political compromises (8–11), and religious beliefs (12).[4] It was as if the most intransigent avant-garde circles of turn-of-the-century Europe had emigrated to China. In fact, Chinese anarchism on the eve of the First World War could be defined as a combination of the most radical theories of the contemporary West and a violent repudiation of Confucianism. Repudiation and modernism—a modernism that naturally meant Westernization—lay at the heart of the May Fourth Movement. But this was no more than the radicalism of a literary club; there remained the question of mass support. Precisely because the real May Fourth Movement was a mass movement, its slogans stopped well short of anarchism. The extreme avant-garde, whether prophetic or Utopian, could never be more than a clique.

The May Fourth Movement

Can we really call the May Fourth Movement a mass movement? We can indeed, provided we concede at the outset that

not an incitement, but a response." A response, that is, to the irresistible pressure and challenge of the West, and one that proved inadequate. Cited in Albert Feuerwerker, ed., *Modern China* (Englewood Cliffs, N.J.: Prentice-Hall, 1964), p. 159.

4 Members of the Heart Society swore they would be vegetarians; abstain from alcoholic beverages; abstain from smoking; not hire servants; not use rickshaws; remain celibate; renounce their family name; refuse all government posts; refuse political office; not join a political party; not serve in the army or navy; and espouse atheism.

the masses in question excluded 95 per cent of the Chinese and came almost exclusively from the tiny educated minority. May Fourth was a movement of intellectuals, and primarily of academics at that; its strength came from students and professors. In the narrowest sense, May Fourth refers to a student demonstration (the May Fourth Incident) staged in Peking on May 4, 1919, to protest the decision of the Paris Peace Conference that transferred Germany's rights in Shantung province to Japan. In its broadest accepted meaning, which is the one used here, May Fourth was a movement of cultural renewal and revolution, a movement that in fact started several years before the demonstration of 1919 and lasted several years after it. Even in this sense, however, the movement had a very narrow sociological base.[5] The most spectacular and most often noted aspect of this intellectual transformation, the "Literary Revolution," was at first just the work of writers and publicists. As for the two steps that contributed most to the movement's success, they affected only the intelligentsia: the creation of a magazine intended for an intellectual audience, and the reorganization of Peking University.

In January 1917 a twenty-six-year-old academic named Hu Shih, who had just completed his thesis for Columbia University, proposed that all Chinese who made their living as writers henceforth use the spoken language (*pai-hua*) instead of the literary language (*wen-yen*). This was the essence of the Literary Revolution. His proposal sounds like a rather technical measure, one that hardly merits such an emphatic description as revolution! In fact, however, a key choice was involved. The Chinese literati wrote in a language that for all its beauties had long been moribund. And they spoke in another, the really living language, the only one understood by ordinary people. All of Chinese literature (with the exception of such despised genres as the novel, which was read only on the sly) was written in

---

[5] But see p. 43 below, particularly note 28 on the broadening of the movement's social base and its coalescence with nationalist currents during the spring and summer of 1919.

wen-yen. The switch from *wen-yen* to *pai-hua* was something like the switch from Latin to the national vernaculars in Europe. In recommending the adoption of *pai-hua*, Hu Shih was pursuing a social goal—that of making works of literature accessible to all. He also urged that literature be tied more directly to the life of the people. In his eyes the Literary Revolution, far from being limited to linguistic reform, implied a new literature, new genres, new styles.[6] In particular it implied the jettisoning of all the outworn literary traditions and stylistic conventions on which the Chinese literati had thrived: extreme conciseness, obscure allusions, classical quotations, and the like. In opposition to this aristocratic literature—literature that allies of Hu Shih would call "pedantic, unintelligible, and obscurantist"—it was high time to promote a popular literature, one that was simple, clear, and meaningful. The "pedants" tried to defend themselves and the classical literary tradition against this violent onslaught, but their efforts were futile: Hu Shih's ideas carried the day, in part because they echoed earlier proposals that had been advanced with increasing urgency in the two decades before May Fourth. By 1920 most writers had adopted *pai-hua*, and periodicals quickly followed suit.

In the front rank of the new periodicals was *Hsin ch'ing-nien* (New Youth; subtitled, in French, *La Jeunesse*), the most important magazine of the May Fourth period. It was *Hsin ch'ing-nien* that published Hu Shih's "revolutionary" manifesto of January 1917 (under the modest title "Some Tentative Suggestions for the Reform of Chinese Literature"), and the following month a warm endorsement of Hu's proposal by the magazine's editor-in-chief, Ch'en Tu-hsiu. Ch'en, who had founded the magazine a year and a half earlier, is one of the most engaging figures in modern Chinese history. Born in 1879, the same year as Stalin and Trotsky, to a family of well-to-do civil servants,[7] Ch'en began a classical course of study but failed to complete it.

[6] He considered language reform and literary vitality related. "A dead language," he wrote, "cannot yield a living literature."

[7] The names of Trotsky and Ch'en Tu-hsiu were often linked later on. As we shall see in Chapter Three, the two men met similar fates.

Instead of preparing for the third and last examination of the traditional cycle, the one that opened the door to the highest posts in the Imperial administration, he opted for a Western-style course of study. He took a French course in ship design in Hangchow, and then at twenty-three left to study in Tokyo. He lived and studied for years in Japan, with occasional intervals in China, where he taught and edited revolutionary journals. Ch'en thus belonged to that class of returned students whose influence we have already noted, those who had been educated in foreign schools and returned to China determined to introduce at home what they had seen and learned abroad.

Ch'en Tu-hsiu was the perfect type of the Westernized radical, a veritable Alexander Herzen of modern China. So pro-Western was he, and so disdainful of the Chinese tradition, that he refused to join Sun Yat-sen's Revolutionary Alliance because he considered it excessively nationalistic. He nonetheless participated in the Revolution of 1911, which led to his appointment as commissioner of education for Anhwei, his native province. He did not keep the post for long; in 1913 he came out against Yuan Shih-k'ai, and when the Second Revolution was crushed fled to Japan. Shortly after his return to China in September 1915, he founded *Hsin ch'ing-nien* in Shanghai. The times had at last caught up with Ch'en's radicalism. For the next twelve years he would occupy the forefront of the Chinese literary and political stage.

At first Ch'en put out *Hsin ch'ing-nien* by himself, but soon many of the most brilliant avant-garde intellectuals joined its editorial committee. In a sense the journal played the role of *Le Globe* for young men who were even more impatient to finish off dead gods than the most hot-headed French Romantics had ever been.[8] Published at a time when strict laws severely curtailed freedom of the press, often forced to suspend publication—sometimes by the authorities, sometimes by lack of funds

---

[8] [*Le Globe* was founded in Paris in 1824 as the literary and philosophical organ of the rising Romantic school. Like the contributors to *Hsin ch'ing-nien*, the French Romantics became increasingly preoccupied with social questions; in 1830 *Le Globe* was sold to the Saint-Simonians, and many of its contributors became important figures in the July Monarchy.—Trans.]

—*Hsin ch'ing-nien* had a devoted student following that took its every editorial pronouncement as an article of faith. These pronouncements were rarely related to the current political scene. For Ch'en Tu-hsiu the illness went deeper and had to be attacked at its roots. The real problem, he felt, was centuries of stagnation, and not such latter-day trivia as the maneuverings of the ephemeral governments then succeeding one another in Peking.

The last important innovation of the era, which was at once the cause and the symptom of the cultural revolution, was the reform of Peking University. Here I am afraid I must burden the reader with yet another Chinese name to remember and a new biographical sketch to read, for this reform was essentially the work of one man, Ts'ai Yüan-p'ei. Even more than Ch'en Tu-hsiu, Ts'ai Yüan-p'ei was a man of two cultures. He acquired his Western education in France and Germany, having already become an accomplished scholar in Chinese. At an exceptionally early age he passed the entire cycle of civil service examinations, a distinction that won him not only a reputation as "the literary genius of Kiangnan" (the collective name for Anhwei, Kiangsu, and Kiangsi, the three provinces of the lower Yangtze), but also the coveted post of Imperial editor. As a revolutionary, Ts'ai resigned from this post after the collapse of the Hundred Days' Reform. As a member of the T'ung Meng Hui, he became minister of education in Sun Yat-sen's government following the Revolution of 1911, only to quit this post, too, when Yuan Shih-k'ai became President. A few years later, when the Peking government offered to make him governor of his native province of Chekiang, he wired his refusal from France. But in December 1916 he accepted the next appointment offered—as chancellor of Peking University. This revolutionary was indeed preeminently an educator; for his accomplishments as chancellor of Peking University, he was known as the Father of the Chinese Renaissance.

Peking University had been founded during the Hundred Days' Reform. Twenty years later, when Ts'ai's administration began, it had left behind the forward-looking circumstances of its founding and was known primarily for its conservatism. Its students, for the most part sons of high-ranking government officials, regarded the university less as an educational institution than as the surest stepping-stone to an administrative career. The professors themselves were civil servants; they were judged not by the quality of their teaching or learning but by their bureaucratic rank, and they were addressed as *Ta-jen*, "Your Excellency." The moral level both of the students and of their excellencies was notoriously low, as is clear from contemporary nicknames for the university: "the gambling den," "the fountainhead of ribaldry and bawdiness," "the brothel brigade."[9]

As a result of Ts'ai Yüan-p'ei's concern with the students' moral well-being, a Society for the Promotion of Virtue was founded at the university in 1918. His great accomplishment, however, was not to restrain license but to bring genuine liberalism to an institution previously untouched by it. Ts'ai defended academic freedom against government pressure, he allowed all schools of thought a voice, and he recruited a heterogeneous but first-rate faculty. One of the first men he appointed was Ch'en Tu-hsiu, whom he made dean of the Faculty of Letters (one of the four schools making up the university). Hu Shih taught the history of Chinese philosophy, and Li Ta-chao, soon to become one of China's first Marxists, was the university's head librarian.[10] The university soon became a forum for debates between traditional literati and modern intellectuals. The result was to bring the latter together and make possible the formation of a group of innovators. It was they who won the students' support. The May Fourth Movement was a youth movement, in which professors in their thirties and their student followers sought with young men's passion to impose young men's values on their society.[11]

---

[9] See Chow Tse-tsung, *The May Fourth Movement: Intellectual Revolution in Modern China* (Cambridge, Mass.: Harvard University Press, 1960), pp. 49–50.

[10] Li had a profound influence on his assistant librarian, Mao Tse-tung.

[11] Ch'en Tu-hsiu, dean of the Faculty of Letters at thirty-eight, was one of the oldest of these ideologists.

The Movement's Direction and Scope

P'o-chiu li-hsin! Down with the old, up with the new![12]

Given its youthful orientation, it is not surprising that the May Fourth Movement was first and foremost an iconoclastic movement. Needless to say, it was an article written for *Hsin ch'ing-nien* by Ch'en Tu-hsiu that contained the most striking example of an attack on tradition combined with an exaltation of youth. Here is the opening of the lead article in the journal's first issue, entitled, unsurprisingly, "A Call to Youth": "When Chinese want to praise someone, they say, 'Even though he's young, he acts like a man of mature years.' What do Englishmen and Americans say when they want to give one another moral support? 'Stay young in heart, no matter what your age.' This is one characteristic difference between Western and Oriental ways of thought." Then Ch'en waxed lyrical: "Youth is like the dawning of spring, the sunrise, new grass and fruit trees in blossom, a newly sharpened blade. It is the most precious time of life. The function of youth in society is the same as that of new cells in the human body: in the metabolic process, the old and rotten is constantly replaced by the new and vital."[13]

Ch'en went on to urge his readers to choose from the world's storehouse of ideas those that were "fresh, vital, and adapted to the present phase of the struggle for survival," and to abandon those that were "old, rotten, and useless" to the process of natural selection.[14] He concluded with six principles to be observed by youth, the cumulative import of which may seem somewhat confused to a Westerner, but which to a Chinese student represented a clear rejection of the model that young Chinese traditionally had been urged to follow: "Be independent, not submissive; progressive, not conservative; outspoken, not reserved; cosmopolitan, not parochial; practical, not formalist; and scien-

---

[12] In August 1966 Red Guards painted these four characters on the walls of Peking, and in doing so revealed their direct descent from the May Fourth Movement.
[13] Adapted from Chow Tse-tsung, pp. 45–46.
[14] Darwinism won a large following in China before and during the May Fourth Movement.

tific, not imaginative." This was to turn upside down Confucian morality, which preached respect for the aged and for tradition, submission to codes and rituals, restraint and obedience.[15] The hateful was no longer audacity and self-expression, but timidity and conformist repression.

Confucianism, classical culture, and traditional society were all one. A lucid madman has revealed to us its true nature, which lay hidden behind the hypocritical façade of words. This madman was the hero of a novella by Lu Hsün published by *Hsin ch'ing-nien* in 1918. Gripped by a persecution mania and the conviction that his family, his neighbors, and the whole world wanted to kill him so they could eat him, Lu's hero wonders if man has always eaten man. He opens a history book; up and down every page are written the words "humanitarianism," "justice," and "virtue." But when he scrutinizes the pages more closely, between the lines he sees two words recurring throughout the book: "Eat men." On the last page of the tale, the author—modern China's most famous writer—made his message even more explicit: "I am party to a history that counts four thousand years of cannibalism."[16]

In a sense the rest of the May Fourth Movement was just a corollary of this fundamental critique, but even if its message can be summed up in a few lines, it was a message that profoundly transformed the lives and ideas of people throughout

---

[15] Contrast Ch'en's extravagant praise of the virtues of youth with the emphasis on the slow maturation of the fully human man exemplified by Confucius himself: "The Master said, 'At fifteen, I set my heart upon learning. At thirty, I had planted my feet firm upon the ground. At forty, I no longer suffered from perplexities. At fifty, I knew what were the biddings of Heaven. At sixty, I heard them with docile ear. At seventy, I could follow the dictates of my own heart; for what I desired no longer overstepped the boundaries of right.' " *The Analects of Confucius*, trans. Arthur Waley (London: Allen & Unwin, 1938), II, 4 (p. 88).

[16] Lu Hsün, *Diary of a Madman*. The title and structure of this novella were taken from Gogol, but Lu Hsün is more often compared to Gorky. Although nothing could be further from Lu's work than Gorky's long, realistic, autobiographical narratives— Lu wrote primarily novellas, short essays, and polemical articles notable for their irony and concealed sensibility—the two men were decidedly similar in general outlook. Both wrote sympathetically of the lives of the illiterate and unfortunate. Neither ever joined the Communist Party, but both supported its attacks on the old order, sometimes as independent critics, sometimes as fellow-travelers. Both died in 1936 and were the object of widespread adulation after their death.

China.[17] Under attack were all the customs that interfered with self-fulfillment: arranged marriages, bound feet, subservience of younger sons. The three sacred bonds that Confucianism had made the basis of social organization—the subordination of subject to sovereign, of son to father, of wife to husband—the May Fourth Movement rejected as responsible for the prevailing despotism of both the family and the state. The movement's leading demand was for the liberation of women, in China as elsewhere the first victims of traditional constraints. Equality of the sexes, the right to love, the kind of generational conflict portrayed in Turgenev's *Fathers and Sons*, hatred for the oppressive and supremely hypocritical family—these were the recurrent themes of post–May Fourth literature, and they were developed with conviction, if not always with talent.

But it was not enough to denounce the misdeeds of Confucianism and combat its continuing destructive effects on the family and society. It remained to subject Confucian dogmas and "sacred history" to the kind of pitiless and unrestrained critique that had been devoted to Christianity in nineteenth-century Europe. Groups that might have taken their inspiration from Renan debated the authenticity of the classics, rejecting those they considered fables handed down from generation to generation and generally contesting the authorship of Confucius. This effort at a critical evaluation of antiquity is a measure of the distance between China's modern intellectuals and the Chinese cultural tradition; in part it also reflected the influence of Western scientific methods of textual criticism.[18] This leads us to the last—the positive[19]—aspect of the systematically destructive undertaking that was the May Fourth Movement.

What were the positive elements in May Fourth ideology?

17 The effects are still being felt today. In certain spheres Communist China is simply trying (and this is no mean feat) to extend to the masses a spiritual revolution already undergone by the intellectuals.

18 The influence of the West was by no means the only one at work. Chinese intellectuals were also following in the footsteps of the great late-Ming and early-Ch'ing philosophers, who earlier had challenged neo-Confucian dogmas.

19 This adjective is not intended to imply a value judgment, but simply to point up the constructive motivation behind a movement whose most obvious result was the destruction of old values.

They were faith in progress, democracy, and science, confidence in the limitless potential of human reason, etc.—in short, the optimistic expectations of eighteenth- and nineteenth-century Europe. The rejection of Chinese ideals and the adoption of European ones were linked: in China pro-Westernism followed naturally from the criticism of Chinese values. The growing conviction that the Chinese tradition was useless led to the search for a foreign substitute. The most vehement denigrators of the national past were the warmest apologists for Western culture. "Chinese thought is a thousand years behind Western thought," wrote the man I have called the Herzen of China. It was the writings of this man, Ch'en Tu-hsiu, that made most explicit the relationship between anti-Confucianism and Westernization, notably in an article of January 1919 in *Hsin ch'ing-nien* written in reply to his critics:

You have accused this magazine of being out to destroy Confucianism, the Sacred Rites, the "national essence," womanly chastity, traditional morality (loyalty, filial piety, chastity), traditional art (Chinese opera), traditional religion (gods and spirits), ancient literature and old-style politics (special privileges and government by individual men).

We admit that all these accusations are well-founded, but we do not plead guilty. If we have committed all these crimes, it is solely because of our support for two gentlemen, Mr. Democracy and Mr. Science. As supporters of Democracy, we are obliged to attack Confucianism, rituals, womanly chastity, traditional morality, and old-style politics. As advocates of Science, we cannot help but oppose traditional art and traditional religion. In the name of both Democracy and Science, we are constrained to deplore ancient literature and the cult of the "national essence." If we consider the question dispassionately, has this magazine committed any crime other than that of supporting Democracy and Science? If your answer is no, then please do not confine your disapproval to this magazine. Be brave and tackle the problem at its roots: take a stand against the two gentlemen, Mr. Democracy and Mr. Science.[20]

Signs of a pro-Western frenzy were everywhere to be seen among modern intellectuals. Popular slogans such as "Total

[20] Based on Chow Tse-tsung, p. 59.

Westernization" were common. Western-language subtitles were given the leading movement journals; for example, the magazine *Hsin ch'ao* (New Tide), second in importance only to *Hsin ch'ing-nien*, bore the subtitle *Renaissance*. Wholesale translations of Western works were undertaken; most May Fourth periodicals were divided into two equal parts, one of which was reserved for translations. Not only did movement writers, notably Lu Hsün, devote much of their time and energy to translating essays and novels from English, French, German, and Russian,[21] but the novel as such was deliberately cultivated by contemporary Chinese writers, in part as a reaction against the orthodox tradition that refused to take the genre seriously, in part out of deference to its importance in Western literature. We have mentioned the leading role of returned students in the cultural revolution; we need only add here that of its three guiding spirits, Ch'en Tu-hsiu returned from Japan in 1915, Ts'ai Yüan-p'ei from France in 1916, and Hu Shih from the United States in 1917. Finally, there were the invitations to such Western philosophers as John Dewey, who arrived in Peking three days before the May Fourth Incident to begin an extraordinarily successful series of lectures that lasted more than two years, and Bertrand Russell, who arrived in 1920 from Moscow and whose books and courses gave him a greater influence on young intellectuals during the last phase of the May Fourth Movement than any other contemporary thinker.[22]

The unmitigated scorn of Ch'en Tu-hsiu and others for their own culture often led to an unthinking enthusiasm for all aspects of Western civilization.[23] These feelings of national inferiority and idolatry for a foreign culture seem hard to reconcile with the spirit of the student demonstration of May 4, 1919, which was a nationalist reaction against imperialism and the annexation of national territory. In fact, however, the two cur-

---

21 This had the effect of further increasing Western influence on their own writings, and through them on the Chinese language itself, whose vocabulary came to include more and more terms of Western origin.

22 A monthly review devoted exclusively to Russell's thought was founded in January 1921.

23 Ch'en's image of France under the Third Republic bore little more resemblance to the original than Voltaire's China bore to the Empire of the early Ch'ing.

rents were in no way contradictory. The May Fourth Movement was opposed to Chinese culture, not the Chinese nation. Indeed, it opposed Chinese culture out of love for the Chinese nation; it was in the name of the living China that youthful patriots wanted to rescue their fellow Chinese from the encumbrance of a dead culture. The passage from Ch'en Tu-hsiu quoted earlier, in which he puts Chinese thought a thousand years behind the West, continues, "If we keep on dreaming about our dead dynasties, our people will be cut off from the twentieth century and will be reduced to living in slavery and bestiality." Elsewhere Ch'en was even more explicit:

We really don't know which if any of our traditional institutions can be adapted for survival in the modern world. I would rather see the destruction of our "national essence" than the final extinction of our race because it is unable to adapt. The Babylonians are no more; what good does their civilization do them today? In the words of a Chinese proverb, "Where there is no scalp, what can the hair adhere to?" The world is constantly moving forward, and it will not wait for us.[24]

Thus the very violence of its revolt against Chinese culture gave the May Fourth Movement its normal, rightful place in the intellectual evolution of modern China from culturalism to nationalism.[25] Just a few years after the Revolution of 1911, the country had entered a new phase. Once the Manchus had been eliminated and could no longer serve as scapegoats, the genuinely national character of China's misfortunes became clear. Hence the furious attacks on Chinese institutions by the most radical critics, or the most farseeing ones. Although the object of the assault may have changed, the motive behind it remained constant: to give China the strength to defend herself against humiliation and exploitation. Anti-Western nationalism and cul-

24 Based on Chow Tse-tsung, p. 46.
25 Culturalism is the term used to describe the Sinocentrism of the Opium War era as distinguished from modern nationalism. These concepts are borrowed from Joseph R. Levenson; see his *Liang Ch'i-ch'ao and the Mind of Modern China* (Cambridge, Mass.: Harvard University Press, 1959), especially pp. 109–22, and also his *Confucian China and Its Modern Fate: The Problem of Intellectual Continuity* (Berkeley: University of California Press, 1958).

tural pro-Westernism were not antithetical, but complementary.[26]

It is not surprising, then, that May Fourth was chosen to symbolize the broad cultural revolution, which surpassed the May Fourth Incident in significance as it preceded and survived it in time. Every contemporary witness—those who deplored and excoriated the new teachers' pernicious influence as well as those who encouraged and supported what seemed to them a movement of great promise—saw the student demonstration in Peking as the direct result and dynamic expression of an intellectual transformation. Shanghai and Canton followed Peking's lead, and within weeks the Peking students' demonstration was transformed into a national movement.[27] Above all, the movement drew the country's different social classes together in a joint effort.[28] Born of a nation's will to live, the May Fourth Movement could count among its legitimate heirs both the Kuomintang, the party of nationalism, and Chinese Communism.[29]

From May Fourth to Marxism

In the twenty years between the Literary Revolution and the Sino-Japanese War, the Chinese intelligentsia moved almost uninterruptedly leftward—to be precise, toward Marxism. This movement picked up momentum in 1927. In nineteenth-century France the decline of Socialist thought coincided with a new, successful phase in the history of the labor movement. In China, by contrast, political defeat—the crushing of the Chinese Communist Party—preceded the triumph of Marxist ideas, whose rapid spread benefited from the counterrevolutionary terror that accompanied the Kuomintang's rise to power. But from the earli-

26 For pertinent remarks on the relation between the two, see Stuart Schram's Introduction to Mao Ze-dong, *Une Etude de l'éducation physique* (Paris: Mouton, 1963).

27 The geographical extension of a political movement had much more significance in China, where regionalism was still a very lively force, than it would have had in a Western country.

28 "Tradesmen's strikes" reinforced and prolonged the student demonstrations. The nascent bourgeoisie participated in the revolutionary movement only so long as its main goal was national independence.

29 For this paragraph and indeed for my entire discussion of the May Fourth Movement, I am heavily indebted to Chow Tse-tsung's standard work on the subject.

est years of the May Fourth Movement, the trend was evident. More specifically, as early as the May Fourth Incident there were certain radical tendencies in philosophy and especially in literature that were simply confirmed by the passage of time. Accordingly, without trying to trace the intellectual history of China between 1919 and 1949, I shall merely touch here on the later fruits of the May Fourth Movement and on a number of philosophical and literary controversies, concluding with a brief balance sheet of the war of ideas on the eve of the Sino-Japanese War.[30]

The triumph of the May Fourth Movement was swift, total, and dazzling. We have seen, for example, how easily *pai-hua* won acceptance. In 1920 the Ministry of National Education issued a decree making *pai-hua* the language of instruction in the elementary schools, thus giving legal sanction to a choice already made by the users of the language themselves. To the four hundred magazines that began to use *pai-hua* in 1919, according to Hu Shih, must be added the hundreds of new magazines that appeared in the next few years. A number of them were the organs of new literary schools, which brings us to another result of the May Fourth Movement: the extraordinary literary effervescence to which the Literary Revolution gave rise. Between 1921 and 1925—to say nothing of later years, when the movement continued to flourish—more than a hundred literary groups were founded. One of the oldest, and the most influential, was the Society for Literary Studies, founded in January 1921 with the explicit intention of bringing together writers favoring linguistic reform. The same year saw the appearance of a rival group, the Creation Society, whose members were equally warm in their support of the Literary Revolution.

This rivalry between two equally "modern" schools of writers gives us an inkling of the price paid for the exuberance of the May Fourth Movement; differences of opinion sprang up among the victors of the day, differences that were quickly followed

[30] The Rectification Campaign (*cheng feng*) launched by Mao Tse-tung in Yenan in 1942 is the most famous, if not the most important, of the cultural developments omitted from this discussion.

by splits. The May Fourth Movement had united all the "new intellectuals" around such vague or general concepts as democracy, science, humanitarianism, liberalism, and reason, and even more around a common desire for destruction. Success having been won—and so swiftly!—it was inevitable that differences should arise; inevitable, for example, that those who were content with a cultural and literary revolution would oppose those who insisted on a political and social revolution as well. In the dangerous days of the May Fourth Incident and the repression immediately following it, the coalition held together reasonably well. Afterward, the men preoccupied with politics moved away from the litterateurs, the radicals from the moderates. On opposite sides of the dividing line were the movement's two leading figures: Hu Shih, who died in Taiwan in 1962, and Ch'en Tu-hsiu, the future founder of the Chinese Communist Party.

In 1918, in an effort to build a mass movement, Ch'en and Li Ta-chao founded a new review, *Mei-chou p'ing-lun* (Weekly Critic), which was more politically oriented than *Hsin ch'ing-nien* and more radical in its politics. The following year Hu vehemently attacked what he called "isms," by which he meant systems of thought with universal claims or appeal, notably Socialism and Communism. He contrasted the "isms" (*chu-i*) with "real problems" (*wen-t'i*). He urged putting aside ideological disputes and attacking concrete problems one by one; in short, he made a Deweyan case for pragmatism, if one dares use an "ism" in discussing Hu Shih. This could not be reconciled with the increasingly Marxian views of Ch'en Tu-hsiu, and in the fall of 1920 the original *Hsin ch'ing-nien* group broke up. The liberals—Hu Shih and Lu Hsün—quit the editorial committee, and the magazine became a Communist publication.[31]

The schism deepened in the next few years. Between 1920 and 1937 Chinese intellectual life was marked by a series of public controversies, whose nature shows both the intellectuals' increasing preoccupation with social questions and the growing audi-

[31] Actually, the Chinese Communist Party was not founded until the following year (1921), but Ch'en, with the aid of a Comintern agent, was already making preparations for a founding congress.

ence for Marxist ideas. Most of the controversies were philosophical: over the relative merits of Eastern and Western civilization, the competing claims of religion and science, the nature of Chinese society, the proper periodization of Chinese history, the value of Marxism, and similar weighty questions. Simply to enumerate this succession of subjects is to suggest the direction the argument took; in about fifteen years the majority opinion, initially pro-Western, became first positivist and scientific and then materialist, and finally was won over to Marxism as such. Hu Shih, who during the first great controversy was part of the modernist majority (indeed, the leading defender of Western societies), gradually stopped participating, not simply because he now belonged to the minority, but because the subjects under discussion had ceased to interest him. This was especially true of the last controversy (1936–37), which I have not yet touched on. This dispute took place wholly within the materialist camp and was aimed at Yeh Ch'ing, who during the preceding quarrel had been Marxism's most conspicuous defender. In his enthusiasm for materialist ideas, it was now claimed, he overrated such outdated precursors as d'Holbach, Helvétius, and Diderot, and thus was guilty of slighting the Marxist classics.

Literature followed a parallel development, conveniently summarized in the title of an article published in 1927 by one of the controversialists: "From Literary Revolution to Revolutionary Literature." Certain landmarks of the controversy are illuminated by the conflicts and regroupings of literary schools. Behind the rivalry of the Society for Literary Studies and the Creation Society in the early 1920's lay a debate between two approaches to literature—a realism oriented toward social questions, as practiced by the first group, and the doctrine of art for art's sake, as arrogantly advanced by the young writers of the second. In 1925, however, the main force behind the Creation Society, Kuo Mo-jo, was converted to Marxism, and the organization accordingly moved to the left of the Society for Literary Studies. "I have now found the key to all the problems that once seemed to me contradictory and unsolvable!" Kuo exclaimed. And a little later: "Literature cannot justify its existence today except by its capacity to hasten the Socialist revolution. . . . We are living in the age of propaganda, and literature is the cutting edge of propaganda." In short, literature was a weapon to be used for lack of anything better, an inferior substitute for direct action. Soon afterward Kuo joined the Northern Expedition as a political commissar in the revolutionary army.

Other writers, however, and not necessarily lesser ones (Lu Hsün, for example), though they identified with the oppressed masses they described, though they may even have prayed for the coming of the revolution, refused to put literature at the service of propaganda. This hurdle was ultimately cleared in 1930, with the creation of the League of Left-Wing Writers and the winning over of Lu Hsün. As late as 1928 and 1929, at a time when he was engaged in bitter polemics against ivory-tower writers who shunned all political and social commitment, Lu had been just as unsparing of naïve young revolutionary writers who showed more enthusiasm than talent. When he suddenly agreed to sponsor the league, then being organized, he was immediately elected president; but he remained isolated among the seven members of the executive committee, which had a pro-Communist majority. During 1931–33 the group's political line was set by Ch'ü Ch'iu-pai, a former general secretary of the Chinese Communist Party.[32] With the founding of the League of Left-Wing Writers, and particularly from 1932 on, the Communist hold on Chinese literature became steadily more pronounced.

By the eve of the Sino-Japanese War, which for a time made patriots of everyone, Marxism had come to dominate not only literature but every sector of intellectual life. Of course certain groups were untouched by Marxism, and others continued to

[32] Ch'ü is a memorable figure. He quit the league's secretariat in January 1934 to become "minister of education" in the Chinese Soviet Republic. Left behind in Kiangsi when the Long March got under way, he was captured by the Kuomintang and sentenced to death. In his autobiography, written in prison, this top-level party official emerges as a romantic and an idealist troubled by the necessities of organization; yet he neither renounced his faith nor sought to minimize his role in the party. He died at the age of thirty-six after writing a final poem, singing the "Internationale" in Russian as the bullets struck. See T. A. Hsia, "Ch'ü Ch'iu-pai's Autobiographical Writings," *China Quarterly*, No. 25 (1966), pp. 176–212.

oppose it. Among the latter was a nationalist conservative movement, which was largely the creation of the ruling regime.[33]
More lively and spontaneous than the conservatives, but deliberately confining its debates to academic matters, was the liberal
school, in which a fairly large number of intellectuals took
refuge. The liberals were oriented toward the United States,
whose educational institutions and influence had supplanted
Europe's in their esteem.[34] By the 1930's a scientific community,
committed to the methods and exacting standards of "Western"
science, was beginning to flourish.

Whatever this rather remarkable flowering may have amounted to—and in the fields of archeology and prehistory, for example, it resulted in the discovery of Peking Man and the excavation
of the site of one of China's first capitals—the intellectual activity
of the country between 1930 and 1937 was indisputably dominated and shaped by Marxism and the hope of revolution.
Among the intellectuals, the Marxists were by far the most active,
the most productive, the most influential. The New Social Sciences Publications series, 70 per cent of whose post-1928 works
were of Marxist inspiration, was increasingly successful. The
most often translated foreign authors were, in descending order,
Marx, Engels, Lenin, and Bukharin. The best-selling literary
works were translations of Russian novels, particularly Soviet
novels. Indeed, popular demand is a revealing gauge of the dominant trend: the prestige of Marxism and the Soviet Union was
even greater among the consumers of intellectual products—
essentially students—than it was among the far smaller number
of creative writers and popularizers. According to a survey made
a few months before the Sino-Japanese War in several Christian
universities,[35] a growing proportion of Chinese students were

---

[33] See Chapter Five.

[34] A considerable number of researchers were educated in American universities or
in the colleges and universities founded in China by American Protestant missionaries,
and many were employed by institutions founded by Americans or supported with
American funds, notably the Academia Sinica, the National Library in Peking, and
the National Institute for Agricultural Research.

[35] Kiang Wen-han, "Secularization of Christian Colleges," *Chinese Recorder*, May
1937; cited in James C. Thomson, Jr., *While China Faced West: American Reformers
in Nationalist China, 1928–1937* (Cambridge, Mass.: Harvard University Press, 1969),
pp. 232–33.

specializing in the social sciences and preferred Marxist textbooks, and religious indifference was spreading; indifferent to
their own intellectual development and concerned only with
participation in a collective struggle, most students looked to
fundamental change, a total upheaval in Chinese society, for a
solution to the country's problems. Such was the dominant state
of mind among those Chinese who were twenty years old in
1937 and in a position to think about something besides the next
day's bowl of rice.

Why was the evolution of ideas so swift, the reversal of opinion
so total? Reason, liberty, progress, democracy—the May Fourth
Movement introduced to China the ideals of liberalism, a young,
vital, conquering liberalism. Wonderstruck, the country's young
intellectuals were impatient to use their new liberty; they could,
they should, try everything. Some twenty years later, the choice
had been made: Marxism ruled almost alone. All possibilities
but one were again ruled out, and the age of liberalism soon came
to seem but a brief intermission between centuries of Confucian
conformity and the reign of a new orthodoxy. "Now that the
slaves of Confucius and Chu Hsi are declining in number,[36] the
slaves of Marx and Kropotkin are taking their place," wrote
Hu Shih at a time when anarchism was still competing with
Marxism for the ear of the intellectuals. The liberals' bitterness
is understandable: scarcely had China awakened to liberalism
when it fell under the spell of a new certainty. The beautiful
blaze they had lit in the name of intellectual freedom to illumi-
nate and purify China had proved just a flash in the pan.

Yet this turn of events seems in retrospect to have been natural
enough. There is, after all, a logical progression from iconoclasm
to revolutionary radicalism. Ch'en Tu-hsiu followed as natural
a route as Hu Shih, a route perhaps less unfaithful to their initial
revolt than Hu Shih's fidelity to liberalism. Moreover, there
have been few historical situations less receptive to liberalism
broadly conceived (a critical outlook, qualified views, a preference for the middle way and gradual solutions) than that of
China from 1919 to 1949. During these thirty years, even more

---

[36] Chu Hsi was a twelfth-century neo-Confucian philosopher.

than during the preceding three-quarters of a century, Chinese affairs were pervaded by a sense of urgency that could not accommodate long delays, patient investigations, careful preparations. From liberalism China kept no more—could keep no more—than the initial euphoria; not the long flowering, but solely the moment of illusion that followed the crucial explosion, the revolt against dogmatism. Liberalism had one hour of glory, one hour of life; whereupon, having accomplished the indispensable work of ground-clearing, it was trampled to death by the hardy children to whom it had helped give birth and whose further growth it could only inhibit.

These rebellious children loomed up on the left, to be sure, but also on the right; before succumbing to the blows of Marxism, liberalism first fell victim to nationalism. At this point the history of ideas, which is never self-sufficient, clearly reflects other pressures. For the moment, it is enough to say that the development of modern China (as I see it, at any rate) was dominated by the interacting pressures of imperialism and overpowering social ills. The force of these pressures permanently eliminated the center as a political power, and in theory the way was left open for two conflicting experiments, one national, the other social. Conflicting, but for a brief period united against the status quo and its defenders,[37] and at the very end united again: as it turned out, the revolution was both social *and* national. The Communist Party appropriated the entire heritage of the May Fourth Movement. Thus the last phase of the ideological struggle was not exactly or not simply the triumph of Marxism over nationalism, but the absorption of the latter by the former. Marxism proved itself the most effective system (the most effective "ism") not only for attacking social iniquities, but also for restoring a national pride that had been sorely tried for a century. Here was a doctrine borrowed from the West that condemned the West, especially with the addition of Lenin's anti-imperialist gloss, a doctrine that put China on the road to

[37] In this sense, the strange alliance of 1924–27 (pp. 23–24 above) is understandable; it was a union of "modern" groups fighting the old China represented by the warlords, many of whom expressly claimed to stand for Confucian ideals.

the modernization she so clearly needed while sparing her the humiliation of aping more advanced nations and forever lagging in their wake.

Moreover, as a philosophy of history, Marxism made it possible to rehabilitate much of the national heritage, which had been condemned *in toto* by the May Fourth iconoclasts. Now that Confucianism was definitely dead, now that it belonged entirely to the past, there was no reason not to consider it "objectively." May Fourth had been a period of invective and sarcasm, of active combat against Confucian "oppression." Once Confucianism was vanquished, however, the victors could be generous and acknowledge that at one time it had embodied the forces of progress. Thus the Chinese cultural tradition did not have to be rejected root and branch; moreover—and this was essential—it could be seen as in no way inferior to the West's.

Japan has copied Western techniques, but it has remained immutably itself, from hara-kiri to kamikaze planes; this persistence of Japaneseness has been generally acknowledged for some twenty-five years. Today, on the basis of such signs as the partial rehabilitation of Confucius and the renewed manifestations of secular xenophobia, one frequently hears an analogous theory about China: that Communist China represents a return to the Chinese past, eternal China rediscovered after a long period of upheaval. According to this theory, the Communist revolution made it possible to loop the loop. With its success, China regained the national pride and unity of the years before the Opium Wars: 1949 was the reply to 1840, the barbarian gauntlet returned. In establishing a new orthodoxy, the revolution was in the most authentic Chinese tradition and indeed constituted an admirable example of historical continuity: after a period of troubles, a new dynasty is always established and the cycle begun again. Or, more precisely, the eternal cycle continues, with Mao founding the nth dynasty.

It is tempting to argue this way. Didn't Stalin's *Ex Oriente Lux* signal the Slavophiles' revenge? But such arguments willfully ignore a fundamental truth: the modernity of the China that emerged from the May Fourth Movement. There was no return to the past, no road back; Communist China has had to face the problems of our century. Not only the "national Communism" of Peking in the 1960's but the conservative nationalism of the Kuomintang itself was fundamentally different from the old cultural Sinocentrism—the former despite its messianic pretensions, the latter despite Chiang Kai-shek's anachronistic attempt to revive Confucian ethics and ideology. After a century of travail, Chinese nationalism is less the assertion of cultural supremacy than the expression of a living creature's will to live. We are much closer to the Bandung Conference than to the Celestial Empire.

The road traveled by the Chinese intelligentsia in the span of three generations, traveled in the sense of experience as well as of accomplishment, runs approximately from the concept of the Celestial Empire to modern nationalism and on to Marxism. Surely this journey represents one of the most prodigious feats of the human intellect—in the strictest sense of the term, an intellectual revolution.

3. The Early Years of the Communist Party

Just 28 years after the founding of the Chinese Communist Party (CCP) in 1921, the Communists were the rulers of China. Their rapid rise to power poses two questions. First, what part in this extraordinary success was played by Marxist doctrine? Second, was the victory a vindication of classical Marxism, and if not, did the Chinese experience represent a key extension of the doctrine or a major deviation from it?

In trying to answer these two questions, let us look first at what happened during the first half of the party's struggle for power, the years 1921–35. I have chosen 1935 as a cutoff date not only because it was the year of the most celebrated episode of this entire history, the legendary Long March, but also because it was the year the Comintern ordered the national Communist parties to adopt the tactic of a united front with socialists and anti-fascist democrats. At a time when Japanese imperialism was tightening its grip, the Chinese version of the French and Spanish Popular Fronts was a policy giving the national struggle top priority. Beginning in 1935 the CCP transformed itself into a patriotic organization; of its traditional program almost the sole remaining vestige by 1937 was anti-imperialism. Up to 1935 the CCP's overriding concern was a more conventionally Marxist one; the party was first and foremost the instrument of social revolution. First it tried to foment risings of urban workers; this was the orthodox stage of CCP history. Then it retreated to the depths of the countryside; this was the peasant stage.

The Orthodox Stage, 1921–1927

During the first six years of its existence, the CCP represented and regarded itself as the party of the working class. It tried to advance the revolution by using the proletariat as its base, and strikes and urban uprisings as its weapons. It also participated in the armed struggle against the warlords, but did not lead it. The party's minority participation in a movement led by bourgeois revolutionaries is a watershed in the first stage of its history. The first phase, 1921–24, saw the very modest beginnings of an autonomous revolutionary party; the second, 1924–27, brought alliance with the great bourgeois revolutionary party, the Kuomintang.

In the party's first years, its following and influence were negligible. Although I have called this the orthodox stage, the CCP was in no way a working-class party, but rather, like most newly founded Communist parties, a party of revolutionary intellectuals of uncertain convictions and extremely diverse views. Two of the twelve men who met in Shanghai in July 1921 to found the CCP later became ministers in the pro-Japanese Nanking government during the Second World War. One of them died in prison; the other was shot by the Kuomintang.[1] There were as many radical or revolutionary anarchists among the delegates as committed Marxists. Indeed, the founding of the CCP can be seen as an extension of the May Fourth Movement. One indication of this is the delegates' choice to head the Central Committee—a man who was not at the Shanghai meeting but who was nonetheless the real founder of the party, the editor-in-chief of *Hsin ch'ing-nien*, Ch'en Tu-hsiu.

These twelve delegates represented an inconsequential organization of 57 members. They were such an unimportant group that in January 1923, when Sun Yat-sen signed his celebrated accord with the Soviet envoy Adolf Joffe in a move designed solely to win Soviet Russia's support,[2] he paid scant attention to

[1] One of the most obscure of the twelve was a delegate from Hunan province, Mao Tse-tung.

[2] On Joffe, the friend and disciple of Trotsky who killed himself in November 1927 following the demonstration of November 7 and the crushing of the Opposition, see Georges Haupt and Jean-Jacques Marie, *Les Bolchéviks par eux-mêmes* (Paris: Maspéro,

the help he might gain from the CCP (which had barely three hundred members as late as the summer of that year), or to the possibility of competition from this tiny group. The collaboration and then merger of the two parties was accordingly an unlooked-for if perilous opportunity for the fledgling Communist Party, an opportunity it quickly moved to exploit.

The merger with the CCP was officially sealed at the Kuomintang's Reorganization Conference of January 1924. As members of the Kuomintang, the Communists could act on an entirely different scale, and the CCP soon emerged as the most dynamic element of a generally dynamic coalition, the one best equipped to organize strikes and ultimately genuine workers' insurrections. One sign of the CCP's progress was the growth in party membership, which was at first very slow (the party's one-thousandth member did not join until spring 1925), then suddenly very rapid. What gave the party new momentum was the May Thirtieth Movement of 1925, thanks to which membership increased tenfold in six months, to 10,000 in November 1925.[3] The May Thirtieth Movement, which lasted throughout the summer, so radicalized Chinese political life that it may fairly be said to have marked the beginning of a truly revolutionary period. From 1925 to 1927 China experienced its first revolution,[4] a revolution that put an end to the warlord period and brought the CCP to the fore as a force to be reckoned with. Its membership tripled in the next eight months (to 30,000 members in July 1926), then doubled again by the spring of 1927 (58,000 mem-

---

1969), pp. 306–11. By the terms of the Sun-Joffe accord, the Soviets in effect acknowledged that since it was too early to establish Communism in China, the nation's most urgent needs were for unification and national independence, which were the goals of the Kuomintang program. Sun sought not only Soviet arms and equipment, but Soviet advice on tactics and organization. Soviet advisers such as Mikhail Borodin, who arrived in Canton in September 1923, were to reorganize the Kuomintang on the Bolshevik model.

[3] The May Thirtieth Movement of 1925 was a series of strikes, boycotts, and anti-imperialist demonstrations throughout China following the killing of ten demonstrators by the police of Shanghai's International Settlement. The proletariat played a very important role in the movement from the beginning. It was against the killing of a worker by a Japanese foreman that the May Thirtieth demonstrators were protesting, and the majority of those killed and wounded that day were workers.

[4] Or second, if one counts 1911. In fact, the years 1925–27 should be defined primarily by their relationship to 1949, which they foreshadowed (as 1905 did 1917 in Russia), rather than their relationship to 1911.

bers in early April). To these figures must be added the membership of the Young Communist League, which was also making rapid strides, and in which the proportion of students, an overwhelming 90 per cent on the eve of May 30, steadily diminished as the proportion of young workers rose. In November 1926, 40 per cent of the Young Communists were workers, 35 per cent students.

Membership figures tell only part of the story. The real strength of the party, particularly in a revolutionary period, lay in its capacity to mobilize the masses. During the summer of 1926, when Chiang's Revolutionary Army launched its offensive, it was the CCP, which organized 1,200,000 workers and 800,000 peasants, rather than the Kuomintang, that really ran the workers' and peasants' movement. The power of a labor movement inspired and led by the CCP was demonstrated several months later by the heroic working-class uprising in Shanghai, which liberated the city even before the Revolutionary Army arrived. A general strike was called on March 21, 1927; by the next day the city was in the hands of the insurgents; and on the twenty-sixth General Chiang Kai-shek, commander-in-chief of the Revolutionary Army, entered the city without firing a shot.

He was saving his blows for his allies—for the bloody double cross of April 12, 1927, one of the episodes of the Chinese Revolution that is least misunderstood in the West (in part because of André Malraux's *Man's Fate*). On the morning of April 12 Chiang's troops launched a surprise attack on the Shanghai trade unions, seizing the workers' weapons and slaughtering them by the thousands. Over the next few months a reign of terror was extended far beyond Shanghai, as Chiang built up his own power while routing his Communist allies and worker and peasant leaders. The party was decimated and driven underground. The first Chinese Revolution was over. For the CCP, it was defeat snatched from the jaws of victory.[5] So ended the orthodox stage of party history.

[5] Conrad Brandt entitles Chapter Five of his book *Stalin's Failure in China, 1924–1927* (Cambridge, Mass.: Harvard University Press, 1958) "A Defeat Out of Victory and A Devil Out of the Machine."

The stage that ended in April 1927 was orthodox in the sense that the party had emphasized organizing the proletariat and preparing for a working-class uprising. What had been less orthodox about it was the merger of the CCP with a bourgeois party. Here we must go back to the way Marxist doctrine had been applied to Chinese conditions, and to the role of the Comintern leadership in the disaster that befell the Chinese party.

The defeat of 1927 was unquestionably a defeat for Moscow. It was Moscow that had decided on alliance and merger with the Kuomintang, and Moscow that had forced the CCP to comply with this decision. The alliance was in a sense a natural one. It accorded perfectly with a thesis formulated at the Second Comintern Congress in 1920, while Lenin was still alive: namely, that during the first, anti-imperialist phase of the revolution, the "national bourgeoisie" in colonial and semicolonial countries is itself revolutionary. Given this belief, it was perfectly conceivable that a Communist party should work with bourgeois nationalists as long as possible, and thus in June 1922, even before any steps toward a united front had been taken in Moscow, the first manifesto of the CCP, speaking as the party of workers and poor peasants, called for an alliance with the "democratic party" or Kuomintang, the party of the bourgeoisie. But this identification of the Kuomintang with the bourgeoisie did not prevail for long, for Moscow had other ideas and soon acted to impose them on the CCP. In Moscow's eyes the Kuomintang was in reality a bloc of four classes—the bourgeoisie, petty bourgeoisie, workers, and peasants. The CCP should not simply participate in joint action with the Kuomintang; it should become an integral part of a revolutionary force that already included the proletariat. Hence the merger of January 1924. As early as June 1923 the Third Congress of the CCP adopted as its own Moscow's strange interpretation of the four-class bloc and acknowledged the Kuomintang as the "central force in the national revolution."

Moscow's directives were followed not only when it was a matter of assessing the nature of the Kuomintang (a problem of doctrinal interpretation) or of deciding on merger (a problem of strategy), but also later on, in the day-to-day application of this strategy (problems of tactics). These last problems became particularly knotty, needless to say, in the revolutionary days of 1926–27.

In this period, two major mistakes were made: the danger represented by Chiang Kai-shek and the revolutionary capacity of the poor peasants were consistently underestimated. A year before Chiang's open attack on the CCP in April 1927, he staged a rehearsal. On March 20, 1926, at Canton, he ordered a surprise attack on a revolutionary naval unit headed by a Communist, a unit that was carrying on the same struggle as he was, against the same enemies. The political advisers attached to this unit were arrested, along with all the Soviet advisers in Canton. Overnight Chiang became master of the city, which was then, the reader will recall, the capital of the revolutionary forces, and he proceeded to eliminate his Kuomintang rivals there, notably the leaders of the party's left wing. On May 15, 1926, a session of the Kuomintang's Central Executive Committee called by Chiang ratified the *fait accompli* and fixed strict limits to the CCP's influence within the Kuomintang. During this session Chiang also had himself named commander-in-chief of the Northern Expedition, which set out from Canton less than two months later to conquer China. In times of war, extraordinary institutions emerge: the government of Canton was transformed into a military dictatorship run by Chiang.

The CCP, forced to follow the orders of the Comintern's Soviet representatives, responded to this unparalleled blow with a timidity almost unique in the history of revolutionary parties. It did not protest any of the steps Chiang had taken, and it acceded to all his new demands. Borodin even went so far as to dismiss the Soviet military advisers that Chiang disliked. Only when the left wing of the Kuomintang (a group of radicals of uncertain ideology, dominated by Wang Ching-wei) established its own government in Wuhan in defiance of Chiang Kai-shek[6] did the CCP have the nerve—or permission—to make

[6] In Hupeh, on the middle Yangtze. Chiang was then in Nanchang, the capital of Kiangsi.

the break with Chiang and join the rebels. The Comintern, which had been slower to take alarm at the Revolutionary Army's ambitious commander-in-chief than the left wing of the bourgeoisie, now ordered the CCP to follow the latter's lead.

Even then, within the Wuhan coalition, the CCP denounced and worked zealously to halt the "excesses" of the peasants in Central China: rioting, pillaging, massacring landlords. Not only did such actions outrage and frighten the officers of the Revolutionary Army, most of whom came from families of *ti-chu* (landlords), but the peasants' refusal to pay rent and land taxes undermined the Wuhan regime's financial base. Clearly a choice had to be made between supporting the Kuomintang, even its left wing, and supporting agrarian revolution. Certainly the choice was not always an easy one. But the major defect of the Russians' strategy was precisely that in a complex and quickly changing situation requiring immediate and difficult choices, they had no concrete knowledge of the reality they were trying to change. They were claiming the right to direct the Chinese Revolution from afar, in accordance with their interpretation of Marxist doctrine. What is worse, the most important decisions, decisions that involved the lives of thousands of Chinese party workers, not to mention much greater numbers of workers and peasants, were made on the basis of Russia's internal political situation. Stalin and his allies of the moment (Bukharin and his followers) were much less concerned with the victory of the Chinese Revolution than with refuting Trotsky's criticisms[7] and assuring themselves of an ally in the Nationalist China then being established. When events proved them wrong, they had the effrontery either to deny what had happened or to claim that they had long foreseen it. Thus all news of the coup of March 20, 1926, was suppressed in the Soviet Union. *Inprecorr*, the official organ of the Comintern compiled in Russia for dissemination abroad, did refer to the event, which

---

[7] Trotsky did not mince words. He compared the CCP's alliance with Chiang Kai-shek to a pact with the Devil: "It is absurd to suppose that the Devil will be converted ... and that he will use his horns not against the workers and peasants, but exclusively for good works." Trotsky, *L'Internationale Communiste après Lénine* (Paris: Rieder, 1930), p. 264.

had been reported by Reuters, but explained it away as a British imperialist maneuver intended to divide the revolutionary camp. In fact, said *Inprecorr* on April 8, 1926, the prospects "were never so favorable as they are now. . . . The province of Kwangsi will shortly form a soviet government."[8]

At this point irony would be cheap. To consider only what interested Stalin, namely results, the total fiasco of his China policy had to be brought to an end. In July 1927 the left wing of the Kuomintang expelled the CCP from its ranks and Borodin hastily fled Wuhan. He left China just when the party he had reorganized on Bolshevik lines was triumphing; the fruit of his work was the Kuomintang that routed the CCP and decimated its ranks, the same Kuomintang that had been admitted to the Executive Committee of the Comintern as a "sympathetic organization."

But we must be fair. The same strategy of merger with the Kuomintang that led to defeat in 1927 had also made possible the quick successes of 1925–26, successes that none of the party's leaders had dared hope for three years earlier. The CCP at first grew like a parasite on the body of the revolution, which then cast it off. More important, both the initial success and the subsequent failure can be explained largely in strategic terms; to be sure, human errors precipitated the debacle of 1927. But does this mean that the objective conditions in 1927 were such as to permit the seizure of power by a party that represented only a small part of the working class, a working class that itself amounted to .5 per cent of the Chinese population? Had the party's leadership shown more independence of Moscow's disastrous orders, would this vanguard have been capable of transforming the China of the warlord period into a workers' state? It certainly would not have been if it had to rely solely on its own forces. Perhaps it might have been (though even here the answer is very doubtful) with the support of the poor peasants, whom, after all, the CCP was also supposed to be representing. But the word support is hardly appropriate here, at least unless

8 Cited in Harold R. Isaacs, *The Tragedy of the Chinese Revolution*, 2d rev. ed. (Stanford, Calif.: Stanford University Press, 1961), p. 97.

one reverses the roles. This must have been the conclusion of Mao Tse-tung, who was eager to steer the party on a different course.

The Peasant Stage, 1927–1935

In 1927 the Chinese Communists embarked on an experiment that was extraordinary in every respect. Here was a party cut off from the proletariat and the cities, crouching in the shelter of a remote and hilly countryside; a party that sought to accelerate the progress of history by choosing as its field of action one of the most forsaken regions (southern Kiangsi) of an underdeveloped country. Moreover, this "party of the working class" was in fact made up of peasants and intellectuals, the former under the thumb of the latter, supplemented on occasion by bandit bands that were also composed of peasants. Guerrilla warfare was the major form of action, not the strike. And a village-based rebel administration made agrarian revolution the heart of its program—a far cry indeed from the Communist Party we know in France, an urban party committed to running for municipal office and to such goals as increasing the number of child care centers, stadiums, and classes in winter sports. This was the key experiment of the Chinese Revolution.

The experiment had Chinese precedents. Putting aside the long tradition of peasant insurrections and jacqueries in a predominantly rural empire, a tradition whose characteristics the Communist revolution in many ways shared and whose stratagems it often adopted,[9] let us consider two contemporary episodes that in different ways heralded or paved the way for the Kiangsi soviets. Mao had a precursor named P'eng P'ai. The

---

[9] One heritage of this tradition was the establishment of a rebel base area in a relatively uncontrolled no-man's-land where several provinces came together, an area that no governor would claim as his once it had become a rebel stronghold. In the Taiping era, the Nien rebels were wont to adopt this tactic of *pien-ch'ü* (border areas). Similar considerations, of course, have determined the location of rebel base areas in other parts of the world besides China. E. J. Hobsbawm tells us, for example, that the Lazzarettist movement was centered in the backward mountainous region (Monte Amiata) where Tuscany, Umbria, and Latium converged. *Primitive Rebels: Studies in Archaic Forms of Social Movement in the Nineteenth and Twentieth Centuries* (New York: Praeger, 1963), pp. 66–67.

son of an extremely wealthy landowner, P'eng had studied in Japan and returned to become a Communist party worker. In 1922 he began organizing the peasants of his native province, Kwangtung, into "peasant associations," radical and militant organizations of poor peasants. In 1927–28 he established a short-lived soviet government in the Haifeng and Lufeng districts of eastern Kwangtung (collectively known as Hailufeng). In 1929, at the age of thirty-three, he was captured and shot by the Kuomintang.

The Kwangtung peasant associations were groundbreaking efforts, but the true roots of the modern peasant revolution lay in the Hunan uprisings of 1926–27. The Hunan movement, which was stronger and more widespread than the Hailufeng movement and had many more members (two million at the end of 1926), also seemed more spontaneous, in the sense that it was not the work of a non-peasant like P'eng P'ai. The only encouraging external factors were the approach and subsequent arrival of Chiang's Revolutionary Army, and of course the revolutionary climate of the day. The Hunan movement was an authentically revolutionary peasant explosion, a violent and radical upheaval that for several weeks made the landowning classes of the entire province tremble.

It had an unsettling effect of a different sort on one particular son of a rich peasant, Mao Tse-tung, who had returned to his native province to conduct an investigation on behalf of the Peasant Committee of the CCP. Five weeks spent in the company of peasants in a state of rebellion resulted in a short pamphlet, the *Report of an Investigation into the Peasant Movement in Hunan*, published in March 1927. This document ranks with the classics of world revolutionary literature. To my mind it is one of Mao's finest works; unlike his later writings, which all too often are ponderously didactic or entangled in dialectics, the *Report* is vibrant with a young man's passion. Disdainful of doctrinal disputes, blithely indifferent to theoretical implications (if not unaware of them), the *Report* started right off on a completely new tack. Its general theme had the marvelous simplicity of the evidence by which Mao had just been struck, which he would never forget, and which would determine the direction of his career and the course of the Chinese Revolution: in a word, revolution in China meant agrarian revolution. It followed that the real force behind the revolutionary movement was the poor peasantry. And from this proposition in turn followed the only possible strategy for the revolution, a strategy that nullified the theses and policies worked out by the party's wise men and rendered all their arguments vain. Finally, the centrality of the poor peasants to the revolution furnished the best, the only, criterion for testing the professional revolutionaries themselves: anyone who opposed "peasant excesses" or even criticized them was a counterrevolutionary, though he be general secretary of the party (Ch'en Tu-hsiu); anyone who supported them, or better still participated in them, was a revolutionary. Where did the true revolutionary party belong? At the head of the unleashed peasants, leading them on to revolution— not in the rear, applying the brakes.

The party leaders did not act on the *Report*'s recommendations, but its author had not lingered to await their decision. Mao Tse-tung had returned once again to his native province, where in September 1927 he led an army of peasants, miners, and soldiers in an uprising whose intended target was the city of Changsha. This insurrection, known as the Autumn Harvest Uprising, was crushed in a week; Mao was arrested and managed to buy his release only hours before his scheduled execution. As a matter of fact, the situation had changed completely in the eight months since Mao's investigation. As a result of Chiang Kai-shek's double cross and the ensuing White Terror, the revolutionary tide had receded almost everywhere. The change was nowhere more marked than in Hunan, where less than four months before Mao's attempted uprising the party's peasant cadres had been systematically massacred.

With what remnants he could gather together (probably about a thousand men), Mao plunged into the Chingkangshan mountains on the border between Hunan and Kiangsi provinces. There, in October 1927, he established the first rural revolutionary base area. After months of hardship and isolation, invaluable reinforcements arrived: several thousand exhausted soldiers, the remains of a defeated revolutionary army, led by a professional military man converted to Communism by China's travails—Chu Teh, later the victorious general of the Civil War. They were followed by a smaller third contingent, a unit of the Kuomintang Army that had rebelled on the appeal of its leader, the future Marshal P'eng Te-huai, who would become one of the most colorful figures in the Red Army and China's minister of defense. Along with two bandit bands, whose leaders would be executed when the situation was less precarious, these men made up the nucleus of the Chinese Red Army, which was to win for Communism the largest population on earth. They were then some 10,000 men in rags, with perhaps one rifle for every five soldiers.

Most important, the establishment of the Chingkangshan base area marked the start of the peasant revolution, led and launched by Communists who turned themselves into farmers, militiamen, and rural administrators in their effort to win over the peasant masses. Little by little these last allowed themselves to be converted—an imposed or coerced conversion in some cases, but more often, it would appear, a spontaneous rallying to the banner of agrarian revolution. An important factor was the growing renown of "Chu Mao," who distributed land and who in the year 1928 alone repulsed three successive attacks by the forces of order.[10] The Communists' success (it being understood that for such an undertaking survival is success) was so great that the heroic days were over by 1929. In that year some opportune civil wars, which called the Nanking government's troops first to South China, then to the North, enabled the Communists to install themselves in a less makeshift and precarious fashion. Henceforth the party and its army were solidly entrenched in their rural districts, which became laboratories for agrarian revolution and Communist administration.[11]

[10] In the minds of the Kiangsi peasants, Chu Mao was an all-powerful personage who wanted to make the people happy. Outside their imagination, he did indeed exist, but in two persons—the military leader Chu Teh and the political leader Mao Tse-tung.

[11] The army numbered some 65,000 men in July 1930, most of them recruited from the peasants of the soviet base areas. (The term soviet, which is used constantly in

The Chinese Soviet Republic and the Long March. November 1931 marked a new phase—the founding of the Chinese Soviet Republic, with Mao Tse-tung as its President and Juichin, in southern Kiangsi, as its capital. Besides the "central revolutionary base area" of southern Kiangsi,[12] the Communists then controlled some fifteen other base areas, more than half of them in the provinces of the middle and upper Yangtze. Their boundaries changed with the requirements of military operations, but almost all of them survived. The central base area, for its part, survived five successive "Extermination Campaigns."[13] The First "Exterminate the Communist Bandits" Campaign was under way by 1930: it failed, as did the next three. Only the Fifth succeeded. Not only did the Nationalists have an even greater superiority of men and arms than in the first four campaigns, but more important, this campaign was finally based on a strategy adapted to an elusive and ubiquitous enemy, a strategy of caution and patience. The Nationalists no longer sent isolated columns into the soviet base area, but on the contrary ringed the area with a veritable wall of small fortifications, from which they slowly and inexorably moved forward toward the center. Among other things this strategy made it possible to effect a ruthless economic blockade. It also deprived the guerrillas of their best weapon—mobility. They were left with only two alternatives: to accept the unequal contest of fixed-position

---

Chinese Communist documents, served primarily to recapture the spirit of an earlier day. The "soviets of workers, peasants, and soldiers" that were organized in territories captured by the Red Army in China bore little resemblance to the similarly named Russian soviets of 1905 and 1917.) The center of gravity of the soviet base areas moved gradually from Chingkangshan to southern Kiangsi.

12 By April 1932 this area harbored a population of almost 2.5 million.

13 Tradition and legend count five Extermination Campaigns, though some writers maintain that there were six or even eight. It is simplest to distinguish between two offensive waves: December 1930–September 1931, corresponding to the first three of the five traditional campaigns, and April 1933–October 1934, corresponding to the last two. See Anthony Garavente, "The Long March," *China Quarterly*, No. 22 (1965), pp. 89–90. Deciding where one campaign ended and another began is both more difficult and less significant for a revolutionary war than it would be for a conventional war. The important thing to remember is that the soviet base areas were subjected to constant harassment, which offered no great threat so long as it remained the work of provincial or local forces but which escalated dramatically whenever the Nanking government's other foreign and domestic enemies gave it enough respite to mount a massive and systematic attack in Kiangsi.

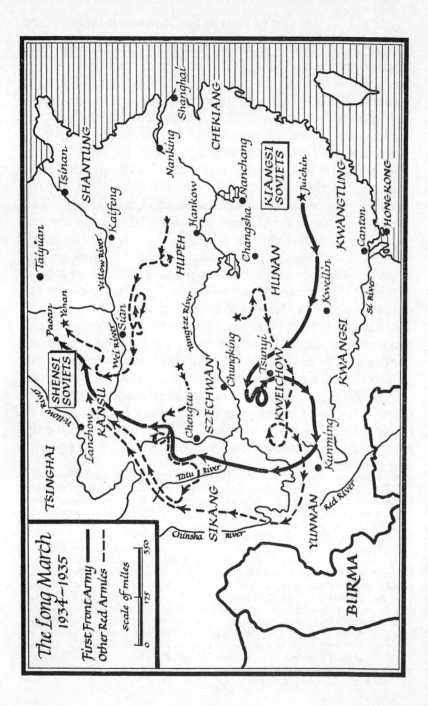

The Long March
1934-1935

First Front Army ——
Other Red Armies ---

scale of miles

0   175   350

warfare or to flee. They did first one and then the other, finally resigning themselves to abandoning Kiangsi when it became obvious that any further attempt at classical warfare would mean the rout of the Red Army. The success of the forces of order was only relative, however; they drove the Red Army from its domain, but they did not destroy it. On the night of October 15, 1934, while diversionary troops sacrificed themselves in delaying actions elsewhere on the front, the main body of Communist forces broke through a comparatively weak point in the Nationalists' encirclement and escaped toward southwestern Kiangsi. This was the beginning of the Long March.

The Fifth Extermination Campaign, which was launched in October 1933, had taken a year to succeed. It would take another long year (October 15, 1934–October 20, 1935) for the Red Army to escape the Nationalists' pursuit and find a haven in a desolate region at the other end of China, in northern Shensi. The Long March from the southeast to the northwest of the enormous country, with a long detour through the southwest (Kweichow, Yunnan), was thus essentially a retreat. Yet it was also an epic—a new Anabasis, not of the Ten Thousand, but of 10,000 kilometers, in the course of which the Communists crossed mighty rivers and soaring mountains, leaving behind thousands who died of exhaustion, cold, hunger, or thirst. It was Napoleon's retreat from Russia on a continental scale, a retreat in which to reach Paris the fleeing French troops had to fight their way across the mountains of the Caucasus and the Anatolian plateau. Instead of the Berezina River, the Chinese had to cross the upper Yangtze (called for this part of its course the Chinsha or Golden Sands River), its subsidiaries and subsubsidiaries (notably the Tatu); instead of the Cossacks, they had to fight not only the Kuomintang Army but also mercenaries in the pay of local warlords and tribesmen of non-Chinese origin who were accustomed to shooting (sometimes with poisoned arrows) at any Chinese intruders. Troops that had been fighting with one another only the day before joined forces in an effort to wipe out the fleeing Communists, who were pursued by the one side as rebels, by the other as invaders, but always and everywhere as "bandits." A skirmish every day, a full-dress battle every two weeks: this is the approximate score for the 370 days of retreat. And here is another and even more eloquent score: of the 90,000–100,000 men who began the Long March,[14] only 7,000–8,000 completed it.[15] The survivors had hardly reached northern Shensi, a region even poorer and more isolated than Kiangsi, when they set about establishing another soviet. A new phase began.

The extraordinary importance of the Kiangsi period obviously lies not only in the Communists' peasant strategy, but also in their military experiment. It was forty years ago, in the rural soviet areas of Central and South China, that the techniques of modern guerrilla warfare were perfected, techniques that would later be applied (though they were not necessarily copied from the Chinese model in every case) by thousands and thousands of other guerrillas in Algeria and Angola, in Cuba and Brazil, and in Vietnam. In China itself, throughout the war with Japan and most of the Civil War, Communist tactics amounted to nothing more than systematic and large-scale application of principles and procedures that had been formulated and tested in Kiangsi, the laboratory of people's war.

The Comintern and the Chinese Soviets. Not only did the decisive Kiangsi experiment owe nothing to the Comintern, but even within the CCP itself it was the work of a minority.[16] From

[14] And 35 women. Among them were the wife of Chu Teh, to whom fell the task of carrying a wounded soldier as well as a rifle on her back, and the wife of Mao Tse-tung, who received some twenty serious wounds from artillery fire and who gave birth to a baby in the course of the Long March. Mao and his wife reportedly left three of their children with peasant families along the way; no trace of these children is known to have been found.

[15] Actually the number of survivors was greater, since some members of the Red Army, including Chu Teh, followed a rival of Mao's still farther west, to Sikang. At the same time, a small number of the 7,000–8,000 men who reached Shensi under Mao's command had belonged to various Communist armies from Central China that joined the Long March along the way.

[16] The following summary is deliberately schematized, though the events in question can in fact be divided into several distinct phases. To describe each of these phases in turn would be to transform the history of the period into an institutional chronicle of the CCP. Just as the historian of early-twentieth-century Russian political forces rightly gives greater attention to the Bolshevik faction of the Russian Social Democratic Labor Party than to the Cadets, the Social Revolutionaries, or even the Mensheviks, so it seems right to concentrate here on the Kiangsi soviets, where real, dynamic history was being made, and pass rapidly over the CCP's official leadership and the party's numerous internal conflicts.

1927 to 1931 the official history of the party was taking place elsewhere. First the lesson of the 1927 debacle was applied; i.e., the man then in charge, Ch'en Tu-hsiu, was found guilty of steering the party down an "opportunistic and rightist" road.[17] Next, in reaction to Ch'en's rightist deviation, the party tried its hand at a number of leftist adventures. In a situation reminiscent of the Russia of 1906 or even 1907, the seers in Moscow detected the approach of a "new revolutionary tide," a "high tide" whose rising flood could already be heard rumbling in the offing, and they concluded from their soundings that the time had come for armed insurrection. The Nanchang Uprising of August 1, 1927, a mutiny instigated by Communist officers and carried out under the banner of the Kuomintang's left wing, was decided on by people on the spot.[18] Not so the Canton Commune of December 11–14, 1927, an urban uprising carried out on the orders of the Comintern under the most unfavorable conditions imaginable and immediately crushed. Canton was in the rebels' hands for two days; it took the government executioners more than four to kill all the captured insurgents.[19] "An uprising in Canton is out of the question at this time," Chang T'ai-lei, the Communist leader in Canton, had warned in response to a telegram from Ch'ü Ch'iu-pai, the CCP's new general secretary, transmitting the Comintern's order.[20] Not only was the order not rescinded, but Stalin sent two personal emissaries to Canton to organize the uprising, and the Soviet consulate there served as the insurgents' headquarters. From Stalin's point of view, his en-

[17] Ch'en, who was expelled from the Central Committee in August 1927, acknowledged his mistakes but refused to take sole responsibility for a policy laid down by Moscow. After joining the opposition, he was expelled from the party in 1929 and led a Trotskyite group until his arrest in 1932. Sentenced to fifteen years in prison, he was freed in the early months of the Second World War and died in 1942.

[18] The mutineers were forced to flee almost immediately. For a time they hoped to take control of Kwangtung province, and at the end of September they actually occupied the port of Swatow, only to be driven out a week later. It was the survivors of this escapade (and several other equally fruitless ones in the next few months) that Chu Teh led to Chingkangshan in the spring of 1928. August 1, 1927, is accordingly celebrated in Communist China as the birth date of the Red Army.

[19] True, to save ammunition they took the time to tie together clumps of ten or twelve men and load them onto boats to be drowned in the Pearl River, downstream from Canton.

[20] Chang, who was twenty-nine, was killed during the uprising.

voys' efforts were not in vain despite the massacre of some 6,000 Communists and Communist sympathizers, for by announcing the initial success of the uprising he succeeded in concealing from the Fifteenth Congress of the Bolshevik Party the truth about the foundering of the Chinese Revolution.

A third leftist adventure was the Red Army's attack on Changsha, the capital of Hunan province, in the summer of 1930.[21] One of the principal aims of this attack was to place the exclusively rural soviet movement under the hegemony of the proletariat; in effect, a Red Army composed of peasants was supposed to take over a large city so as to profit from the leadership of that city's working class. The Red Army did indeed take Changsha in July 1930, but its presence failed to incite any working-class uprising whatever. At the end of a week the army could only quit the city, which it was in no position to hold against approaching government troops. And again there followed massive retaliation. Li Li-san, the CCP's general secretary, was convicted of "putschism" and disgraced.[22] Chou En-lai, one of Li's leading collaborators in the ultra-leftist policy, admitted his own "rotten opportunism" and remained on the new Central Committee that condemned Li.[23] By 1932 the entire Central Committee had left its clandestine headquarters in Shanghai and moved to Juichin, the capital of the Chinese Soviet Republic. The Kiangsi soviets had proved their worth, and the party's nominal leadership was thus reunited with its "real power."[24]

The Comintern did not oppose the "peasantist" minority within the CCP. Its leaders were at first unaware of what was happening in Kiangsi, then decided to tolerate it. They were badly informed and slow to grasp the significance of this new ex-

21 Attacks on Nanchang and Wuhan were also envisioned. Mao, who was reluctant to risk his painfully built-up army in such an uncertain venture, ignored the Central Committee's order to attack Wuhan.

22 Li was called to Moscow, where he acknowledged his errors. He stayed in the USSR throughout the Second World War and reappeared in Manchuria in 1946.

23 Chou is the only CCP leader to have held uninterrupted membership in the Politburo for over forty years (since 1927), the only one to ride with every curve in the party line.

24 Benjamin Schwartz, in a close study of the conflicts among the different CCP factions, describes the isolated minority current represented by Chu Teh and Mao as "the Real Power Faction." *Chinese Communism and the Rise of Mao* (Cambridge, Mass.: Harvard University Press, 1951), p. 180.

periment in "soviet" government. They were particularly ill-informed about the man behind the experiment, this Mao Tse-tung who had been dropped from the Central Committee in November 1927 after his Autumn Harvest Uprising was crushed. One of the first references to Mao in a Comintern document appears in a letter of June 1929 from the Executive Committee of the Comintern to the Central Committee of the CCP. The letter sharply criticizes Mao's excessive moderation toward the rich peasants; in short, it imputes pro-kulak tendencies to Mao at a time when the kulaks were being officially denounced in the Soviet Union as the very incarnation of the counterrevolution. But it would be misleading to make much of this one reference. The truth is that no one in Moscow gave Mao much thought. In 1927 he did not have the stature of a top-rank leader, and after 1927 he was too deeply entrenched in the Chinese interior to attract the attention of the outside world, even the Communist portion of it. When news of the Red Army's first major successes reached Moscow, the Comintern attributed them to "Comrade P'eng Chu-mao," who was even more of a composite personage than the Kiangsi peasants' legendary Chu Mao, being a trinity composed of P'eng Te-huai, Chu Teh, and Mao Tse-tung. Finally, on March 13, 1930, *Inprecorr* ran a laudatory obituary of the peasant leader "Mau," reportedly dead of tuberculosis after a long illness. To say the least, Mao's policies were devised and carried out without the assistance of the Comintern! Indeed, there is a striking contrast between the effectiveness of the peasant experiment and the failure of the Moscow-inspired urban adventures in Canton and Changsha. The Comintern intervened constantly in China from 1921 to 1930, making one mistake after another. Only after 1931 did its direct interventions become rare and comparatively discreet, to the great benefit of the CCP and the Chinese Revolution.

Beginning in November 1931 the Comintern's leaders were forced to focus on the President of the Chinese Soviet Republic. Ritual homage was paid Mao with every reference to the "great Chinese Communist Party" or "the world's most powerful Communist Party outside the USSR." The homage, however, was not wholly unreserved. Mao was hailed as the unrivaled leader of the Chinese soviets, but his relationship to the party was obscured. Where exactly the CCP was—in the soviet base areas or the "White areas"—was left unclear. That way, depending on whether Mao succeeded or failed, he could either be acclaimed as the triumphant leader of all the Chinese Communists, both urban and rural, or be repudiated as a peasant leader who had failed to grasp the fundamental role of the proletariat.[25]

At least he was left reasonably free to carry on his experiment (not that the Comintern was really in a position to put a stop to it), though not completely so: after the Central Committee moved to Juichin, the influence of Mao and his supporters in the central soviet base area, if not directly thwarted, was decidedly circumscribed. Even before the transfer, Chou En-lai had reproached Mao (or at least the policies adopted at Mao's behest for the central soviet base area) for lacking offensive spirit, and had particularly deplored the Red Army's failure to attack the main cities of the Kan Valley;[26] and in May 1933 this critic of Mao the temporizer became political commissar of the Red Army, a position Mao had lost shortly before.[27] But Chou En-lai was a much less formidable opponent for Mao than the "28 Bolsheviks," young Chinese Communists who, after completing their studies at Sun Yat-sen University in Moscow, had returned to Shanghai and captured control of the Politburo in January 1931. They were given a number of important posts almost the moment they set foot in the Kiangsi soviet base area later that year.[28] The arrival of these intruders forced Mao to tread care-

[25] See Charles B. McLane, *Soviet Policy and the Chinese Communists, 1931–1946* (New York: Columbia University Press, 1958), pp. 29–34.

[26] The Kan is the largest river in Kiangsi province. Its middle and upper course ran in some places through the very heart of the soviet base area, and in some places along its edge.

[27] In fact, Mao had been political commissar of the First Army, the largest of the armies of the central soviet base area; Chou was given this post as well. Obviously, it is pointless to speculate about the working relationship of Mao and Chou in 1971 on the basis of their difficulties in 1932–33. The polemics and insults exchanged by Lenin and Trotsky in 1904, for example, did not affect the way they worked together in 1917 and afterward.

[28] It was their party rivals and adversaries who ironically dubbed them Bolsheviks, presumably because their revolutionary experience was limited to what they had read in books and because they were unrelenting advocates of a hard line. The name stuck

fully, and as a result his freedom of movement, which had never been absolute, was further diminished. As a general rule, he noisily applauded directives he disapproved of and then paid no attention whatever to them, a practice that led to his being violently attacked as "two-faced." For all his maneuverings, however, he was almost certainly in disgrace in 1934, on the eve of the Long March.

It was only during the Long March that Mao finally took command as the undisputed leader of the Chinese Communists. At a historic meeting held in Tsunyi (Kweichow province) in January 1935, the Politburo, which had been enlarged for the occasion, elected Mao Tse-tung chairman. During the Red Army's hegira, it had no contact with Moscow; on its own, the Chinese party had chosen, or rather recognized, its leader.

An Asian Marxism?

In the eventful history of the Chinese Communist Party, the Kiangsi period is the period of wandering in the wilderness, the period of sacred history. Even today there are very few major figures in China who did not participate in the crossing of the desert. "Crossing" should be understood in a temporal rather than a spatial sense; it is a question not so much of the Long March as of the preceding years of heroic and primitive struggle.[29] Yet if the leaders of this period are still in power in Peking, it is because the Kiangsi years (which ended, let us not forget, in failure and flight) were soon followed by the Second World War, during which the CCP made decisive advances. In making these advances, the party did not limit itself to exploiting the misery of the rural masses and decrying the unjust lot of the peasant, as it had in the Kiangsi period. On the contrary, it gave

---

and is still used. This group of returned students retained control of the party machinery for several years, thanks in part to the influence of Pavel Mif, at the time Stalin's chief expert on Far Eastern questions.

[29] Among those whose commitment to the Chinese Revolution can be traced as far back as the soviet experiment in Chingkangshan are Ch'en I, currently minister of foreign affairs, and Lin Piao, Mao's heir-designate. At the time both men served under Chu Teh—Ch'en I as a political instuctor, Lin Piao as commandant, at age twenty-one, of a 900-man column, one of the five in Chu Teh's army.

much less emphasis to social revolution than it did to national-ism.[30]

Nor is it enough to say that the Kiangsi period was not imme-diately fruitful for the Chinese Revolution. It must also be add-ed that the peasant strategy represented just one element in an as yet incomplete formula; other ingredients were added to the recipe worked out between 1927 and 1935, among them the de-velopment of a large armed force. Nonetheless, it is worth our while to pause for a moment on this unique aspect of a particu-lar period of the Chinese Revolution. For if the peasant road to revolution, a road laid down and followed without the assistance of Moscow and in opposition to Marx, was not in itself the secret of the Chinese Communists' success,[31] it did constitute the first major reworking of Marxist doctrine. If the term Asian Marx-ism has any meaning, the Holy Land of this new religion is two adjoining provinces in the Chinese interior—Hunan, where the prophet had his peasant vision, and Kiangsi, where his faith first began to move mountains.

The peasant revolution being carried out by a section of the Third International in China's remote and almost unknown so-viet districts was precisely contemporary with the "final solu-tion" of the kulak problem being ruthlessly pursued, also in the name of soviets, several thousand miles to the north and west.[32] From the sarcasm of Marx, Engels, and Trotsky toward "the class that represents barbarism within civilization"[33] to Stalin's bloody expeditions against the "blood drinkers" who resisted forced collectivization, Marxism was in theory as in practice the deadly antagonist of the peasantry. Among other things, Marx-ism may be seen as an ideological expression of the age of urbani-zation and industrialization.

---

[30] See p. 53 above and especially Chapter Six.

[31] And if, on the other hand, what has been called the Sinification of Marxism has continued since 1949, and does not refer simply to a strategic innovation in the seizing of power.

[32] Kostas Papaioannou, "La Prolétarisation des paysans," Part II, *Le Contrat Social* (Paris), Vol. VII, No. 2 (March–April 1963), p. 90.

[33] Marx, *Class Struggles in France* (London: Lawrence and Wishart, 1935), in the celebrated passage (p. 74) on the peasant insurrection of December 10, 1848.

Yet at the same time it has become clear that whether or not the world revolution is led by avowed Marxists, it is becoming more reliant on the poor peasants every day. While the working class in capitalist countries, which only yesterday found its cause in reformism, is increasingly adopting an attitude that reflects its relatively privileged position, the peasantry is rising up in places where the situation is really revolutionary—in the preindustrial countries. Is the peasantry replacing the working class? And if so, is this radical innovation attributable to the Chinese Revolution, the most celebrated example of peasant revolution? From Mao's *Report on Hunan* to Lin Piao's statement in September 1965 on the encirclement of cities by the countryside, from Mao's remarks on the peasant essence of the Chinese Revolution[34] to Liu Shao-ch'i's assertion that Mao has nationalized Marxism,[35] there are many indications of the development of such a theory among the former comrades-in-arms now opposing one another in China. The relationship between Chinese or Sinified Marxism and peasant messianism is perhaps nowhere more manifest than in the work of young Communist Chinese historians, for whom glorifying Chinese peasant revolutions of earlier eras is an indirect way of glorifying the national past. For these historians, the Chinese peasantry has become the revolutionary class *par excellence*, a class with a more distinguished tradition of struggle than any Western proletariat. They have even managed to discover a united front directed by the peasantry in feudal China.[36] In theoretical terms, it follows from

[34] In *On New Democracy* (1940); a modified version is in Mao's *Selected Works* (Peking: Foreign Languages Press, 1961–65), I, 339–84.

[35] In his report to the Seventh Congress of the CCP (May 1945); cited in Hélène Carrère d'Encausse and Stuart R. Schram, *Marxism in Asia* (London: Allen Lane, 1969), pp. 259–61. (Liu was then the third-ranking member of the Central Committee, after Mao and Chu Teh. He became Chairman of the People's Republic in 1959 and was Mao's heir apparent until 1966, when he became a major target of the Cultural Revolution.) To be sure, "nationalization" takes in much else besides the adaptation of Marxism to a peasant society. But what a document like this one shows is precisely the development of a theory that, starting from a divergent view of the role of the peasantry, results (or claims to result; that is the question) in a Sinification of Marxism.

[36] See James P. Harrison, *The Communists and Chinese Peasant Rebellions: A Study in the Rewriting of Chinese History* (New York: Atheneum, 1969). National and social themes are once again inextricably mixed. It is a question not of the peasant as a social

their analysis that the peasantry is capable of assuming the revolutionary role of either the bourgeoisie or the proletariat, depending on the historical period. And this is the class on whose disappearance Marx was banking, a class whose disappearance would be its first, last, and only service to the cause of revolution and hence of historical progress! At this point, need we continue asking whether the peasant strategy represented a new departure for Marxist doctrine?

Is there any need either to take seriously the question of heresy? During both the Kiangsi period and the Second World War, while the CCP's leaders lived and worked among the peasants, contemporaries were calling Mao's undertaking a heretical break with Marxist doctrine.[37] Some called it heretical in order to condemn it—Trotskyites, for example, like Ch'en Tu-hsiu, who made ironic remarks about "mountain Marxism," and Trotsky himself, who said the rural soviets had no future and compared the Chinese party to the Russian Narodniks. Others called it heretical in order to praise it, including sympathetic missionaries, who were moved by the suffering of the peasantry, and liberal journalists, who were hostile to the dictatorship in Chungking (the Nationalists' wartime capital) and prone to idealize its adversary, or at least to impute to the Communists views that conformed to their own ideal. In the eyes of a good many reporters and of most outsiders who dealt with the ingratiating Chou En-lai, the party's grand master of public relations, the Chinese Communists were nothing more than agrarian reformers. Stalin himself seemed close to sharing this view in 1944, when he jeeringly remarked, "The Chinese Communists are not real Communists. They are 'margarine' Communists."[38]

---

type, but of the Chinese peasant; this glorious peasant tradition is presented as peculiarly Chinese. In departing from the dogma of peasant apathy, these historians also deviate from another Marxist principle, internationalism.

[37] We return now to the historic experiment discussed in this chapter, i.e. the Communist-led peasant agitation of the Kiangsi period. With respect to the ideologists of the triumphant revolution, suffice it to say that the views of contemporary Chinese historians on the peasantry, views whose doctrinal implications I have considered briefly above, differ markedly from the conclusions of the existing serious studies of peasant revolts in Imperial China.

[38] Cited in Herbert Feis, *The China Tangle* (Princeton, N.J.: Princeton University Press, 1953), p. 140.

The two views were equally wrong.[39] Despite the illusions of one side and the fears of the other, the Chinese Communists were neither misguided revolutionaries who had taken a disastrously wrong turn nor reformers disposed to accept a pluralist approach to the transformation of Chinese society. At no time did they become prisoners of a peasant mentality; at no time did the pressures of the moment cause them to lose sight of the "grand design." As Benjamin Schwartz emphasizes, "However immersed they may have been in a peasant environment, the leaders of the party never for a moment doubted that they were the chosen instruments of History, destined to lead China on the road to an industrialized socialism." They fully shared "the Hegelian-Marxist faith in a redemptive historic process and the Leninist faith that the Communist Party is itself the sole agent of historic redemption."[40]

The policy the Chinese Communists have followed since coming to power confirms their Marxist faith; they have used the peasants to force the progress of history, without wasting much time on the narrow-minded aspirations of the rural masses. This course of action implies not a change of heart but a remarkable consistency. The Chinese Communists did not transform themselves into peasants. They simply recognized and exploited two things the peasants had to offer: a reservoir of discontent great enough to overthrow the old regime, and a reservoir of labor great enough to make possible the primitive accumulation of capital.

Are we faced, then, with something that is neither a new application of Marxism nor a heretical departure from it? In fact, that is asking the wrong question. Our task is neither to clear the Chinese Communists of charges of heresy nor to deride their claims to innovation, but to establish exactly where their originality lies. Between 1927 and 1935 Mao was not inventing a theory; he was finding his way along a road that had to be traveled. What he discovered cannot be separated from the act of putting it to the test. What he was following was not the

---

[39] Possibly Stalin, who was speaking to American ambassador Averell Harriman, was being deliberately deceptive.
[40] *Chinese Communism and the Rise of Mao*, p. 202.

model of a theoretician, but the intuition of a political leader. We turn again to Benjamin Schwartz, who in his book characterizes "Maoist strategy" as a "heresy in act."[41] "Strategy" implies a contribution relating to the technique of seizing power, on the same level, if you will, as Lenin's recommendation of a highly organized and disciplined party. "Heresy in act" assumes that this strategy is worked out in action rather than in words; it is thus the direct opposite of an explicitly formulated doctrine whose novelty is loudly asserted. A Trotsky would have hastened to spell out the theoretical implications of the peasant strategy, to use the experiment and the concrete situation as a basis for generalization, and to proclaim the new doctrine to the world as Marxism's latest creative advance. Mao, by contrast, seemed constantly preoccupied with disguising the originality of the policy he was following,[42] with giving an unorthodox practice the appearance of orthodoxy. The Chinese Soviet Republic of which he was President was defined as a "democratic dictatorship of the proletariat and peasantry." In the legislation of this democratic dictatorship, few laws were so elaborately worked out, and none given so much publicity, as the laws on working conditions, which instituted the eight-hour day for the Republic's nonexistent proletariat. The novelty lay in the facts, not in the professions of faith; at the second congress of soviets, held in January 1934, there were eight urban workers out of 821 delegates.

The creator of the peasant strategy did not have to be a pro-

41 *Ibid.*, p. 191. Schwartz's views have been challenged by Karl Wittfogel in the *China Quarterly*, Nos. 1, 2, and 4 (1960), and more recently from the opposite point of view by John E. Rue in *Mao Tse-tung in Opposition, 1927–1935* (Stanford, Calif.: Stanford University Press, 1966), pp. 286–87. Neither of these two critiques seems to me very pertinent.

42 Except of course for the period when he was writing the *Report on Hunan*, which as we have seen represents an exception in his work. At the same time we must admit that Mao's circumstances were hardly comparable to Trotsky's (Trotsky, too, knew how to keep quiet when the struggle required it). Mao disguised his most daring innovations, hoping above all not to provoke the displeasure of the Executive Committee of the Comintern; it was bad enough that he was not following the Comintern's advice. Over and above the difference in circumstances, however, there remains a fundamental difference in character: Mao (the practitioner of 1930, not the divine prophet of the 1960's) did not try, as Trotsky did, to interpret the history he was making.

found thinker, and in fact was not. Later Mao would become a mediocre theoretician, but in the years when he was working out the peasant strategy and putting it into effect he rarely ventured into the domain of abstraction. Significantly, his ventures in this domain came after his self-confidence had been bolstered by his success in action.

Mao's greatness lies not in his writings, but in his deeds. What value his thought has derives directly from its practical base. It is a reflection and extension of Mao's day-to-day problems; without them it would have no substance. In this sense he is the highest type of Marxist, scornful of the world of ideas and of a doctrine that is not at the same time a guide for action. "Marxism-Leninism," he reminded the party's intellectuals in 1942, "has no beauty, no mystical value; it is simply very useful." And he added, for the benefit of "those who regard Marxism-Leninism as a religious dogma": "Your dogma is less useful than excrement. We see that dog excrement can fertilize the fields and man's can feed the dog. And dogmas? They can't fertilize the fields, nor can they feed a dog. Of what use are they?"[43]

Needless to say, I am not seeking to diminish Mao's stature indirectly by emphasizing that he is preeminently a man of action. We are trying to understand a historical figure, and through him the originality of a revolution. Mao is a man who was graduated from a normal school at twenty-five and discovered the rudiments of Marxism two years later, at an age when Trotsky was adumbrating his concept of permanent revolution in *The Balance and the Prospects*; a man who heard of America for the first time at seventeen and read his first newspaper at eighteen, when he moved to the capital of his native province. That a man's education was belated or incomplete does not mean that he cannot make important contributions to theory; my point is at once more modest and more sweeping. By repeating some well-known facts about Mao's life, I am trying to convey a situation that is all the more difficult to conceive of for being the polar opposite of the comfortable, carefully planned

[43] Boyd Compton, ed., *Mao's Chin : Party Reform Documents, 1942–44* (Seattle: University of Washington Press, 1952), p. 22.

life pattern of Western intellectuals. To take these truisms a step
further, is it at all surprising or unexpected that the man who
made the Chinese Revolution should be more of a fighter than
a thinker? No enterprise ever had less use for the contemplative
virtues. But what heroism, what toughness, what audacity, were
needed in the leader of a hounded band of Chinese revolutionaries for him to persist in his "crazy" schemes against the whole
world! Of the many kinds of courage Mao had to demonstrate
as a Marxist revolutionary, perhaps the greatest was the courage
to free himself from dogma, to perceive reality as it was even
when it called into question Marxism's most sacrosanct maxims.
Seen in forty years' perspective, Mao's strategy seems to represent the triumph of common sense, indeed to have been dictated by Chinese reality itself. What point can there be now in
labeling as heresy or innovation what was inherent in the nature
of things? Mao, or the greatness of common sense—only the
frivolous could read irony into this formulation. It is a rare virtue
to perceive the essence of a situation, an even rarer one to act on
one's perception. This is what Mao, and under his leadership the
CCP, did repeatedly in the years from 1927 to 1949.

That Marx has been proved wrong by his own victory, that the
doctrine has not emerged intact from the movement's success—
these statements are not new. It seems to me pointless to rehearse
Marx's errors once again. It seems even more pointless to cite
some passage or other by Marx to prove that he foresaw everything, or to appeal to the spirit of Marxism against the letter.
Suffice it to repeat that among other "anomalies" in the development of the Chinese Revolution, the roles of the proletariat
and the peasantry were reversed.[44] This does not mean that the
Peasantry with a capital P has replaced the Proletariat in the
vanguard of the revolution. All it means is that in China a more

[44] Some of these anomalies are only extensions of certain characteristics of the first
Communist revolution: a revolution that broke out in a "backward" country and failed
in the advanced capitalist countries; an expansion of the elite's role at the expense of
the revolutionary class (which would unquestionably have disturbed Marx and Engels);
an implicit identification at times between party and class—to name a few. Extensions
is an inadequate term; since in certain cases the Chinese developments carry to the
point of caricature (or to their logical conclusion) trends first observed in Russia, one
can scarcely regard them as mere accidents.

realistic strategy, one better suited to local conditions, made use of peasants; elsewhere, in societies with different economic systems, workers have proved the more effective revolutionary troops. Let us not bedeck the wretched peasantry in its turn with virtues to which it can lay no claim. With the Chinese Revolution, the myth—for myth it is—of the messianic role of the proletariat collapsed. Let us not replace it with another.

One can argue that the peasant strategy accorded with Lenin's views, that Maoism did not substantially modify Leninism.[45] This is true, but not terribly important. Maoist practice derived not from a theoretical outline that it applied or developed, but from objective conditions to which it responded. To understand it, to understand the Chinese Revolution, we must cease talking on this level. To juxtapose doctrine and practice, to compare the development of ideas in men's minds with developments in the real world, is a necessary undertaking but one whose potential is quickly exhausted; such comparisons suffer from a certain lack of depth, an externality with relation to the phenomena being compared, that tends to distort our conclusions. I do not mean to defend particularity, or historical "matter" as opposed to ideas, but simply to warn against a temptation to which I find historians prone. In studying societies whose contemporary development is related to (and in part determined by) a dominant ideology, they are tempted to give excessive attention to the ups and downs of that ideology, as if these ups and downs were in some sense history itself. At least this is what happens in discussions of the history of contemporary China. So as to avoid this pitfall, the following chapter attempts to take a searching if somewhat fragmentary look at what was actually happening in China in the 1920's and early 1930's.

[45] Lenin did not challenge the orthodox view of the peasantry, but saw no reason why a revolutionary party should not exploit peasant discontent.

4. Social Causes of the Chinese Revolution

China's basic social conflict was rural. The two opposing sides were the peasant masses and the landed upper class. Alongside the dire poverty and exploitation suffered by immense numbers of peasants, all other problems seemed minor. Nevertheless, urban social problems were never negligible and at times became critical, both for the working class and for the course of Chinese politics.

The Condition of the Urban Classes

The limited and geographically restricted development of modern industry in twentieth-century China gave rise to a class that lived and worked much as other nascent proletariats had done—150 years earlier in England, a hundred years earlier in France, fifty years earlier in Russia. A long workday, infrequent days of rest (one day a week was exceptional), extensive use of ill-paid female and child labor (especially in the textile industry), a high incidence of crippling accidents and occupational diseases, endemic tuberculosis, arbitrary deductions from wages, harsh rules and regulations, an almost total absence of welfare legislation, an extremely low standard of living, and for many workers chronic indebtedness — all these features of Chinese working-class life are straight out of the social history of nineteenth-century Europe.

To these must be added the special features of China's many precapitalist enterprises:

Some of the match factories and carpet factories, the ceramics and glass works, and the old-style silk and cotton factories could well have served as an inspiration for even Dante's description of the infernal regions. Pale, sickly creatures move around there in almost total darkness, amidst indescribable filth, and breathing an atmosphere that is insupportable to anyone coming in from outside. At ten o'clock at night, or sometimes even later, they are still at work, and the feeble light of a few oil lamps lends the factories a still more sinister aspect. A few breaks are taken to snatch some food while still at work, or to eat a meal in a courtyard covered with excrement and filth of all kinds. When the time to stop work finally comes, these miserable creatures doss down in any place they can find—the lucky ones on bales of waste material or in the attics if there are any, and the rest on the workshop floor, like chained dogs.[1]

Little by little, however, the workers' lot was improving. Progress was most marked from 1936 to 1946, when real wages rose appreciably, the workday was shortened (though in 1946 it was still about ten hours), child labor almost completely disappeared, and the gap between men's and women's wages diminished.[2] On the eve of the revolution, the problems of the working class had become less acute—and they still affected only 1 per cent of the Chinese population.

The smallness of China's working class did not in itself prevent it from becoming a great, indeed *the* great, revolutionary force, the more so since it was concentrated in a small number of industrial centers that were also among the country's leading political centers. (In similar circumstances the workers of Petrograd and Moscow played a more decisive role in 1917 than Russia's tens of millions of muzhiks.) After such promising beginnings as the Hong Kong strike of 1922, the Chinese labor movement grew so rapidly and spectacularly that it became a major force in the revolutionary upsurge of 1925–27.[3] Yet the proletariat played a negligible role in the last and decisive phase of the revolution. Neither major strikes nor urban uprisings paved

[1] Cited in Jean Chesneaux, *The Chinese Labor Movement, 1919–1927* (Stanford, Calif.: Stanford University Press, 1968), p. 86.

[2] The average workday in Shanghai was nine hours, 56 minutes, according to a report prepared for the city's Social Affairs Bureau. Cited in A. Doak Barnett, *China on the Eve of Communist Takeover* (New York: Praeger, 1963), p. 79.

[3] See pp. 55–56 above and Chesneaux, *The Chinese Labor Movement*.

the way for the Red Army as they had twenty years earlier for Chiang Kai-shek in Shanghai. There were very few workers in the triumphant Red Army; it was composed essentially of peasants and officered by other peasants and intellectuals. Why did the proletariat default at the decisive moment? No one has offered a satisfactory explanation. One can cite structural causes, notably the weakness of the proletariat's social base, but the proletariat's class enemies were scarcely more numerous and even more heterogeneous.[4] To confine ourselves to direct causes, the main reasons for the noninvolvement of the working class seem to be simply political—the repression of 1927–28 and the organization of semiofficial unions.[5] In the year following the formation of the Nanking government, union leaders and active union members were systematically killed off. The crippled and decimated labor movement was supplanted by a syndicalist system that was sponsored and controlled by the government.[6] For two decades the unions established under this system carried out only one progressive function, the only one they were

---

[4] The Chinese proletariat was not only small in size, but inexperienced and close to its peasant origins (many workers were seasonal migrants who returned to their village at harvest time). As a class, Chinese workers were more strongly influenced by regional and guild traditions than the *dévorants* and *gavots* of France under Charles X. [The *dévorants* and *gavots* were two of a number of competing mutual-aid societies of a type that originated with a medieval carpenters' association and gradually spread to other professions. These associations generally were limited to a specific occupation, carried on elaborate rituals, and by negotiation or violence acquired a monopoly in a given town. Under the Restoration they filled the vacuum left by the suppression of the guilds and were responsible for many short-lived, uncoordinated strikes.—Trans.]

[5] It remains, of course, to go beyond the direct causes. Why did the coordinated policy of repression and government syndicalism succeed? Did its success show the strength of the Chinese bourgeoisie, as represented by Chiang and the Nationalist regime? Probably not. In any case, given the dearth of research on the Kuomintang, any such hypothesis must be purely speculative. Equally hazardous (or at least premature) is any effort to attribute working-class passivity in 1946–49 to deteriorating economic conditions. From the little we know about economic conditions in those years, we can just as well argue the opposite case; it is a fact, for example, that the rare instances in which the proletariat seemed to throw off its lethargy (notably in early 1947 and early 1948 in Shanghai) coincided with periods of severe economic crisis.

[6] Union officials had to be members of the Kuomintang, and in some cases were directly appointed by the party. In big factories, membership in the government unions was obligatory. Since union funds came not from dues paid by the workers but from a special tax paid by the employer, financial dependence was a further guarantee of docility.

permitted: negotiating specific improvements for the workers. The results obtained by their pragmatic opportunism were necessarily won at the price of accepting the political and economic status quo.

Alongside these sham unions, which had more in common with the corporations of fascist Italy than with real labor unions, a free labor movement survived; but it was persecuted and weak, had no real hold on the working masses, and signaled its existence only in sporadic and quickly suppressed explosions. Outside CCP-controlled areas, there was no unofficial labor movement worth the name. Consider, for example, the great port and industrial center of Tientsin, which had one of the country's largest working-class populations. In the spring of 1948, during the Sixth Congress of the "Pan-Chinese" (pro-Communist) General Union, which claimed to represent 2,660,000 blue- and white-collar workers in both the "White areas" and the Liberated Areas, Tientsin was in the throes of an economic slump;[7] a number of factories had closed, and unemployment was widespread. Yet despite the fact that this slump was known to have been caused by deliberate government policy,[8] and the fact that Communist armies were only thirty to forty miles to the north, west, and south, no sign of strikes or subversive activity disturbed the calm on Tientsin's labor front. The Chinese Communists were wise to build up the military power of their peasant armies rather than count on the revolutionary ardor of the urban proletariat.

China's bourgeoisie, for its part, was for a time won over to revolution by its nationalist sentiments, as the bourgeoisies of other colonial and semicolonial countries had been. But for this class to rise in protest against China's political and social sys-

[7] In Communist terminology, the Liberated Areas were the areas that had fallen under Communist control during the war. The term later was applied to all the territory over which the CCP gained control between 1945 and 1949.

[8] Twenty-one of the city's 54 soap factories and 36 oil refineries were shut down in January 1948, after the government issued a decree limiting imports entering the port of Tientsin to 7.8 per cent of the country's total imports (as opposed to an average of 18 to 20 per cent before the Second World War). This quota was fixed as part of a general policy of discriminating against North China, which was in imminent danger of falling to the Communists. A. Doak Barnett, *China on the Eve*, pp. 57–58.

tem, it would have had to be impatient to throw off the yoke of the traditional ruling class,[9] like the French bourgeoisie under the Old Regime; and it was not. One might even suggest that the Chinese bourgeoisie was starting to transform itself peacefully into China's new privileged class.[10] And yet despite its rising fortunes, in comparison with its French counterpart it was lacking not so much in motivation as in strength. This ascendant class was still extremely small and rather marginal to the Chinese world; it was not a class to lead or inspire a revolution.[11]

One small segment of the bourgeoisie, if the term is conceived broadly and not limited to its economic connotations, did play a crucial role throughout the Chinese Revolution—the intelligentsia. But like the capitalists who sided with the revolution, the "modern" intellectuals did not consider social questions as such to be decisive, at least not directly or exclusively. For the most part, China's left-wing intellectuals came from the upper social strata.[12] They had their economic problems, to be sure: unemployment struck many young university graduates in the early 1930's, and inflation had even more serious effects during and after the Second World War.[13] Yet it was not their difficult material situation that made intellectuals into revolutionaries, but ideological commitment and a feeling of malaise. Social factors contributed to this malaise, tellingly in many cases, but most intellectuals regarded social ills as but one element in "the Chinese crisis," which they saw chiefly in nationalist terms. The mi-

---

[9] In the Chinese case, the landed upper class, whose influence was declining.

[10] The entrepreneurial class, which on the whole prospered from 1911 to 1927, continued to flourish under the Kuomintang, but at the price of trimming its sails and becoming to some extent a party to the regime. In some ways its relations with the government recall the *kuan-tu shang-pan* system of the last decades of the Manchu dynasty ("Direction by officials, management by merchants"). The "Great Families" of trade, industry, and banking were given extraordinary privileges by the government bureaucracy as a result of their close ties, and in some cases identity, with the ruling political class.

[11] It ended up joining the revolution when inflation and maladroit administration (see pp. 196–97) had driven it to desperation.

[12] Their families belonged either to the landed upper class or to the commercial bourgeoisie.

[13] A seeming paradox is that engineering undergraduates were particularly hard-hit by unemployment. As in many other underdeveloped countries, and for the same reasons, the two main careers open to returned students were politics and teaching.

nority who gave social questions top priority were moved much more by the situation of the masses than by their own problems. Their concern was first with the urban poor, and then, increasingly, with the rural masses.

The Misery of Peasant Life

The peasants up and down the valley [in West China, on the borders of Szechwan and Shensi] lived and died in their special fashion. ... The father of one family died. Since his wife had been failing and the family was very poor, they decided not to bury him right away. Perhaps the old woman would die, too, before really warm weather came and the old man began to smell. Then they could save by burying both with one funeral. The old lady agreed, so they stored the coffin in their darkest, coldest room, the old woman's sickroom, and piled stones on its lid to keep the dogs out.[14]

A historian's job is not to report cases of individual hardship, and certainly not to gratify a taste for the sordid and horrifying. It is not even primarily to recapture the life of the past; a poor historian it would be who forsook the world of ideas and the search for effects and causes. Nevertheless, I shall here cite other vignettes gleaned from the press and from memoirs and eye-witness accounts, vignettes that I think bring us closer to the heart of our subject (how the Chinese Revolution was born) than discussions of the interpretation and application of Marxism in China. The source of the revolution, the real strength of the CCP, must be sought in the living conditions that prevailed from one end of rural China to the other, where poverty, abuse, and early death were the only prospects for nearly half a billion people.

Dire poverty is evident in the passage quoted above, along with the kind of brutalization it led to. Moreover, for the Chinese sensibility, permeated by the importance of ancestor worship, the bitterest aspect of this situation is not the fate of the widow but that of the unfortunate dead man, who is condemned to wander, a prey to evil spirits, until he has been prop-

14 This passage comes from Graham Peck's fine book *Two Kinds of Time*, rev. ed. (Boston: Houghton Mifflin, 1967), p. 208.

erly buried. The last sentence in the passage alludes to the dogs who devoured corpses, a not uncommon sight in the Chinese countryside; in periods of famine, they attacked not only the dead, but also people who were still alive but too weak to defend themselves. And in mountainous regions, if one can take Lu Hsün's word for it,[15] wolves made quick work of babies that overworked mothers left unattended for an instant.

The second document I shall quote, consisting of excerpts from the correspondence of an American missionary couple, takes us to the other end of China, to a hospital in northern Kiangsi whose patients suffered from strange complaints:

Another desperate case that we treated for nothing [was] that of a young man who looked like a skeleton. One would have said there was nothing but skin on his bones. . . . His family was so poor that they had been obliged to sell him. . . . He was accordingly sent . . . to a family that had no sons. When, six years later, a son was finally born, his new family simply threw him out. And the poverty is so great in the region that one month spent begging and homeless brought him to death's door.

Another patient:

A young conscript was not yet familiar with the demands of military life and did not answer the sentinel's challenge fast enough: he paid for it with a bullet in the lung.

Still another:

A man who was attacked by a panther in the Kuling mountains, ten miles from here [the hospital was in Kiukiang, on the southern bank of the Yangtze]. This is the fourth such case that I have treated. This one I was able to cure; the last one did not survive the panther bites.[16]

Once again, in these simple medical notes, we read the familiar message of poverty and brutalization. Even extreme poverty

---

[15] In *Benediction*, which I consider one of his finest tales.

[16] Letters from Georgina and Edward Perkins, dated February 25 and August 22, 1931; in the archives of the Methodist Episcopal Church, Interchurch Center, New York.

rarely led to the selling of a son, as in the first case reported here, though the sale of daughters was common. As for brutalization, after a boy spends six years living with a family as their adopted son, the birth of a baby makes him superfluous and he is sent packing. His adopted family could not afford the luxury of being pitying, or, in rich men's language, humane. The doctor's notes show the brutality, too, of military life; the army treated its recruits, almost all of whom were peasants, with the same contempt, cruelty, and disregard for human life that characterized its relations with peasant civilians, who were constantly subjected to forced labor and arbitrary taxation, constantly brutalized and plundered. The last case, of the man wounded by a panther, reminds us of other factors making rural life precarious. The insecurity of the Chinese countryside in the twentieth century (an insecurity to which both wild animals and bandits contributed) was comparable to that of settled clearings in early medieval Europe, with their surrounding forests full of wolves and outlaws. In China, danger began with the first stretch of uncultivated high ground. It lay in wait, too, along roads, rivers, and even railroads; many a passenger in wagons, boats, and trains was attacked, robbed, or held for ransom, and more than a few were killed.

A final vignette, the last to be quoted here:

Everywhere one sees people beseeching the gods, praying for rainfall, putting up altars, burning incense, and staging processions in honor of the Dragon King. The most tragic of all are the peasants who offer themselves as sacrifices to make the rain come...; in Ningpo, ten peasants hurled themselves into the Dragon's Pond in hopes of appeasing the monster.[17]

This passage evokes an enemy that periodically assailed the Chinese peasant—drought. But above all it again evokes the mental universe of the early medieval West. Peasants led by tragic superstitions to drown themselves in the hope that the dragon

---

[17] Excerpt from an article in *Ta-kung-pao*, one of the country's leading daily newspapers, published on July 14, 1934. The area referred to is a hundred miles south of the mouth of the Yangtze, in Chekiang province.

who dispensed rain would at least spare their families—it is indeed our medieval ancestors that these contemporaries, these future soldiers of the Red Army, call to mind. The similarity in outlook reflects their equal helplessness before the forces of nature, the equal precariousness of human life, a precariousness heightened in the Chinese case by semifeudal oppression.[18]

The word oppression immediately leads us to ask whether the Chinese peasant's wretchedness was due primarily to injustice and exploitation, or to such objective factors as the backwardness of the economy and the relationship between available wealth and the number of mouths to be fed. Was the maldistribution of wealth to blame, or was there too little wealth to distribute? Chinese Communist historians naturally stress human responsibilities and relentlessly denounce the landowners' exploitation of the peasantry. This denunciation, though manifestly called for, is to my mind inadequate. I believe that objective conditions, i.e. economic and demographic conditions, were in themselves sufficient to make the distress of the vast majority inevitable.[19] But because human actions arouse more indignation, they are more useful in inciting peasant revolt; the excess comfort of a privileged few, their arbitrary and oppressive conduct, seem less bearable than a general scarcity of resources. That is why, in discussing the social causes of the Chinese Revolution, I have chosen to give relatively more extensive treatment to the exploitation of man by man than to the objective givens of the Chinese situation, which have defied and will long continue to defy the policies and programs of the People's Republic.

Demography and Economy

One of the most remarkable facts of world demographic history, a fact whose full consequences are still to be felt, is the extraordinary growth of the Chinese population in the last few

---

[18] "Semi" should be emphasized; modern Chinese society, as we shall see, was very different from feudal Europe.

[19] Needless to say, it is only for analytical purposes that we distinguish between natural and man-made causes of peasant suffering. Obviously this suffering resulted from a total situation, in which political and social organization and the heritage of a long history weighed heavily.

centuries. If the official figures can be believed, shortly after the People's Republic was founded its population was ten times that of the last dynasty, the Ch'ing, three centuries earlier; mainland China had 580 million people in 1953, as opposed to ten million households or 50–60 million people in 1651. The Chinese population today is reasonably estimated at 750–800 million. The contemporary population growth is not particularly astonishing; similar increases have occurred in most underdeveloped countries and can be convincingly accounted for by demographers. What is harder to explain is the earlier growth of the Chinese population, and particularly its rate. There were 432 million Chinese by 1851, according to official estimates. If we make only the most rudimentary corrections in these estimates—the one for 1851 may be a bit high, whereas the one for 1651 is probably no more than half the true figure—we must still conclude that China's already vast population tripled in 200 years, from 120–140 million in 1651 to 350–430 million in 1851. In the eighteenth century the population seems to have more than doubled in less than a hundred years, from some 150 million in 1700 to 313 million in 1794. And all this growth came *before* any real contact with the West, *before* the beginning of industrialization.

Whatever the causes of this phenomenon, which belies the classical view of population growth in premodern societies, its effect in our time is clear.[20] On the eve of the revolution, the

[20] In the last two centuries China may have been paying the price of the extraordinary successes of earlier centuries. For nearly a thousand years, according to Ho Ping-ti's classic demographic history, China's food situation was appreciably better than Europe's. A series of advances, some of them revolutionary, made possible increase after increase in the acreage under cultivation and in per-acre yield, and every increase helped to feed an expanding population. Some advances, such as the introduction of early-maturing strains of rice, dated from the Sung dynasty (960–1279). Another advance, the southward spread of grains grown in northern China (wheat, barley, millet, and kaoliang), had been favored by the Sung emperors but did not have its full effect until centuries later; the introduction of new food crops from America (potatoes, maize, and sweet potatoes) had an even greater delayed impact. With these native and imported crops it became possible to cultivate soil too dry or too light for rice, and thus to achieve a new equilibrium between food supply and population; in the eighteenth century, settlement of the highlands of Central China went hand in hand with population growth. See Ho Ping-ti, *Studies on the Population of China, 1358–1953*, Chapter Eight. (The estimates given in the previous paragraph are also taken from Ho's work, pp. 270, 281, and *passim*.)

pressure of population on land in China was greater than it had ever been before. According to several inquiries carried out between 1930 and 1935, the average peasant family plot was 3.3 acres. It goes without saying that there were marked variations in average plot size, depending on the region, the climate, and the fertility of the soil. In a village in Yunnan (the province bordering Indochina) studied around 1940 by one of China's great rural sociologists, the average family had the use of slightly less than one acre. A whole village in Yunnan was then roughly equivalent in size to a single family farm in the American Middle West, and the two were also equivalent in production. In the one case the land fed the five or six members of an American family, in the other the five or six hundred inhabitants of a Chinese village.

One last point by way of emphasizing demographic pressures on agriculture and peasant life. A plague as common as drought, which was responsible for more deaths than floods, locusts, and outlaws put together, can of course be explained by geography and climate. But demographic pressure is an even better explanation, for it brought to the Great Plain of North China a population density unknown in any other semi-arid region of the world. Rainfall there was, but nowhere near enough to grow food for so dense a population.

In the 1930's Japanese farms were even smaller than Chinese farms, but though the Japanese peasant was far from living a life of ease, he was much better off than his Chinese counterpart. The reason was Japan's relatively advanced science and technology, or, to put it another way, China's relatively backward economy.

Chinese agriculture was by no means primitive. The Chinese farmer's refined techniques and infinite painstakingness (the only resource he never stinted on was his own labor) have been compared to the highest form of gardening. But the Chinese farmer's art belonged to a prescientific era, which meant that no matter how untiring and ingenious his efforts, he could never hope for more than a modest yield. As I have suggested, the per acre yield obtained with such great effort in Yunnan should be compared to that of the large mechanized farm of the American prairie.

The methods of the Chinese farmer were prescientific. His choice of seed was generally left to chance; as readily as not, he might plant an arid slope with a variety of grain that required irrigation, or even the flood conditions of humid bottomlands. Even if the Chinese farmer had had some knowledge of modern agronomy, the crudeness of his equipment would have kept him from applying it. Deep plowing was not possible with the plows used in many provinces. The inadequately tilled and aerated land was subjected to exhausting demands: one or two harvests a year, without fallow periods or crop rotation, for hundreds if not thousands of years. After the harvest, the land was stripped of straw, grass, leaves, and other bits of organic material, which was carefully hoarded for use as fuel.[21] And if much was required of the land, little was given it in return. As much fertilizer as possible was applied, but at most it was far too little. Animal manure was rare in a country where men had to be fed before any thought could be given to raising animals. Chemical fertilizers were out of the question; almost no such fertilizer was produced, and even if there had been more, the peasants would not have had the capital to buy it. They compensated for the soil's deficiency as best they could, not only with human excrement, which they collected systematically and measured out by the spoonful for each plant,[22] but with all the low-quality, low-cost soil-enriching materials that they could find or fabricate—low-cost, that is, provided one disregards time and toil. The laboriousness of some of their methods seems almost insane to one who is not driven by necessity to the same extremes. Some peasants actually removed soil from canals and riverbeds

[21] Wood was lacking because of the deforestation that had occurred earlier, notably during the eighteenth century (*ibid.*, pp. 146–48). This, too, had stemmed from the need to bring new fields under cultivation, and had in turn caused further suffering by aggravating the effects of floods. Coal was also scarce. We know now that China has abundant coal deposits; but the size of these deposits was undreamed of until recently, and those that were known were only sporadically and inefficiently exploited.

[22] The practice had tragic consequences. Among the occupational diseases of the Chinese farmer, the deadliest ones came from working barefooted in plots fertilized with night soil.

as soon as a thin layer of fertilizing alluvium had been deposited on it, and carried it off to apply to their fields.

The peasant's plight was further complicated by all sorts of psychological, social, and cultural patterns and practices, not all of them the consequences of material penury. Among these were a propensity to adhere to established routine, which inhibited the adoption of new techniques and plant varieties; the practice of ancestor worship, which required that space be set aside for graves on plots of land that were already too small; and the absence of hygiene measures, which resulted in numerous plant diseases and killed large numbers of silkworms. Another example was the extreme parcelization of land, the result of a long-standing system of inheritance that did not favor the eldest child. Among other things, parcelization led to wasteful duplication of effort, obstructed both drainage and irrigation, and prevented an effective attack on destructive insects.

The Chinese peasant accepted poverty as his fate. How could he escape when there were so many obstacles, each related to others that were still more unmovable? With apparently equal resignation, he accepted the fact that other men were rich and lived off his misery.

Village Class Structure

Economic development in this economy of scarcity was further hobbled by the Chinese social structure. Although much of China's arable land was divided into plots too small to be economically viable, the heart of the agrarian problem lay not in parcelization but in the prevalence of tenant farming. To be sure, tenant farming and land rent are by no means the whole story of the exploitation of the peasant by the landed upper class. Before we discuss this question in detail, it should be made clear that on the eve of the Communist revolution, China had very few large landowners; even the richest man in a village rarely owned more than 50 acres.[23] We are dealing, then,

[23] And in some cases only two to five acres. A district in Kwangtung province, for example, was investigated in great detail in 1933. On the average, resident landlords

with a society of poor people in which even the well-to-do had very little property.[24] It should also be pointed out that a little more than half the Chinese peasants owned the land they tilled. (The proportion was much higher in the North, and decidedly lower in Central and South China, particularly near cities, rivers, and ports, where the impact of a money economy and Western influence appears to have favored tenant farming.) Moreover, the majority of tenant farmers were landowners as well; that is, they worked both their own tiny plot, which was too small to support their family, and land belonging to someone else. Only about 20 per cent of Chinese peasants were tenant farmers pure and simple, though the figure rose to 75 per cent or even higher in the South.

With these stipulations in mind, let us look at the approximate division of landownership in China proper at the end of the Second World War:

Social class	Percentage of rural families	Percentage of landholdings
Upper class	3%	26%
Rich peasants	7	27
Middle peasants	22	25
Poor peasants	68	22

Our table shows that 10 per cent of the rural families owned slightly more than half the land.[25] This disproportion was least marked in the North and greatest in the South, where close to half the land belonged to large landowners and tenant farming was much more prevalent.

It is not patently absurd to compare the Russian aristocracy in the waning years of the Empire with the French nobility of

---

owned 16.7 *mou* or just over two and a half acres (a mou is .1518 acres). Absentee landlords, who were fewer in number, were slightly better off.

[24] Sun Yat-sen once quipped that Chinese society was composed of only two classes: the very poor and the less poor.

[25] Taken from Ch'en Han-seng, *The Chinese Peasant,* Oxford Pamphlets on Indian Affairs, No. 33 (London: Oxford University Press, 1945), p. 13. Excluded from the tabulation are the Northeast (Manchuria), which was recently settled and therefore atypical, and the Northwest (Tibet, Sinkiang, Outer Mongolia), which had a more archaic social structure than China proper.

the Old Regime, different though the dramatis personae of Chekhov and Beaumarchais may be. But we must immediately discard any notion that the class against whom the Chinese Revolution was made resembled the old guards of 1789 and 1917. Still less was it like the hereditary nobility of the medieval West.²⁶ China's landed upper class was *sui generis*. In some respects it must be ranked higher, in some respects lower, than its closest European counterparts. It did not have anything like their wealth; hence the term gentry would adequately convey its economic position. But to its limited economic power—which was not all that limited in a Chinese village, where it made possible the inordinate privilege of leisure and sometimes even a superfluity of possessions—were added intellectual prestige, as prized in China as noble blood was elsewhere, and political power, a monopoly of the educated elite. For centuries these privileges had enabled the large landowners to dominate and govern Chinese society. The upheavals of the early twentieth century had begun to undermine the landlords' dominant position, but though they lacked the vitality as a class to adapt to the twentieth century, they were still strong enough to defend their threatened privileges.

What role did the upper class play in rural economic life in the twentieth century? As landowners they received land rent from their tenants.²⁷ As the holders of all sorts of local administrative responsibilities, they received various fees and gratuities. As grain merchants (for land rent was often paid in kind and led to marketable surpluses), they were almost automatically speculators under the market conditions then prevailing. Finally, they were of necessity the local moneylenders, for they alone, or almost alone, had money to spare in a land where borrowers were legion and interest rates high. Rarely did the same person fulfill all these functions. The moneylender might be the brother

---

²⁶ In China there were neither ties of personal dependence nor hereditary membership in a closed caste. As for the tastes and values of the professional warrior, the very idea would have horrified the Chinese scholar-official.

²⁷ Although land rent was far from negligible, it was not so great as is sometimes thought. In Szechwan in 1940, for example, land rent less taxes yielded a return on capital of 8 per cent. Other estimates range from 10 to 11 per cent.

or uncle of the local landowner, the grain merchant the steward of the great absentee landlord. It was the upper class as a whole that dominated all four sectors of the rural economy.[28]

The large landowners were almost the only villagers who did not till the soil. With few exceptions, all the other classes participated in productive work of one sort or another.[29] One of these classes, the rural proletariat, does not appear as such in the table on p. 95 for the simple reason that it owned no land.[30] This marginal class, composed of paid farm workers, temporary or itinerant hired hands, peddlers, and vagabonds, had certain characteristics that in less deprived societies define the subproletariat. From its ranks were to come some of China's most dedicated revolutionaries.

By definition much larger in size than this marginal class were the social classes that were a more integral part of village society: the peasants properly speaking. No single criterion satisfactorily distinguishes the rich peasants from the poor and middle peasants;[31] at the very least, both the land owned or worked and the work force employed on it must be taken into account.[32] Let us designate as middle peasants those peasants who could make ends meet in a normal year without either hiring anyone else or working for anyone else. Those who continuously employed paid workmen from outside their family during the busy season and had under cultivation an amount of land greater than the average middle peasant holding in the same village were the rich peasants. Either one of these two criteria may suffice to define the rich peasant—for example, if his landholdings were at

---

[28] Sometimes they had competition from rich peasants. When Mao Tse-tung's father became a rich peasant, he also became a grain merchant.

[29] In some cases a substantial proportion of the small landowners (30 per cent in the village of Lutsun, in Yunnan province, according to Fei Hsiao-tung) did no work at all. In an economy with no real capacity for expansion, to work hard at getting rich was regarded as taking the bread out of someone else's mouth. Fei Hsiao-tung and Chang Chih-i, *Earthbound China* (Chicago: University of Chicago Press, 1945), p. 84.

[30] Actually, the rural proletariat is counted in with the poor peasants there.

[31] As we have seen, even tenant farming was less a matter of social class than of geography.

[32] Twenty mou of rented land may be taken as roughly equal to eleven or twelve mou of land a peasant owned himself. The ratio differs from region to region, and even from district to district, with variations in land rent rates.

least twice those of the middle peasant. Poor peasant families, by contrast, were those who depended on the wages of one or more members for their subsistence, who had less land of their own than the middle peasants, or both. This classification established, it would be wise to use as a control—and a corrective—such criteria as indebtedness, which was chronic among the poor peasants, generally seasonal among the middle peasants, and rare and temporary among the rich peasants.[33]

These distinctions are tedious but fundamental. They are the very ones used by the Communists from the Kiangsi period on,[34] the basis of their agrarian revolution—and of the Chinese Revolution itself. As difficult to define as they are to distinguish, these social categories correspond not only to real divisions in the village class structure but to the self-perception of the people in question, who saw themselves spontaneously as rich, middle, or poor peasants. Between these categories there was no unbridgeable chasm: a rise in status was always within the realm of possibility,[35] and falls were common. Nonetheless, there were at times marked inequalities. In one district on the Kwangtung coast, for example, the average rich peasant family owned two-thirds as much land as the average member of the upper class (who, to be sure, had other sources of income) and something like ten times as much as the average poor peasant![36] It is no surprise that rich and poor peasants were not equally receptive to the speeches and suggestions of professional revolutionaries. The class that listened to the revolutionaries, the class they cultivated, the back-

---

[33] Adapted from Ch'en Han-seng, *Landlord and Peasant in China: A Study of the Agrarian Crisis in South China* (New York: International Publishers, 1936), p. 8.

[34] With the qualification that the CCP's basic criteria, though they have varied with shifts in the party's agrarian policy, have been stricter for each class than the ones proposed here, and in my judgment have suffered from excessive rigidity and narrowness. See, among other discussions of the subject, Mao Tse-tung, "How to Differentiate the Classes in the Rural Areas" (1933), *Selected Works*, I, 137–39.

[35] Even, though the odds against it were enormous, from the peasantry to the upper class, since literati status was traditionally defined by the passing of government examinations.

[36] According to my source (Ch'en Han-seng, *Landlord and Peasant*, Table 11, p. 127), which unfortunately fails to distinguish between poor peasants and the relatively small rural proletariat, the average family holding of the two classes combined was one-thirteenth that of the rich peasants (.87 mou as opposed to 11.33 mou). Here and elsewhere the word "district" is a translation of *hsien* (often translated "county"), an administrative unit that usually had a population of several hundred thousand people.

bone and flesh of the Chinese Revolution, was the poor peasant class, which is to say the backbone and flesh of China herself.

Land Rent, Land Taxes, Usury

The only social categories that can be defined with precision cross-cut others: e.g. the prosperous tenant farmer,[87] the small landowner who worked his own land and was on the brink of destitution. The categories do, however, enable us to see more clearly the victims of the ills that struck the peasant masses, of which the two leading ones were land rent and land taxes.

It is hard to say just how much land rent amounted to, the more so since it varied considerably from one place to another and payment took many different forms.[88] On the eve of the Second World War, land rent probably averaged around 45 per cent of the total harvest. Although this figure is somewhat lower than the ones given in most books on China, it still represents an enormous burden on the tenant farmer. What was left after he paid the rent was scarcely enough to keep his family alive in a year when no extraordinary natural or man-made disaster upset the precarious balance. Refusal to pay land rent was an increasingly common occurrence, as was the practice of dodging the landlord's collection agent when he made his customary rounds. But it was difficult, and dangerous to boot, to try to evade the rent collector. Not only was the legal arm of the government always at the landlord's disposal (recalcitrant tenant farmers were promptly clapped into prison), but the landlord could also take back his land and rent it to a more docile tenant.[89] Omnipresent land hunger and the resulting competition among

[87] Such cases were of course most common in the South. In the coastal Kwangtung district mentioned earlier, one rich peasant in six owned no land whatever.

[88] Rent was most often paid in kind, less often in money, and on rare occasion in work. Sometimes the rent was a fixed amount, but sharecropping arrangements were more common. In some cases the sharecropper paid the owner a percentage of all the crops harvested, in others a percentage of the main crop only; the variations were legion.

[89] This was not true at all times and in all places. In some places the tenants had tenancy rights (the so-called surface rights) and the landlord only ownership rights (subsoil rights), which meant that he could not force the tenant off the land. Elsewhere the tenant's rights to the land were fixed not by law but by practice; the owner could not evict the tenant except for cause. As in medieval and early modern France, practice varied from province to province and sometimes from district to district, which makes generalizing difficult and all generalizations partly false.

tenant farmers reinforced the landlord's position,[40] just as the plethora of would-be factory hands on the outskirts of London and Manchester favored the manufacturer in the early nineteenth century.

Certain widespread practices of more or less recent origin further aggravated the tenant farmer's plight.[41] Among them were the practice of exacting advance payments on land rent, and that of requiring a deposit (ranging from 10 to 200 per cent of the total rent!) on conclusion of the rental agreement.[42] Tenants who could not pay the deposit frequently borrowed part or all of it, at interest, from the landlord himself. Another relatively new practice, which was particularly prevalent in the fertile river deposits (*sha-t'ien* or sand fields) of the Sikiang delta in South China, was the subleasing of land. Land-renting companies leased clan holdings of several thousand acres and divided them into a great many plots; the tenant farmer on each plot paid a rent twice the amount paid to the clan. Some exceptional customs, most commonly found in the western provinces, recall the forced labor and services of feudal Europe. When the master's family sought refuge in the mountains from the summer heat, the tenant farmer was sometimes transformed for a week or two into an unpaid coolie who helped the family with the move. It does not follow that tenant farmers were in any sense subjects of the landlord. Outside Tibet and a few other areas, the tenant farmer was unquestionably a free peasant who was not subject to any sort of legal servitude. His servitude was economic.

Land taxes were the second great torment of rural life. The land tax was by no means comparable in amount to land rent; indeed, it was relatively moderate. But the peasant had no idea what the legal tax rate was, and no collector was held to it.

---

[40] There were even cases, notably on clan holdings, of tenants bribing the official in charge of land rentals in hopes of getting a slightly larger plot.

[41] Nor did the costly customs of earlier times die out altogether. Many a tenant in the 1930's was still constrained to supply certain obligatory meals to his landlord and various gifts—e.g. chicken, wood, straw sandals, and fish—to his landlord's agent.

[42] In two districts in Kiangsu province, the percentage of farms rented with an advance deposit rose between 1905 and 1924 from 73 to 88 per cent in one case, and from 25.5 to 62 per cent in the other.

Often the theoretical amount of the tax was doubled by so-called surtaxes, and sometimes it was increased tenfold.[43] Originally a given surtax was imposed for a specific purpose—to pay for a new canal, school, or road, for the taking of a census, for an anti-bandit campaign. But the local administration rarely renounced a source of additional revenue once the original purpose was accomplished. From the administrator's point of view, the repeal or reduction of a tax was justified only when popular protests promised to make it inordinately difficult to collect.

After surtaxes, the most striking abuse was collection of the land tax long before it theoretically fell due, a practice begun under the Empire. Sometimes local administrators, but more often military potentates, would collect taxes due years or even decades later so as to pay the back wages they owed their mercenaries or to finance an expedition against a neighboring warlord. The record is held by Szechwan, which was fought over by rival warlords in the 1930's: in one district the taxes due in 1971 were assessed in January 1933, and in another those due in 1974 were assessed in April 1933. Elsewhere, eleven years' land taxes were collected in a year and a half (October 1931 to March 1933).

The last abuse—the last one to be mentioned here, that is, for the subject is inexhaustible—was the monopoly on tax collection sometimes held by a hereditary caste, which kept its account books closed even to the district magistrate. In a district near Nanking, monopolistic tax collectors are believed to have turned in less than a third of the sum they actually collected in 1932. The profits of the farmers-general under the Old Regime in France pale by comparison.

Finally, precisely as in France under the Old Regime, inequities of all sorts were accompanied by numerous inconsistencies and irregularities. A piece of land might be subject to double taxation because it had been counted twice in the last census; elsewhere, no land survey had been made and some families

[43] In Chekiang province in the early 1930's the various surtaxes amounted on the average to one and a half times the land tax, but there were districts in neighboring Kiangsi province where surtaxes were twenty times the nominal tax, and even fifty times (in 1933)!

paid no taxes at all. The tax rate varied from one district to another, as did the timing and frequency of collections. The peasant, never knowing when the next payment would be due, tended to think of the land tax as an arbitrary exaction, something he had to pay because he was in no position to argue with the revenue officials. The tax-collecting agency was a powerful one; it could not only arrest delinquent taxpayers but also punish them, and frequently did so. The overlapping powers of tax collectors, the many abuses of those powers, and the general muddle had an effect that went beyond the purely fiscal (here again one thinks of 1788). All these difficulties were evidence of an ineffectual and arbitrary judicial system that did not fall with equal weight on all.

The peasant often had to take out a loan to pay his taxes. In rural China, as in every society of small producers, the problem of credit was a constant, unremitting torment. To pay land rent and land taxes, and to buy the necessary minimum of equipment and essential items that the family could not produce itself (perhaps a quarter of its total consumption), the peasant's main and sometimes only source of income was his small marketable surplus. Marketing conditions were highly unfavorable to the small producer. His lack of capital and his primitive means of transport, not to mention numerous tolls and local taxes, generally kept him from selling his produce in distant markets; add to this the absence of a unified national market and a general ignorance of prices paid elsewhere, and it is clear that everything conspired to put the peasant farmer at the mercy of the grain merchant, the man who could stock up, acquire information, and wait.

Having sold his surplus produce (and sometimes a little more) right after the harvest, when prices were at their lowest, the peasant could earn no more until the next harvest. If he had no other way to subsist, he begged a loan from the village moneylender or from one in the neighboring town.[44] Alternatively, he

---

[44] According to a 1933 investigation of twenty-two provinces by the official Committee for Agricultural Research, nearly 90 per cent of all loans to peasants came from traditional moneylenders, either individual lenders (large landowners, 24 per cent;

could go to the pawnbroker, whose rates were also extremely high (provided he had something to pawn, which was not always the case), sometimes to a neighbor who was a little less hard up than he, or to his landlord. It was not unheard of for a landlord to lend money at moderate interest or even to advance small sums at no interest. The professional moneylender's rates varied considerably, depending on the season, on whether the loan was in money or in grain (grain was much more costly), on whether the harvest had been poor or abundant, etc. For a cash loan, annual interest of 20 to 30 per cent, deducted in advance, was common, but annual interest was known to reach 100 per cent or more. In hard times, interest rates rose to incredible heights. Combined with the concurrent rise in grain prices in such times, a food loan stripped many a family of its land. Borrowing was the classic road to dispossession, to the point where many peasants were resigned to selling their children rather than mortgage their land. Nonetheless, investigations in 1929, 1934, and 1935 revealed that almost half of all peasant families (44 per cent)—poor, middle, and "rich"—were in debt.

Although I have not exhausted the list of serious, even tragic rural problems, it is perhaps worth mentioning again a plague that was almost as serious as usury, namely chronic insecurity. The extortions of soldiers and bandits[45] are political problems, to be sure, but their relation to socioeconomic conditions is obvious. The condottieri recruited their mercenaries from a starving peasantry. Banditry arose from the kind of conditions depicted in a dispatch from the American consul at Foochow describing the impact of famine on two districts in Fukien province and estimating the number of deaths from starvation and suicide. He sums up the survivors' fate as follows: "The strong have become bandits and the weak beggars."[46]

---

merchants, 25 per cent; rich peasants, 18 per cent) or businesses that lent money at interest (village shops, 13 per cent; pawnshops, 9 per cent). Modern banks accounted for only 2.4 per cent of peasant loans.

[45] The line between soldiers and bandits was not always easy to draw; some men switched from one category to the other depending on whether or not their wages were paid on time.

[46] United States, Department of State, 893.00 PR Foochow/68 (dispatch of Sept. 2, 1933).

Was the Peasant's Condition Deteriorating?

At this point the reader may object that the picture given here of the extreme poverty and exploitation of the peasant masses is essentially timeless. How is it that comparable albeit different social conditions persisted for generations and even centuries without apparently compromising a political stability that is traditionally presented as unique in world history?

This objection raises two orders of questions, the first concerned with changes in the peasant's condition, the second with the peasantry's capacity for revolution. On the first point, we know that even apart from the disruptions caused by imperialist penetration, the peasant's standard of living declined during the modern era simply as a result of population growth; a Chinese peasant's existence in the early twentieth century was more precarious than his eighteenth-century ancestor's.[47] It is possible that things got still worse in the decades immediately preceding the Second World War, but we cannot be certain.[48] One can easily construct a systematic "proof" to this effect, citing such evidence as increases in land rent, concentration of landownership, a drop in agricultural prices, and an increase in female agricultural laborers, which last is an indication that more and more men were leaving the land to seek a living in cities or foreign countries.[49] But there is almost equally impressive evidence tending to prove the opposite. Before any overall hypothesis can be

[47] Ho Ping-ti, *Studies on the Population of China.*
[48] Most writers on the subject conclude that the peasant's condition was continuing to worsen, but the evidence even of such serious scholars among them as Fei Hsiaotung, R. H. Tawney, and Ch'en Han-seng is not conclusive. Their writings either express an *a priori* conviction, or use continued deterioration as a working hypothesis, or offer generalizations too broad to be supported by their investigation of one sector of peasant activity or a single geographic region. It may well be that the men writing in the thirties mistook for symptoms of steady rural disintegration what were in fact temporary, though undeniably acute, reflections in China of the worldwide depression. (I am indebted to Mme. Marie-Claire Bergère for suggesting this last idea to me.)
[49] For example, it can be argued that the increasing concentration of landownership was turning more peasants into rural proletarians, causing widespread unemployment that led to a drop in agricultural wages, etc. Other economic factors can be adduced in making such an argument: for example, that the appearance of a capitalist sector in the Chinese economy led to the concentration of landownership; that international economic competition undermined two supplementary sources of peasant income, silkworm breeding and rural handicrafts; that the worldwide economic crisis caused a

proved or disproved, new monographs (for which there are abundant materials) will have to be written. Not everything in the arguments presented in note 49 is wrong, yet only one thing is certain: developments were neither so simple nor so uniform as these arguments suggest.

Nevertheless, we must not let the conflicting facts distort our perspective. Whether or not rural misery was increasing during the twenties and thirties, it was surely in ample enough supply to fuel a revolution. Whatever the overall picture, there were many instances of increasing distress. By way of conclusion, it is worth mentioning two new developments of the revolutionary period that are symptoms—or perhaps causes—of difficulties unknown to previous eras. The first was demographic: the settlement of the Northeast, thanks to which the population of Manchuria tripled in thirty years.[50] This remarkable result seemingly reproduces on a Chinese scale the success of Norway, which also undertook to populate its northern frontier regions at the beginning of the twentieth century. But in Norway the impetus to settlement was bolstered by positive advantages, not the least of which was the parcel of land given each new settler; and though the Norwegian venture was much less risky than crossing the Gulf of Chihli or the Great Wall, it had all the glamour of a pioneer expedition. When a peasant left for Manchuria, by contrast, he was impelled, or more precisely compelled, to leave by purely negative factors, if only the simple inability to survive in his native place. The name given these settlers is eloquent testimony to this: *nan-min*, literally "refugees" or "disaster victims." The settlement of Manchuria, then, was much more of an exodus than a pioneering movement; its purpose was not so much to develop Manchuria's virgin lands as to escape the blighted areas of Shantung and other Yellow River provinces.

The other new feature of the prerevolutionary period lay in

---

fall both in land prices (from 30 to 80 per cent in various places between 1929 and 1933) and in grain prices; that a continuous rise in land rent forced the tenant farmer to exhaust the soil by double-cropping in order to survive; and finally that social disintegration made for a decline in production (by causing people to abandon land that had once been cultivated, etc.).

[50] Kungtu C. Sun, *The Economic Development of Manchuria in the First Half of the Twentieth Century* (Cambridge, Mass.: Harvard University Press, 1969), p. 21.

the domain of social relations, specifically relations between members of the landed upper class and their tenants. Under the Empire, in part because of Confucianism, these relations were what might be called paternalistic.[51] In the twentieth century they became more distant, less human. Absentee ownership increased, and once in the city the landlord acquired new values that tended to undercut his feelings of obligation to his tenants. More and more landlords left the management of their lands to a steward, and this new class of professional intermediaries was much harder on the tenant farmer than the traditional landowner had been.[52] The contract binding the owner and the man who actually worked the soil became increasingly impersonal, to the point where some tenants no longer knew who their master was. In several districts of the lower Yangtze Valley, for example, land rights became the object of routine transactions worked out in town rather than on the site itself; a company sold land rights and took the responsibility for rent-collecting. In these circumstances it is not surprising that the landlords' traditional prestige was on the wane. Though it remains an open question whether or not material conditions were steadily deteriorating, and if so to what extent, it is clear that supporting social arrangements had begun to change.

This statement brings us back to the second question raised earlier, that of the peasantry's capacity for revolution. Our answer this time is briefer, but much more immediately relevant to the subject of this book. Peasant insurrections had occurred throughout Chinese history, but even the successful ones resulted only in a change of dynasty. One of the great new facts of the contemporary era was the existence of an organized revolutionary movement, a movement that knew where it was going and was ready to exploit, channel, and transform discontent arising from social problems. We saw the movement at work in the previous chapter; we shall encounter it again. To say that it

---

[51] In hard times, for example, land rent was waived or deferred and grain was distributed to the starving. Confucianism also stressed *kan-ch'ing*, the feeling of mutual respect and trust among men, which acted as a check on exploitation.

[52] Also, this meant there was one more class living off the land without contributing to production.

played an indispensable role in the dynamics of the revolution is to suggest that the revolution was not made by social ills alone.

In political consciousness and coherence of action, the Chinese peasantry did not constitute a revolutionary force commensurate with the seriousness of its problems. To the extent that the non-Communist peasant movements I have studied can be characterized in general terms, they seem to me diffuse, sporadic, and lacking in coordination and firm leadership. Above all they seem defensive: peasants may arouse themselves to protest an assault on the status quo, but they almost never attack the deeper causes of their exploitation and misery.[53] The peasants who made the Chinese Revolution were not ready to make it on the eve of the Second World War. One is struck by the contrast—which is in no way peculiar to China[54]—between the seriousness of the peasant problem and the weakness of the movement to which it gave rise. Thirty-five years ago, the few serious observers of the Chinese scene would all have agreed that the peasant problem required speedy resolution, and that it would not be resolved without upheavals. But upheavals were one thing; revolution was another. What did the peasant masses contribute to the Chinese Revolution? They supplied the pool of forces from which Communism drew its sustenance. Discontent and the bankruptcy of rural society created an inexhaustible supply of potential revolutionaries, but it was the Chinese Communist Party that gave this blind force purpose and direction.

[53] Peasants might rebel because the exactions of local army troops exceeded current (one might say "normal") standards, or because a new surtax was levied the same year that locusts ruined the harvest. But it was highly unusual, for example, for a united and concerted peasant movement to challenge the very principle of land rent. See Lucien Bianco, "Les Paysans et la révolution," *Politique Etrangère*, No. 2–3 (1968), pp. 117–41.

[54] Otherwise the peasants of northeastern Brazil, for example, would long since have risen in revolt.

5. Reform or Revolution?

Before turning directly to the agrarian revolution, we must first assess the efforts to remedy the situation within the system. In appraising the chances of reform in China, one naturally thinks first of the period of Kuomintang rule. Not that the party's program or ideology was reformist in any sense of the word; indeed, as early as the turn of the century, when Chinese students and émigrés in Tokyo were rent by disputes almost as bitter as those dividing Russian socialist émigrés halfway around the world, it was the nationalist Sun Yat-sen who stood for revolution, in opposition to K'ang Yu-wei's most important disciple, the reformer Liang Ch'i-ch'ao. The Kuomintang came to power by violent revolution, and never thereafter showed the slightest sign of the moderation and restraint that rightly or wrongly tend to be associated with a commitment to reform. Yet the Kuomintang by no means stood for the total break with the past represented by the CCP: we all know there was only one Chinese Revolution, and that it took place in 1949.

With this axiom as a starting point, the Kuomintang era can be seen to represent the last chance for gradual change in a situation that hardly encouraged the harmonious development of political pluralism. For all its manifest inadequacies, the Nanking government was, in John Fairbank's words, "the most modern government that China had known." It was fitted out with a real Ministry of Finance, a Ministry of Railroads, a Ministry of Industry, and so forth. Scores of surveys, plans, and programs based on other countries' experience were turned out by its enlightened young bureaucrats. What seemed to be coming into being in Nanking impressed many contemporaries, including foreign observers who ordinarily put little stock in the Chinese. They reported to the world that something had changed in the land of immobility; here at last was a regime determined not to perpetuate the errors of the past.

How valid was this claim? And just how great was the Kuomintang's capacity for responding to China's ills in a positive, progressive way? To be fair, our assessment of the regime should be limited to the years 1928–37, or what Fairbank calls "the Nanking decade."[1] For if the Kuomintang ran out of time, the regime itself was not entirely or even primarily to blame. Beginning in 1937 foreign invasion and civil war eliminated all possibility of long-term reforms.

The Failure of Reform

To make China into a modern country, to build what needed building, to introduce a minimum of social justice—these goals are easy enough to list, but no government of China, past or present, has successfully met their tremendous challenge. The historian who would render a verdict on the Kuomintang era must make allowances not only for the immense complexity of the tasks the party faced but for extenuating circumstances of all sorts; he must further concede that in some ways any judgment is premature. And yet when all is said and done, he will find it hard to avoid concluding that the Nationalist regime was a failure.

Social and Economic Reforms: Limited Progress. In what follows we shall not look at every sphere of government activity or draw up an exhaustive balance sheet of the regime's assets and liabilities. All we shall do is briefly consider, or reconsider, some of China's major social, economic, and political problems in the 1930's, beginning with what I regard as the fundamental social problem, the condition of the peasantry. In this critical area, the Kuomintang's failure was well-nigh total.

[1] Whenever necessary, however, we shall refer in this chapter to events occurring after the war broke out and even to wartime trends.

This is not to say that the regime made no effort to improve the peasants' condition, or even that its efforts were altogether fruitless. A number of government agencies charged with improving the agricultural economy and peasant life were set up, especially after 1933 in response to the Communist challenge in Kiangsi.[2] These new agencies cooperated with others in such activities as taking socioeconomic surveys, promoting technical improvements, launching irrigation and reforestation projects, and trying to improve peasant health and hygiene.[3] But all these measures affected only a few areas, and those only superficially. How paltry the government's efforts were in comparison with the country's needs is clearly indicated by the percentage of the national budget allocated to rural reconstruction: in 1931–32, .2 per cent; in 1933–34, .5 per cent; in 1934–35, 3.9 per cent (most of which went to the National Economic Council in Kiangsi); in 1935–36, 3.7 per cent.[4] Furthermore, most of the government's measures were concerned with the rural economy as such, not with the deeper problem of social relations. Some of its programs seemed to be based on the assumption that the peasant problem came down to the need for agricultural modernization, others on no assumption whatever. As a result, whereas there was limited progress of sorts in different directions, no concerted attack was made on the problem as a whole. Almost nothing was done to satisfy the peasants' most basic needs: no steps were taken to protect them against exactions and violence on the part of the military, to eliminate usury by reforming and expanding the system of agricultural credit, or to reduce the misery caused by land tax and land rent.

[2] It was in Kiangsi that the most ambitious government projects were launched. Among the new agencies established by the government were the National Economic Council, the Rural Rehabilitation Commission, and the National Bureau of Agricultural Research.

[3] The proposed technical improvements covered a very broad range: from the use of artificial fertilizers and the diversification and rotation of crops, to measures for the control of insects and blight and the scientific selection of seeds.

[4] These figures were computed by Franklin L. Ho, as cited in Thomson, *While China Faced West*, p. 123. Expenditures on rural reconstruction made up a much larger proportion (one-sixth) of provincial budgets, but they were financed by land tax surcharges and were thus an added burden on the peasant. *Ibid.*

Let us consider briefly this last point and the related problem of landownership. Agrarian reform was one of the traditional planks in the Kuomintang platform. Before Sun Yat-sen's goal of "land to the cultivator" could be reached, there was to be a transitional stage in which land rent rates would be set by the government. At the Reorganization Conference of 1924, the Kuomintang came out in favor of a 25 per cent reduction in land rent; and in 1930, after coming to power, it fixed the maximum rent at three-eighths of the main harvest. But with very rare exceptions the law of 1930 was never enforced.[5] The most striking example of the regime's approach to rural social policy came in Kiangsi in 1934-35; as the Red Army retreated, the status quo was restored and the large landowners' holdings returned to their former owners. Since the old landowners had fled during the period of Communist control and all deeds to property had been destroyed, it would have been relatively simple to redistribute the land by statutory reform. This was the period, moreover, when Kiangsi was supposed to be a laboratory for rural reconstruction, and when the League of Nations experts called in by the Chinese government were urgently recommending just such a statutory redistribution of the land. But then other supporters of the regime, including men as untouched by Communist sympathies as Hu Shih, had been urging the same thing for years. All of them came up against the obstinacy of Chiang Kai-shek, whose personal predilections in this matter seem to have been decisive. For one brief period Chiang seemed worried—in 1933, when he was embarking on his most important Extermination Campaign. He declared at that time that his task was only three-tenths military and seven-tenths political, which would seem to mean that once the roots of peasant discontent were destroyed, the battle against the Communists would be two-thirds won. The same year he had Ma-

[5] Enforcement of the law would certainly have run into numerous hurdles, notably the obstructionism of the landlords, who insisted that all disputes over land rent and sharecropping agreements be taken to court; this effectively settled the issue, since sharecroppers could not put together the money required to bring suit. But the significant point is that the government never seriously contemplated forcing recalcitrant landlords to obey the law.

dame Chiang sound out American missionaries on their willingness to undertake a massive rural reconstruction campaign in Kiangsi at the Nanking government's expense.[6] By 1935 this reformist zeal was a thing of the past. Military means had proved adequate for routing the Red Army, and the Generalissimo appeared to lose interest in political programs.

If this attitude of Chiang's was obviously shortsighted, it was in some ways inevitable, as I shall try to show later in this chapter. For now, let us simply note this deliberate refusal to confront the issue. It is not enough to say that the Nanking government was unable to solve the country's major social problem. It did not even want to.[7]

The government's rural reconstruction efforts emphasized economic progress at the expense of social change, to the point of promoting agricultural modernization as a substitute for agrarian reform. But even from a purely economic point of view, the results were extremely disappointing.[8] Between 1932 and 1936, the last year before the war (1931 is excluded because it was a year of catastrophic floods), China's total agricultural production increased less than 1 per cent. Since the Chinese population must have increased by at least .5 per cent a year during this period, or two or three times as fast as agricultural resources, there was presumably less food available per capita on the eve of the Sino-Japanese War than there had been five years earlier.

So far as nonagricultural production is concerned, estimates range from stagnation (Douglas S. Paauw), to a slight increase

---

[6] The highly Americanized Madame Chiang Kai-shek, a graduate of Wellesley College, regularly acted as the Generalissimo's go-between with the English-speaking world. She often served as his interpreter during interviews with English-speaking journalists and political figures.

[7] This conclusion is not intended to slight the efforts at rural reconstruction mentioned earlier. They are simply irrelevant in this connection, not because they were inadequate, not even because they were poorly coordinated, but because they carefully skirted the heart of the problem.

[8] The following discussion is by no means a survey of the Chinese economy in the Kuomintang era, or even a complete review of the economic policies of the Nanking government. It is simply an attempt to shed light on the main trends and consequences of the regime's economic and financial policy by means of selected examples. Here as elsewhere one must guard against attributing economic developments too directly to government policy; the development of the Chinese economy during the Nanking decade was only minimally affected by government measures.

of 5 per cent between 1931 and 1936 (T. C. Liu), to a more marked increase (John K. Chang). At least in the modern sector of industry, impressive strides were apparently made, with an annual growth rate of 8.4 per cent between 1928 and 1936. But this sector still amounted to only a little more than a quarter of all industrial production, including handicrafts, or scarcely 3 per cent of the gross national product; and its contribution to the country's overall economic growth remained negligible.[9] Had there been no war or civil war, would the modern industrial sector eventually have carried the rest of the economy along with it? One can only ask the question, and note that in 1937 it was a long way from doing so.

Communications and credit are two top-priority sectors on whose growth industrial development—and indeed all development—depends. The Nationalist regime launched a number of new projects in both areas. Railroad mileage doubled between 1926 (7,700 miles) and 1949 (15,500 miles). This was a great improvement, to be sure, but it still left the vast expanse of China with less than two-thirds the railroad mileage of France. The province of Szechwan, which was larger in both area and population than France, still did not have a single mile of track in 1949. Not only was railroad mileage far too low, but rail lines were unevenly distributed and often discontinuous. Much of the rest of South and West China was as barren of track as Szechwan.

Another difficulty of the Kuomintang era was that improvements were limited almost entirely to visibly modern means of transportation: railroads and great cross-country highways. New highways were built out of Shanghai and Nanking in several directions, and others linked up the large cities of the interior, but except in the lower Yangtze basin (Kiangsu, Anhwei, Chekiang), where connecting roads were built to the back country, these highways did little for the regions they crossed. There was no extension or significant improvement of water routes, and

---

[9] This was all the more true because this sector, particularly mining and metallurgy, was to a noteworthy extent under foreign control, and because such products as tin, antimony, and tungsten were produced almost entirely for export.

no real effort to break the virtual monopoly on water-borne trade that foreigners had acquired in the heyday of imperialism. (As late as 1936, two-fifths of all China's coastal and river cargo was carried under the British flag.) The regime cannot be blamed for a lag that dated from many years before, but neither can it be given all the credit for what progress there was. Much of it was the work of the imperialists; almost half of the 15,500 miles of railroad that the People's Republic inherited in 1949 was in the Northeast, which was in Japanese hands until 1945.[10]

In the financial sector, the new measures introduced by the government seem at first sight more impressive. Eager to control internal resources and to break free of imperialist domination, which was even more marked in this sphere than in coastal and river traffic, it created or expanded four State Banks. By 1935 these banks held 56 per cent of the deposits and 40 per cent of the capital reserves of the country's modern banking institutions. A monetary reform measure of late 1935 further consolidated the new system's position relative not only to foreign financiers but also to locally controlled provincial banks, which were thereafter required to accept only the national currency issued by the State Banks and to reject the various local and regional currencies that had circulated previously. But this modern financial instrument—a centralized credit institution with a monopoly on the issue of currency—did little to stimulate economic life. Worse, it helped perpetuate such deep-rooted practices as speculation. The State Banks financed the government deficit in the most costly possible way, by issuing bonds on which they paid astronomical rates of interest (sometimes as high as 40 per cent); many of the bondholders were high officials in the Nanking government. Nor was the power elite content to make speculative profits on loans for the maintenance and equipping of the central armies;[11] it also gradually extended its control over

[10] There was a comparable imbalance in the overall development of modern industry; if the Northeast (which was Japanese from 1931 on) is omitted, the annual growth rate for the years 1926–36 drops from 7.6 to 6 per cent.

[11] "Power elite" is to be taken in its narrowest sense. The most powerful financial dynasty of all was the Soong family, the family of Madame Chiang. Her brother, T. V. Soong, was a government minister; so was her sister's husband, H. H. Kung. It is

the other key sectors of the economy. Here again it took advantage of the unrivaled power of the State Banks, which were in the hands of a small number of ministers and high officials. The slogan *"T'ung-chih ching-chi,"* or "controlled economy," meaning an economy run by the state, was much in evidence. In fact, however, after a series of maneuvers and manipulations, various government-controlled sectors of the economy became the private domain of certain members of the Kuomintang, who built vast personal fortunes from government monopolies and the management of public funds. To convey clearly the everyday attitude of most public officials during the Kuomintang era, we should probably cast doctrine aside and recall the famous toast that under the Empire automatically associated opulence and administrative office: *"Sheng-kuan fa-ts'ai,"* "Become an official and get rich!"[12] To be sure, the regime did introduce modern financial practices, and in general accomplished much more in the financial sphere than its predecessors; we cannot censure it as categorically on this question as on the question of agrarian reform. But censure it we must, if only for misdirecting potentially productive investment capital toward speculation and toward enormous military expenditures.

From Tutelage to Dictatorship. The democratic tide sweeping the world is like the Yangtze: "nothing can stop it." Sun Yat-sen was undeniably sincere in this affirmation of his basic optimism and his democratic convictions. However, he went on to say, just as the Yangtze "makes crooks and turns, sometimes to the north and sometimes to the south," before reaching the Eastern Ocean, China would reach democracy only at the end of a long, hard

---

not reducing history to the level of a family chronicle to mention Madame Kung's prodigious aptitude for exploiting state secrets to carry out enormously profitable business transactions. Compared with her gigantic operations, those of Le Château in France a century earlier (recounted by Stendhal in *Lucien Leuwen*) were no more than petty swindles. The "central armies" were the armies under the direct control of Chiang and the Nanking government, as opposed to the various regional military forces. Nɯarly half the Nanking government's expenditures were on national defense—from 40 to 48 per cent between 1929 and 1935, according to Chou Shun-hsin, *The Chinese Inflation, 1937–1949* (New York: Columbia University Press, 1963), pp. 41 and 70.

12 See John K. Fairbank, *The United States and China,* rev. ed. (Cambridge, Mass.: Harvard University Press, 1958), p. 220.

journey.[13] Along the way the country would pass through two intermediate stages: first, military unification under the leadership of the Kuomintang; second, a period of political "tutelage," leading in the end to a mature democracy.

By 1928 unification could be considered an accomplished fact, and in accordance with Sun's schema the victorious revolution inaugurated the period of political tutelage. But the last stage of the journey was never completed.[14] The only discernible movement was toward dictatorship, or more precisely toward increased dictatorship, for from the start the Nanking government interpreted tutelage to mean dictatorship by the Kuomintang over the rest of the nation. The party's grip on the nation tightened steadily until no meaningful distinction existed between the party and the government.[15] At the same time, power within the party came to be increasingly concentrated, first in the leadership as a whole and then in the hands of a single leader. The Kuomintang had adopted the Bolshevik principle of democratic centralism, and, as one might expect, in practice centralism prevailed over democracy.[16] The Kuomintang also adopted Bolshevik techniques of action, organization, and recruiting, but there its imitation of the Bolsheviks stopped. Methods introduced by the Soviet adviser Mikhail Borodin were con-

[13] *The Three Principles of the People*, trans. Frank W. Price, ed. L. T. Chen (Shanghai: Institute of Pacific Relations, 1927), pp. 179–80.

[14] In 1948, on the brink of final defeat, the government decided to inaugurate the third stage, i.e. democracy, but under conditions that deprived the experiment of any real impact.

[15] Some ministries (notably Information and Social Affairs) ended up taking orders directly from the party, rather than the government.

[16] The group of men dominating the Central Executive Committee were always in a position to control the delegates to the party congress, and thus to perpetuate their own power. There was a steady tightening of control: first by the Central Executive Committee over the party congress, then by the Central Executive Committee's standing committee, which met every week, over the rest of the Executive Committee, and finally, from 1938 on, by the *tsung-ts'ai* or party leader (Chiang Kai-shek) over the standing committee. Still, it would be rash to draw a direct parallel between this pattern and the gradual concentration of power in the Bolshevik Party, or even the trend that resulted in the dictatorship of the Committee of Public Safety under the Convention. China in the 1930's was not going through a revolution. The progressive concentration of power in a group (and later in a man) reflected not so much a logical necessity of the revolutionary situation as the natural consolidation of a regime that had never conceived of any but an authoritarian form of government.

verted to the service of an increasingly resolute anti-Communism. In his choice of authoritarian methods, Chiang came much closer to Germany and Italy, whose achievements he greatly admired, than to Soviet Russia. By way of example, the men who controlled the party machinery made use of a fascist-style secret police, the Blueshirts, to suppress their internal enemies—whether they were simply liberals or men suspected of Communist sympathies.

In short, despite the publication of a draft constitution in 1936 and the creation in 1938 of a consultative assembly (the People's Political Council), tutelage never evolved into democracy. An episode that brought China to the brink of civil war a few months before the Japanese invasion illustrates the tragic absence of democratic traditions. In the Sian Incident of December 1936, a dissident general kidnapped Chiang Kai-shek with the explanation that there was no other way of obtaining a change in China's policy toward Japan (he did in fact obtain the change by his exploit).[17] During Chiang's captivity, censorship and the deliberate dissemination of false information by the official press agency made it impossible for the Chinese to find out what was really happening, though their fate depended on the outcome. The resulting uncertainty and confusion left a handful of generals and politicians free to make self-serving decisions in the name of the state.

Despite the ruling party's strict control over political life and the absence of democracy, it would be wrong to see the government of China on the eve of the Second World War as another manifestation of the totalitarianism then sweeping the world. At several centuries' remove from Stalin's Russia and the major fascist states of Europe, Chiang's China was totalitarian only in intention. Not only did it lack the efficiency of a "strong" regime, but it was even more impotent—and in its way more addicted to idle talk—than a parliamentary republic. The regime's inept performance demonstrates its essential powerlessness, and at the same time confirms the persistence of an imme-

17 On the Sian Incident itself, see pp. 146–47.

morial China that the Nationalist "revolution" had scarcely
touched. Few of the practices inherited from the Empire seemed
as hardy as corruption. Two works published in the United
States by the scholar Chung-li Chang have shown just how
small the nominal salary of a late-Ch'ing official was in proportion to his total income. In the Kuomintang era extortion and
other perquisites of office made some administrative posts so
lucrative that they were in effect put up for sale.[18] The sale of
offices was illegal, of course, but under at least one provincial
governor it was such an open and accepted practice that prices
were fixed in advance. In Kiangsu, between 1931 and 1933, a
three-month appointment as district magistrate cost 3,000 dol-
lars.[19] In the same orderly fashion, the toll collected by local
bandits for passage along a given road or through a given valley
was known to all.

But was there nothing new in district- or village-level administration and politics? Apart from an attempted reorganization
of local administration in 1939, which wartime conditions foredoomed to failure, the Kuomintang's main innovation was its
reintroduction of the traditional *pao-chia* system in an effort to
get the peasant masses under more effective control.[20] Even this
"innovation" was adopted from the oldest Chinese traditions;
it at once served the regime's authoritarian tendencies and gratified its consciously past-oriented nationalism. From the peasants'
point of view, it simply added police control to the tyranny of
local administrators and military officials; it had little impact on
the way they lived. For the government, *pao-chia* made the suppression of Communism much easier (it was applied primarily
in Kiangsi), but it did not and could not solve the crucial problem of making the regime's will obeyed as law in the far reaches

[18] Our earlier discussion of the traditional connection between administrative office
and high income involved only parasitism and tendencies toward bureaucratic capitalism. Here the issue is corruption, a corruption that was acceptable so long as it remained
within bounds. An "honest" official was one who did not extort more than a certain
sum; a "corrupt" official was one who exceeded what were considered reasonable limits.
[19] United States, Department of State, 893.00/12485 (Peck dispatch of Sept. 5,
1933).
[20] Under the *pao-chia* system, peasant families were officially grouped in units and
made collectively responsible for all infractions committed by anyone in the group.

of rural China. For behind the government's inability to win acceptance of its authority lay the excessive independence not of the peasants but of their masters,[21] and the insubordination not of the governed but of the governing class, including members of the Kuomintang's local branches.

Little by little the Nanking government fell into the habit of running the country by words alone, governing in a void, issuing decrees that were more often misrepresented than enforced and still more often ignored altogether. In addition to the law limiting land rent, which the government itself had no intention of enforcing, many other laws and administrative measures remained a dead letter despite the government's wishes. Thus, when the government decided to abolish the notorious internal tax known as the *likin*, it expressly forbade local authorities to reinstate this tax under another name; but many a local warlord hastened to do just that.[22] As one Shanghai newspaper put it, many reform projects sounded extremely attractive when they were being discussed, but no sooner had a decision been made to enact them than "they were never heard of again."[23]

The paradox of an authoritarian government that is unable to impose its authority is certainly not peculiar to China. Indeed, as we shall see later in the chapter, the reasons for the Kuomintang's failure to impose its will were by no means all of its own making. For the time being, however, the point is simply that it failed. Perhaps the best measure of the regime's failure is its superficiality, its poor grasp of reality. If the regime strikes us as a mere epiphenomenon, it is because the Kuomintang made no real effort to transform China. On the morrow of the Revolution of 1911, Lu Hsün declared that despite the change in regime nothing had changed in the countryside. When he died in 1936, he must have had the bitter conviction that his earlier judgment could still stand. At the risk of caricaturing the China of the 1930's by grossly exaggerating her basic features, we might

21 Once again, masters is not used in its juridical sense (since the peasants were free), or even in its economic sense (since we are not talking about landowners as such), but in its political sense: the men who wielded authority on the local level.
22 There are several instances recorded in the American diplomatic archives for 1931.
23 *Hsin-wen pao*, Dec. 26, 1933.

choose as a symbol of the regime a private prison in the Italian concession in Tientsin, run by a general who was also a provincial governor. Its occupants, all personal enemies of the general, were kept under round-the-clock surveillance by 21 uniformed guards. If we pursue the analogy further, the modernity of Kuomintang China once again becomes just a matter of words. When the Italian authorities discovered the prison and freed the prisoners, the general's son denounced their "imperialist" interference.[24]

The Success of Conservatism

The problems just discussed would have been the fundamental problems for any government of China. They were difficult and complex; above all, they would take a long time to solve. But there were also more immediate problems, problems that a man might hope to solve in his lifetime. The most obvious of these was to unify the country and impose the authority of the central government on the many greater and lesser autonomous provincial potentates—precisely the sort of "duty" Chiang understood best. Neither the actions, nor the speeches, nor the writings of this traditionally educated soldier show any real understanding of such matters as economic modernization. But was China's most urgent need for a modern-minded statesman, or for a tough, determined, relentless military leader? We must bear in mind China's persistent centrifugal tendencies and in particular her incessant civil wars, which the Japanese threat made more dangerous than ever. It was a rare period that did not see the hatching of a new revolt or the culmination of an old one. In some cases warlords with strong regional bases and sizable armies joined forces with a prestigious politician or a popular political cause; thus in the North China war of 1929–30 the warlords Yen Hsi-shan and Feng Yü-hsiang were allied with Wang Ching-wei, a leading figure in the Kuomintang and a rival of Chiang's. Even during times of truce or respite—there were no times of genuine civil peace—local potentates continued

[24] United States, Department of State, 893.00 PR Tientsin/38 (Atcheson dispatch of Aug. 4, 1931).

to defy the authority of Nanking. In October 1928, when Chiang sent a delegation of seven emissaries to a warlord in eastern Shantung to urge him to recognize the authority of the central government, the man had all seven stabbed to death.[25]

Chiang's response to such acts of defiance was characteristically energetic. In turn wily and cruel, he defeated or disarmed his enemies one after another. Dividing his opponents (within the Kuomintang as well as without) had long been his chief occupation; and his talents in this sphere were indisputable. Small wonder, then, that military struggle and political intrigue took precedence over the sufferings of the peasantry or the problems of economic development.[26] The man the Chinese press called "the super-warlord" had all the characteristics, and all the strength, of the founder of a dynasty.[27] With rare determination he pursued a single end, or rather two ends that in his eyes merged into one—the establishment of his own authority and that of the state. To the extent that he compelled recognition of his own authority, he made real (if limited) progress toward extending the authority of the central government in the provinces.[28] What did the Kuomintang accomplish in the ten years before the war with Japan monopolized its energies? Essentially, the unification of the country.

To this top-priority task the regime sacrificed others that it considered less urgent. To this task it brought the wealth of the

[25] *Ibid.*, 893.00 PR Chefoo/6 (Webber dispatch of Oct. 18, 1928). Two outstanding books, published while the original French edition of this book was in press, have brought us a wealth of new material on the role of the warlords in Republican China, as well as new interpretations of the warlord period: James E. Sheridan, *Chinese Warlord: The Career of Feng Yü-hsiang* (Stanford, Calif.: Stanford University Press, 1966), and Donald G. Gillin, *Warlord: Yen Hsi-shan in Shansi Province, 1911–1949* (Princeton, N.J.: Princeton University Press, 1967).

[26] The odd ring of "economic development" in this context tends to bear out the "naturalness" of Chiang's concerns, given the pressures of the time and his circumstances.

[27] In Chiang's case this strength was a result of courage, self-discipline, determination, and cleverness. These qualities were reinforced by pride, stubbornness, callousness, and a lack of scruples.

[28] Up to the outbreak of war, and even during and after the war, there was only pro forma recognition of the central government's authority in some regions. The Cultural Revolution has demonstrated the continued strength of centrifugal forces even in Communist China, particularly in the outlying provinces.

country, or as much of the wealth as it controlled. Given the need to build a modern army to fight Japan, and the even more pressing need to finance campaigns against the warlords and their successors and allies (not to mention the costly campaigns against the "Communist bandits"), it is scarcely surprising that the capital drained off by the four State Banks was not productively reinvested, and that military expenditures absorbed almost half the government budget. Even the modernization of the banking system was not intended primarily to stimulate the economy, but to establish the government's financial supremacy, which in turn was only an instrument for establishing its political supremacy. The priority given to political unification goes a long way toward explaining the dearth of economic achievements in the Kuomintang era, as well as the regime's indifference to social problems. But the consequences of this emphasis were profound and far-reaching.

To preserve at any cost the power they had paid so dearly to acquire thus became the ruling passion of the comrades and disciples whom Sun Yat-sen had chosen to lead the Chinese people to the promised land of progress and democracy. The preservation of power for its own sake had an inherent logic. Driven by fear of the forces they had set in motion, men who rose to power as revolutionaries became not just conservative but reactionary.[29]

This point, however, requires serious qualification. The Kuomintang's increasing conservatism was due only in part to its decision or need to give priority to military pacification and political unification; in part it had limited its options by the way it came to power in the first place. Although popular support and revolutionary fervor helped assure the success of the Northern Expedition of 1926–27, the Kuomintang victory owed

---

[29] It may be objected here and elsewhere in this discussion that Chiang Kai-shek was a conservative from the outset, that he was not forced to act against his own better judgment or adjust his aspirations to what was realistically possible. From many points of view this is so. But the development we are concerned with here is not that of a man but that of a party, and we must accordingly ask why was it Chiang who became the man of the hour? Why Chiang and not one of his rivals in the party, someone with greater prestige, longer party service, and a more progressive outlook?

much to compromises with warlords, some of whom were simply taken into the Kuomintang at the top level.[30] With the expulsion of the Communists it became both easier and more common for warlords to rally to the Kuomintang banner. By the time the new regime was established, the center of gravity within the Kuomintang coalition had already shifted markedly to the right, with the warlords and their traditionalist supporters replacing the ousted revolutionary wing.[31]

From the logic of attaining power by compromise to the logic of preserving power at any cost, the difference is primarily chronological. Given the Communists' predictable eagerness to use peasant discontent as a weapon against their former ally, it may at first seem surprising that the Kuomintang should concede so important a point by deliberately deciding to tackle symptoms rather than causes with measures that were clearly incapable of preventing a further worsening of the peasants' plight. But the party's attitude is perhaps best explained by the dynamics of conservatism. Real agrarian reform would have caused a profound upheaval in rural life by calling into question centuries-old social relationships and privileges. To put it plainly, lowering the land rent or even redistributing the land would not have been nearly enough; the government would soon have been

---

[30] Sheridan, *Chinese Warlord*, pp. 15, 240. See also his analysis in Chapter Nine, especially pp. 224–30, of the dealings that led General Feng Yü-hsiang to come down on the side of Chiang Kai-shek against the Wuhan "government," and his reasons for doing so.

[31] This shift was accentuated with the Kuomintang's accession to power. Large landowners with any political authority flocked to the new dominant party, just as they had earlier served as the pillars of Confucian orthodoxy and of the Imperial administration. There is no implied value judgment in this observation, and no disguised irony. For the landed upper class and for traditional China (there lies the problem: the Kuomintang was still in large measure traditional China), the association of landlord and government was a matter of course. Ten years after the revolution of 1926, the members of the Kuomintang in any given locality were almost invariably the village head and government officials, which is to say members of the privileged landlord class. In breaking with the Communists, in governing with whatever support came to hand, and finally in giving first priority to short-run objectives that fell far short of a revolutionary program, Chiang was the spokesman of "reality" within the Kuomintang and the revolutionary movement, the realistic appraiser of the weight of objective conditions. In this sense the Communists after 1927 were not fighting to carry the revolution into its second, or social, stage. It had still to enter its first, or political, stage, which Realpolitik or intractable reality had prevented it from doing.

driven to attack the privileges, economic monopolies, and political dominance of the large landowners. In short, the logic of agrarian reform would have required the government to become the implacable foe of the landed upper class, to destroy its resources, its authority, its prestige, its very reason for existing.[32] Not only would such a policy have cut off the regime from the class that owned or controlled everything in village China, but by overturning the complex sociopolitical edifice on which rural "order" rested it might well have brought down the government itself.

The Nanking government was understandably unwilling to run this risk, even though its refusal meant shirking its most urgent task and having to deal interminably with agitation in the countryside. "Understandably" might not be said of an energetically reformist or revolutionary regime, but it is properly said of a group of men, and one man in particular, whose overriding goal was to remain in power. It is understandable, in this sense, that Chiang's passing interest in agrarian problems coincided with the peak of his efforts to dislodge the Communists from Kiangsi and dropped off on the morrow of the Long March; to put the matter somewhat crudely, Chiang was interested in finding a solution to the agrarian problem only as a way to deprive the Communists of their trump card.

Conversely, by the same logic, sacrificing peasant interests might be regarded as the price that had to be paid to obtain allies against the Communists and other potential troublemakers.[33] From this point of view, it is not enough to describe Chiang's agrarian policy as a prudent refusal to intervene for fear of setting off a dangerous explosion. The rejection of reform is not a policy. Once the decision against reform was made, it was imperative to go one step further and attempt a consolidation of the status quo, if only to prevent disorder. Chiang was not content simply to spare the large landowners, to refrain from

---

[32] At least in the large landowners' own view, as determined by their upbringing.

[33] Of course, Chiang did not see the problem in these terms. That what he did made the peasants' condition still worse may be the "objective" truth. In his eyes, however, there was not so much a peasant problem as a problem of maintaining order, and this was the problem that preoccupied him completely.

attacking their economic position; he actually reinforced their position. Indeed, in the end he did his best to make the class that had most reason to fear the Communists into a pillar of the regime.[34]

The bond between the Kuomintang and the landed upper class helps explain not only why agrarian reform was eschewed, but also why Nanking's efforts to increase political and administrative centralization so soon ran aground. Ultimately the regime could not assert its full authority over those who ruled in its name because the class that prevented the enforcement of government directives on the local level was the same class that had the political power to guarantee order in the countryside.

Here lies the social problem at the heart of the political problem. It is no great distortion to say that the Kuomintang in the mid-1930's was striving to preserve its rule by supporting the political, economic, and social dominance of the large landowners, while the CCP was seeking to win power for itself by opposing that dominance. But of course things were not that simple or clear-cut. The government drew equal support from the commercial bourgeoisie, which it took pains to encourage in the ports and cities where it existed and helped create in other cities. More important, the limited modernization measures the regime did succeed in carrying out could not help but threaten vested interests in the long run. Perhaps it would be nearer the

[34] Perhaps the plural, class*es*, would be more accurate here, since a Communist-led agrarian revolution would be made at the expense of the rich peasants as well as the upper class. With the aid and protection of the government, China's rich peasants might well have become the agents of a conservative social order. And in fact the government's rural reconstruction projects did serve the interests of the least deprived peasant farmers, or at any rate the most solvent. The National Economic Council established its "centers for promoting rural welfare" in the most prosperous districts of Kiangsi, and the cooperatives, which had some 300,000 members in 1935, offered assistance and loans only to those who could supply collateral. What was involved here, however, was not so much discrimination against the poorest peasants as an effort to ensure the success of these pilot projects, on which government propaganda was focusing public attention. More significant is the fact that at no time did the government try to favor the more prosperous peasants at the expense of large landowners. As we have seen, in Kiangsi land confiscated by the Communists was returned to its former owners by the Kuomintang. And in some places "rural reconstruction" meant simply the recruitment of peasant laborers who were paid little or nothing to build roads used only by landlords and military convoys.

truth to say that the Kuomintang era saw the beginning in rural China of significant political, economic, and social changes, changes that shook the traditional structure of society by bringing catalysts of modernization into a still largely unchanged reality. Even so, the struggle between the old and the new, between the archaic and the modern (to which, by giving undue weight to Nanking's innovative impulses, one can assimilate the struggle for influence between the local landowners and the central government), seemed to affect only one class, the privileged class, with one wing desperately defending the status quo and the other eager to exploit new fields of activity and new sources of wealth.

To put the best face on the Kuomintang's policies, we can say that the party relied on the traditional upper class's more dynamic faction, which was wealthier and more open, and that members of other classes—notably, since we are discussing rural China, the peasants—were simply not involved in the debate. The peasant masses continued to be supernumeraries as they had been throughout Chinese history, the anonymous human dough that suffered and submitted, the governed whom one rounded up or counted for tax purposes. In this fundamental sense, nothing had changed. Government continued to be the exclusive province of the upper class. As it had been under the Empire, this privileged class was shaken by internal conflicts; and like a chronicler of the Empire, the historian of modern China is tempted to see these conflicts as the very stuff of history, since only on this basis can he put the official actors at the center of the stage. The illusion does not bear scrutiny. What difference does it make, after all, whether a given landlord was a conformist or a nonconformist, with the current or lagging behind it? In the government's eyes, every member of the privileged minority had a well-understood role.[35] What really mattered was this minority's collective domination of the rest, the formless and numberless rest.[36]

[35] In this respect the social base of the Republican regime was only marginally broader than the Empire's.

[36] I have stressed the ties between the Nanking government and the traditional ruling class, i.e. the social aspect of the political problem. In addition, of course, some

There is something unreal about an ostensibly modern government that is at once so impotent and so conservative as to perpetuate such an archaic state of affairs, a government that deliberately remains as out of touch with the Chinese people as the Imperial bureaucracy was in its time. And indeed the superficiality and conservatism of the Kuomintang were faithfully reflected in its ideology. It is in this realm, in fact, that the characteristics emerging as the hallmarks of the regime can be seen most clearly—or, to put it another way, that Chiang Kai-shek's personal influence and basic predispositions were expressed most directly. This influence is nowhere more apparent than in the New Life Movement, which Chiang thought up and tried to popularize as an antidote to Marxism.[87] The New Life Movement, in the mind of Chiang and the writings of his propagandists, who were more often cynics than dupes, was both a moral doctrine and the key to the country's salvation: China would be saved by giving her people a new soul. In fact, the most ambitious formulations of the doctrine are just what one might expect a traditionally educated army officer like Chiang, and a puritanical and ascetic officer at that, to propose as a remedy for social injustice and economic stagnation. The 96 sections of the propaganda pamphlet entitled "On the New Life" (55 sections on conduct, 41 on hygiene) invest battalion-level rules of conduct with the status of philosophy: "Be clean. Do not spit in the streets. Button your suit properly. Stand up straight. Do not eat noisily." Also such injunctions as "Do not drink, dance, or gamble" and "Shun high living and dissipation." The police and fanatical adherents of the movement attacked with equal fervor people who smoked, women with permanent waves, and

---

of the regime's purely political tendencies can be attributed directly to the logic of remaining in power, without reference to social questions. A case in point is Nanking's ambivalent attitude toward local conflicts among the warlords (for example in Szechwan and Shantung in 1932). Nanking wanted the country to be at peace, and popular opinion concurred. But these private wars were more a scourge of rural populations than a direct threat to the central government, which was not greatly distressed to see the belligerents sapping each other's strength. After all, Nanking's strength derived to a large extent from the weakness of potential rivals.

[87] Thus he chose Nanchang, the capital of Kiangsi and his headquarters during the Fifth Extermination Campaign, for the formal inauguration of the movement in February 1934.

people who threw orange peels in the canals, which ordinarily were aswarm with rats and from which, in the big cities, the corpses of the latest victims of starvation were fished out every morning.[38] Despite such unpleasantnesses, the New Life Movement's precepts furnished intellectuals with an inexhaustible source of amusement, as well as some gratifyingly specific criteria for evaluating the conduct of government administrators. As for the peasant masses, in the words of the important daily paper *Ta-kung-pao*, they would gladly have forgone the new life being urged upon them in return for some assurance that the only life they had would not be snuffed out.[39]

In addition to an ideal of Spartan simplicity and the assumption that virtue is more important than rice, the New Life Movement embodied an explicit return to the traditional moral imperatives of Confucianism.[40] Its preachments to this effect were but one of many ways in which the regime and its leader vaunted the morals of the ancestors, the national tradition, and Confucian wisdom, which were seen as essentially interchangeable.[41] Chiang encouraged his officers to read the Four Books, which had been composed or compiled shortly after the death of the Sage;[42] he made Confucius's birthday a national holiday, and in

38 It is only fair to mention that the movement also worked at killing off the rats. Between these hygienic, ascetic, and puritanical tendencies and the campaigns against rats and flies in Communist China (and the Red Guards' intolerant righteousness), there is an unmistakable thread of continuity.

39 "It is true," the paper went on to say, "that peasants sometimes lead disorderly and even impure lives; but they really cannot be any more frugal or live any more simply than they do already." *Ta-kung-pao*, March 10, 1934.

40 Among many other things. This syncretic movement also embraced several features borrowed from Christianity (to which Chiang had been converted), and gave almost equal weight to techniques borrowed from German and Japanese militarists. Its version of Confucianism stressed four venerable virtues that with the passage of time had become rather vague: right conduct, righteousness, integrity, and sense of shame. Translation impoverishes these concepts, in part by making them too precise; they cannot be understood apart from the philosophy from which they derive.

41 In 1935 Chiang addressed leading members of Szechwan's landlord class on the "Causes and Cure of Rural Decadence." The main cause was a falling away from the morality of the ancestors; the cure was to restore this morality to a place of honor.

42 The Four Books (among which the best known are the *Analects*, a rather disorganized collection of the conversations of Confucius with his disciples, and the *Mencius*) are part of the Thirteen Classics, the canon of traditional Chinese culture.

1934 he reinstated Confucianism as the state religion.[43] "China's own philosophy of life," he was to write a few years later,

developed by Confucius, amplified and propagated by Mencius, and further explained by the Han scholars [206 B.C. to A.D. 220], automatically became a lofty system, superior to any other philosophy in the world.... The glories and the scope of our ancient Chinese learning cannot be equaled in the history of any of the strong Western nations of today.

These assertions appear in Chiang's book *China's Destiny*, which at the time of its publication in 1943 was heralded as the most important Chinese work since Sun Yat-sen's *Three Principles of the People* and was immediately included on required reading lists in schools throughout China.[44] But the disciple preserved almost nothing of the master's revolutionary ideology except anti-imperialism, and even his latter-day version of anti-imperialism was strongly tainted with chauvinism. To Chiang, one thing explained all China's ills, from civil wars to famines, from opium-smoking to personal self-aggrandizement and corruption: imperialism, as embodied in unequal treaties, extraterritoriality, and foreign concessions. Yet simple-minded as this explanation is, the passages describing and denouncing the imperialist penetration of China are perhaps the least false in the book, which quickly came to be known as the Chinese *Mein Kampf*.

The comparison is pertinent, for it suggests not only the antidemocratic and anti-liberal bias of the work, but also the conservative nationalism that lay at the heart of Chiang's thought and of the official ideology that bore his stamp. The distance the Kuomintang had traveled since coming to power can be measured by the homage it paid the life and thought of Tseng Kuofan, a general and statesman of the Ch'ing period; in the 1920's

[43] This was also the year in which the New Life Movement was launched—and fifteen years after the May Fourth students' denunciation of "Confucius & Sons."
[44] The quoted passage is from the English edition by Philip Jaffe (New York: Roy Publishers, 1947), pp. 95–96.

the Kuomintang had claimed kinship with the Taiping rebels, whom Tseng had crushed. An American historian, writing on the evolution of Kuomintang ideology after the 1924 Reorganization Conference, aptly entitled her article "From Revolution to Restoration." The article compares Chiang's ideology with that of the T'ung-chih Restoration of 1862–74, whose leaders— among them Tseng Kuo-fan—tried to practice selective Westernization while preserving an orthodox Confucian base.[45] A policy that was foredoomed to failure as an anachronism in the second half of the nineteenth century was reinstituted by Chiang in the twentieth.

The Middle Way

Studying the reformist impulses of the regime that preceded Mao's may gratify the historian, but what of the contemporary observer who is concerned with the practical problems of the choice between reform and revolution that yesterday faced China and today faces other countries? That the Kuomintang proved to be a very conservative regime does not answer the question of reform versus revolution as such so far as China is concerned. What would have happened if a team of genuine reformers— sincere, intelligent, dedicated men—had tried to introduce the necessary reforms in China?

There was not one such team, but many. The industrial cooperatives (*kung-ho*), for example, set up by the New Zealander Rewi Alley during the war with Japan, were an experiment in industrial decentralization; they sought to develop new domestic markets at the same time as they increased production.[46] Earlier, various other groups had addressed themselves to the most imperative needs of rural China. Indeed, rural reformers made

---

[45] For the T'ung-chih Restoration, the subject of an important book by the same author, Mary C. Wright, see pp. 5–6 above.

[46] The idea was first given currency by the well-known American journalist Edgar Snow. The founders of the industrial cooperatives started from the assumption that the industrial revolution would never get off the ground in China until there were more Chinese in a position to buy manufactured goods. Thus the experiment was of both social and economic interest—and political interest as well, for the first cooperatives were started in the unoccupied Northwest in 1938, at a time when the industrial centers of eastern China were in the hands of the Japanese invaders.

up the majority of the troops mobilized between 1920 and 1945 to carry out the various economic, social, political, educational, and medical missions that men of good will were calling for. This is scarcely surprising; it shows the growing concern of at least a small segment of the intelligentsia with the country's leading social problem. A consideration of these rural reform efforts, which were increasing rapidly in number on the eve of the war, may help us to appreciate the difficulties of a middle course.[47] We cannot describe all these efforts here or even enumerate them, but will simply list some of the most important:

(1) The China International Famine Relief Commission, founded in 1921 to coordinate and put on a permanent footing the work of the various relief agencies that had just helped keep the death toll of the 1920–21 famine in North China to the relatively low figure of 500,000. This charitable organization qualifies as a reformist movement because of its broad definition of its task; it spent much less money distributing rice in periods of famine than on preventing future famines by digging wells, building dikes, setting up agricultural credit unions, and even building roads that would make it possible to convey supplies by truck to distressed areas when famine struck again.

(2) The Mass Education Movement (*Ping-chiao-hui*), which started in Ting Hsien, a rural district near Peking. The man behind this movement, James Y. C. Yen, quickly realized that there were more urgent tasks than teaching peasants to read, and consequently broadened the scope of his activities.

(3) Rural reconstruction projects run in two other northern provinces (Honan and Shantung) by a renowned intellectual, Liang Shu-ming.[48]

(4) Finally, the many different projects launched by Chris-

---

[47] If I dwell on the rural or agrarian case, it is partly because I have access to primary sources on this subject and not on others, and partly because I am convinced that of all the social issues confronting China, this was the most important.

[48] The term "rural reconstruction" designates both the theories of Liang Shu-ming, one of whose books, published in 1937, bore the title *Theory of Rural Reconstruction* (*Hsiang-ts'un chien-she li-lun*), and all the activities undertaken by rural reformers. As we have seen, it also encompasses government activities on behalf of agriculture or the peasantry. The expression owed its currency to widespread recognition of the need to "reconstruct" a society that was falling apart.

tian missionaries—or rather Protestant missionaries, for the great majority of Catholic missionaries made little effort to remedy the evils that surrounded them.

These efforts, along with many others, represent an important and insufficiently known aspect of the Kuomintang period.[49] They cannot be dismissed lightly as being permeated by foreign influence or motivated by naïve American Christian piety. The foreign influence is indisputable but hardly surprising, given the shortage of competent technicians in any underdeveloped country; under the circumstances, a desire to do good works was less an indication of naïve piety than of farsightedness, seriousness, and selflessness. When the missionary Samuel H. Leger asserted in 1932 that "the Christian Church is becoming rural-minded," when the American Board of Commissioners for Foreign Missions decided to dedicate the same year (1932–33) both to rural areas in general and to China in particular, their grasp of China's main problem was as precocious as it was profound. Others, too, among them Hugh W. Hubbard and Chang Fu-liang, deserve a place in history analogous to that of the first French socialists. Or rather, since theory and prophecy interested them less than practical accomplishments, let us call them the Considérants of our century, not the Fouriers.[50] Whether they were Chinese literati like Liang Shu-ming or young men from New England, they had no more in common with the peasants they chose to live among than the Comte de Saint-Simon and the polytechnicians of his school had with the "barbarians" living in the working-class suburbs of France's earliest industrial cities.

In one sense these private projects continued a long Chinese tradition. Under the Empire, the literati had made it their business, among other things, to repair dikes and roads, launch am-

---

[49] Outside archival sources (the Missionary Research Library and the Interchurch Center, both in New York), and papers by American students and researchers, the only detailed study of this subject is Thomson's *While China Faced West*.

[50] [Charles Fourier was an early-nineteenth-century socialist theoretician who advocated among many other things the reorganization of society in cooperative settlements of 1,620 persons. His leading disciple, Victor Considérant, made unsuccessful efforts to launch such settlements in France and Texas.—Trans.]

bitious irrigation projects, and establish charitable granaries from which they distributed grain in lean years. The rural reform efforts of the 1930's, however, differed in an important way from this traditional paternalism. The large landowners had sought to make tolerable for the masses a social order whose costs were borne by the masses and whose benefits accrued to the landlords, which as a class considered this order legitimate and immutable. The reformers of the 1930's, by contrast, considered the social order unjust, and were impelled by a desire to change it as quickly as possible. This disinterested impulse first introduced them to rural suffering and then plunged them further into it. Soon they were working desperately, racing against the clock to stave off catastrophe.[51] Far from congratulating themselves on successful projects, they were dismayed by what a small dent their efforts made and by the depths of corruption and misery their very successes brought to light. Against violent revolution, these were the real partisans of reform.

In a sense they were also the real representatives of the West, of the West that was democratic and optimistic because it had been freed—or had freed itself—from the ills that assailed China. The fact that many used traditional Chinese approaches in such matters as economic preferment and local action belies their motivation: what inspired most of them was the American model. Whether they were American or Chinese, whether or not they had studied in the United States like James Yen,[52] they shared the faith of America's Founding Fathers in the value of education and persuasion. What they did can be seen as the last chance

---

[51] Some of them were explicit on the form this catastrophe would take; they saw agrarian revolution as inevitable if their own efforts failed. Symbolically, perhaps the most important of the organizations coordinating the missionaries' work in rural areas, the Christian Union of North China for Rural Service (Hua-pei Chi-tu-chiao Nung-tsun Fu-wu Lien-ho-hui), adopted a constitution on November 1, 1931—just a few days before the founding of the Chinese Soviet Republic. There was no third course: the Christians had to do what the Communists were doing to keep the Reds from carrying the day, and to preserve the chances of the Kingdom of God.

[52] Of the nine Chinese famine-relief officials mentioned by Andrew J. Nathan in his *History of the China International Famine Relief Commission* (Cambridge, Mass.: Harvard University Press, 1965), pp. 23–24, eight had studied in the United States and the ninth in England.

for the West in China, the last chance for the West to be accepted as the embodiment of its own ideals.

This tireless, clear-sighted devotion ended in almost total failure—a failure that could largely have been predicted.[53] If the judgment seems harsh, here are some of the reasons behind it, beginning with the most debatable and proceeding to the most obvious. In the first place, these reformers, like the French utopian socialists to whom I compared them earlier,[54] believed that the success of their isolated experiments would automatically trigger other programs of the same sort; on the contrary, their work was simply swallowed up in the vastness of rural China. Second, many of the rural reformers were idealistic intellectuals who tended to see the basic problem as moral and cultural. They responded to the symptoms of rural suffering rather than its causes; they attacked ignorance, filth, poor health, and adherence to routine rather than the maldistribution of land and inequities in the land tax and land rent.[55] Some had the naïveté of populists, e.g. the students who tried to promote hygiene by handing out color pamphlets on the use of toothbrushes to Hopei peasants, people who could not afford even one toothbrush for a household and who did not remove their clothing for months at a time in winter because their houses were so cold.[56] Other reformers refrained from attacking the root causes of rural distress

[53] As we shall see, these men were not altogether immune to wishful thinking. But they were more clear-sighted than most.

[54] A man like Liang Shu-ming should be compared rather to Frédéric Le Play. Both were conservative theoreticians concerned with social questions. Le Play wanted to preserve the principle of authority and the Christian religion in French society. Liang hoped his work in rural reconstruction would preserve the Confucian aspect of Chinese society. In the dispute over the relative merits of Eastern and Western civilization mentioned in Chapter Two, Liang was one of the East's most ardent defenders. Always swimming against the stream, he was a defender of the old China before he became a precursor of the new.

[55] This summary is necessarily unfair. Not only does it loosely classify as symptoms certain problems that were causes as well as expressions of the peasant's plight (and in this sense serious obstacles to his liberation), but also, and more important, it seems to blame the reformers for failures they could hardly have avoided. By way of justification, I can only say that my concern here is not with making a value judgment about well-intentioned men but with assessing what they could have done and what they did.

[56] Letter from Agnes M. Moncrieff, secretary of the Peking Student Christian Movement, March 13, 1934, cited in "Peiping Students and Rural Reconstruction," a manuscript in the Missionary Research Library, New York.

not from any failure to grasp their importance, but simply to avoid open conflict with the established order.[57] This leads us to a third criticism, namely, that many projects were destroyed by compromises with the regime—witness Lichwan, a district in eastern Kiangsi, where Protestant missionaries were put in sole charge of rural reconstruction in 1934 but ended up collaborating with the authorities.[58] Sometimes political collaboration went even further: the reformers dreamed of a bureaucracy that would not sabotage their most important projects, and during the time the regime was supporting their efforts, some actually agreed to serve as magistrates of their own model districts. What did they actually accomplish in the end? All in all, their achievements were extremely, almost laughably, meager.[59] Unquestionably the reformers themselves expected their projects to have long-term rather than immediate results, and unquestionably the Japanese invasion snuffed out many a promising project in its infancy. But this very lack of time and this very precariousness of national independence were facts that must in retrospect be counted against the reformist approach.

In short, if we have not been wholly fair to the reformers, neither was history, which in the end eliminated any possibility of a middle course and forced a choice between the Kuomintang and the Communists. The man in charge of the Lichwan experiment became a publicist for the New Life Movement;[60] and Rewi Alley, who ran the industrial cooperatives, for years lived in the People's Republic, where works of political edification have been published under his name. The fate of these pioneers of rural reconstruction and industrial decentralization is

[57] Once again, with the exception of usury. Agricultural credit, which the reformers sought to make available to much of the peasantry, would in time have become an effective weapon against usury.

[58] Thomson, *While China Faced West*, Chapter Five.

[59] The credit unions are a good example. Considered one of the great successes of rural reconstruction, they were its most highly vaunted achievement, and justly so. They grew at a remarkable rate; there were more than 25,000 of them in 1937. At that time they were nowhere more widespread than in Hopei, where the credit union movement was born in 1923. But in Hopei on the eve of the war, traditional money-lenders still accounted for more than 80 per cent of loans to peasants (almost the same proportion as in China as a whole).

[60] Thomson, *While China Faced West*, Chapter Eight.

symbolic.[61] In the same connection, we could point to the misapprehensions and reservations with which a man like Hu Shih must have gone over to the Kuomintang and a man like Lu Hsün to the CCP. We could bemoan or mock the misadventures of democrats, of liberals, of the lukewarm, and of nonconformists of every stripe—those, for example, who later formed the Democratic League[62] and after furnishing martyrs under the Kuomintang became fellow travelers in Communist China, where their political careers ended with public recantation (and in some cases suicide). Was it their inescapable fate to be either hollow shells or victims of persecution? All the historian can say is that such was in fact their fate, beginning with the execution in 1931 of Teng Yen-ta, the founder and general secretary of the Third Party, the first organization that tried to map a middle course between government by the CCP and government by the Kuomintang.

But let us go beyond what we know to some of the reasons—proceeding this time from the most obvious to the most debatable—for *believing* that the middle way never had a chance. One reason for the weakness and futility of reformism was the narrowness of its social base. Perhaps "narrowness" should be "nonexistence"; at times one had the impression that reform did not express the interest of any social class,[63] that it was as bereft of support as the leaders of the political Third Force[64] were of troops, with no roots in Chinese reality and no hold on it.

A second cause of the reformers' failure was the attraction of the inessential. Even when a reformer did not deliberately choose a marginal or futile project (the kind best calculated to yield quick results), the force of circumstances condemned him to futility. He might think he was grasping the substance; in fact he was grappling with the shadow. A village on the border of Szechwan and Shensi was chosen as the site of several industrial cooperatives. A stroke of luck for the village and the whole

---

[61] The concept of industrial decentralization was revived by the Communists in the heyday of the People's Communes in 1958.

[62] See p. 192.

[63] Except at most a fraction of the intelligentsia, which was itself a tiny minority of the Chinese people.

[64] The term refers to the Democratic League and other minor parties.

valley? Not at all; the only ones to benefit from it were refugees from the Japanese. None of the native villagers had either the competence or the capital required to join any of the cooperatives.[65] It was as if the masses whose life had to be changed were beyond reach, as if the best efforts of men of good will must perforce help only the privileged.

The attraction, or curse, of the inessential and the lure of wishful thinking—such were the inevitably recurring temptations of this Sisyphean enterprise. For finally, no matter how profound a man's insight into the problem might be, where could he find the strength to pursue to the bitter end the implications of a heartbreaking, desperate situation, the strength to deny all hope? Few men knew the problems of the Chinese peasantry as well as the ethnologist and sociologist Fei Hsiao-tung. And yet what a contrast between his diagnosis of the disease and his prescription for a cure. To demonstrate the futility of some remedies he proposes, we need only refer to his own farsighted criticism. Thus, when he expresses the hope that the landed upper class will voluntarily give up its land, we need only recall that he elsewhere describes this class as incapable of meeting the challenge of history. If Fei proposes impractical or unrealistic solutions, is it not because he could not bring himself to abandon all hope? There is another point to be made here. Fei's proposal that the privileged class divest itself of its privileges is not only unrealistic, it is revolutionary: its intent is to expropriate the rich and privileged. All the proposal lacks is violence—which would have made it realizable, but which this gentle man was incapable of recommending.[66] In some situations an informed reformist like Fei is impelled to propose revolutionary remedies.[67]

Could the dominance of the Chinese ruling class have been

[65] Graham Peck, *Two Kinds of Time*, p. 219.

[66] This is the problem raised by Mao in a celebrated passage of his *Report on Hunan*: "The revolution is not a dinner party; it is not put together like a work of literature, a drawing, or a piece of embroidery. . . . Revolution is . . . the act of violence by which one class overthrows another."

[67] Though Fei, as one might expect, was far from being a Communist or a Marxist, he chose to stay in Communist China, where at first he was highly honored. During the Hundred Flowers period, however, he made the mistake of calling for a liberalization of the regime, with the result that he was made a scapegoat during the Antirightist Campaign of 1957.

brought to an end peacefully when it took so many forms, when it was so deeply rooted in the past as to be second nature to exploited and exploiter alike, when it was so closely related to all sorts of truths and ideas of truth, so much a part of rural China's institutions and everyday life? Was a mere adjustment— a painless crumbling away of the old and grafting on of the new—a real possibility in a complex society with so long a history, a society in which all the crises of a rapidly changing world were coming to a head at once, along with other crises peculiar to China? Once again, to pose such questions is not to answer them. For my part, however, I cannot think of any gradual solution that would have stood a chance of success. The problems were brutal and exigent; so were their solutions.

Insurmountable as the task facing the reformers was, the Kuomintang's was hardly less so. A balanced assessment of that regime would find its shortcomings less appalling than its problems, and would even grant it the enormous virtue of having established some semblance of order where chaos had reigned.[68] For a time Chiang's regime represented a step forward in the development of modern China. Of Sun Yat-sen's Three Principles, it preserved one—the first. It scorned democracy and the "people's livelihood," but it remained faithful to nationalism. Unfortunately for the regime, it was not even able to establish a truly national government. Had it done so, history would doubtless have allowed it to survive, if not absolved it altogether.[69] Even an unpopular, conservative government unable

[68] Even this fragile order, this modicum of political stability, was a blessing for the peasant. Though it seems immoral to say so, the Kuomintang by its very conservatism, and almost despite itself, did more in the short run to improve the lot of the masses than all the good will of the reformers.

[69] Here it is instructive to compare the two antagonists, the former rulers of China and the present ones. The source of the CCP's strength against the Kuomintang is today the source of its weakness—namely, the circumscribed nature of what a historical movement can in fact achieve, the inevitable gap between aspiration and accomplishment. This is an elementary truth, of which those who offer present-day China as a model for the world must constantly be reminded, as must those who see nothing but the inevitable dark side of Communist China and unthinkingly condemn everything Chinese. China's leaders are tackling their country's problems in a certain order: national greatness and independence before social justice and individual self-fulfillment. How could it be otherwise?

or unwilling to tackle China's fundamental problems could easily have maintained itself in power by putting down the forces that were pulling the country apart. The assault on Chinese nationalism by Japan was what made it apparent that the negative had carried the day over the positive—which is to say that China's need for the Kuomintang and a political leader like Chiang Kai-shek was a thing of the past. The Japanese invasion and the war, by giving explosive force to the contradictions born of China's unresolved basic problem, put an end to whatever slight chances there may have been for a gradual modernization of the country.[70]

[70] One ironic consequence of the war with Japan was that government officials whose sole allegiance was to nationalism came for a time to be regarded as traitors.

6. Nationalism and Revolution

The importance of nationalism to China's Communist revolution is by now a commonplace. Since the Communists' triumph in 1949 the newspapers have reminded us of it constantly; before that, China specialists repeatedly made the same point. In a sense the whole history of modern China can be seen as a reaction to imperialism, to an outside force that threatened the country's very existence. Modern Chinese history in this view culminates in the birth—after an extraordinarily painful labor—of the Chinese nation. Never was the pain greater, or delivery closer, than during the Sino-Japanese War of 1937–45. It is with these eight years, the period of the Second World War in Asia, that this chapter is primarily concerned. But first we must turn briefly to the only constants in the drama that began with the Europeans' intrusion into the Celestial Empire: imperialism and the nationalism to which it gave rise.

Imperialism and Nationalism

The introductory summary in Chapter One begins, it will be remembered, with China's brutal initiation into the concert of nations. This initiation was a result of the Opium Wars, i.e. of imperialism. Unequal treaties, the rush for spoils, the first steps toward dismembering Imperial China in 1895–98—all these were also the work of imperialism. So was the heavy Boxer indemnity, which the richest nations in the world imposed on one of the poorest. The control of customs collections by foreigners, their enduring predominance in finance and the key sectors of industry, their ill-concealed contempt for the "Celestials" (as expressed in the famous sign outside a Shanghai municipal park, "Dogs and Chinese not allowed")[1]—these are but a few aspects of a familiar and endlessly engrossing story.

China is not the only country to have suffered from the white man's arrogance in the past hundred years. Elsewhere economic exploitation may have been more thoroughgoing, political domination more direct; but the people smugly dismissed as "natives" elsewhere rarely had the same self-conscious pride in a brilliant civilization, or were as quick to scorn the European barbarians for confusing tools and weapons with refinement and culture. In some countries, such as neighboring Japan, nationalism was quicker to become an effective force. But if nationalism lay behind Chinese as well as Japanese imitation of the West, the very inadequacy of China's progress toward modernization made Chinese nationalism the more important of the two as a revolutionary force. This was particularly true from the beginning of the twentieth century on, as we might guess from these lines from a favorite song of revolutionary students of that time:

We are only afraid of being like India, unable to defend our land;
We are only afraid of being like Annam, of having no hope of
    reviving....
We Chinese have no part in this China of ours.
This dynasty exists only in name!
Being slaves of the foreigners,
They force us common people to call them masters![2]

The main shortcoming imputed to the dynasty, then, was servility toward the "white devils." In fact, what the dynasty lacked was not the will to resist but the strength.[3] The Manchu

[1] And also in an article in *L'Echo de Chine*, "journal of French interests in the Far East." The editor compares the Chinese who watched Russian, English, and German detachments parading through the streets of Tientsin in the aftermath of the Hundred Days' Reform to cattle watching a passing train. His article ends with this sensitive remark: "May the cattle be forgiven!" *L'Echo de Chine*, Oct. 12, 1898.

[2] From C. T. Liang, *The Chinese Revolution of 1911* (New York: St. John's University Press, 1962), p. 12. The author of these lines, Ch'en T'ien-hua, killed himself as a protest against the Ch'ing dynasty's repression of nationalist students.

[3] Its will to resist is clear from its suicidal policy of stirring up the Boxers in 1900.

dynasty was no less nationalistic than its Chinese opponents. Its fault lay in being powerless to meet aggression and helpless to convert humiliation into vengeance; this was its unforgivable sin and the reason for its fall. To the revolutionaries of 1911, overthrowing Imperial institutions or even the "foreign" domination of the Manchus was less important than adopting a political system that would make the country strong. If Chinese of that time aspired to a democratic republic, it was not because they loved liberty or hated absolutism, but because they wanted China to be strong. If Chinese were ardent readers of the *Social Contract*, it was because they considered Rousseau's work one of the inspirations behind the French Revolution—the revolution that made France the leading nation in Europe. The validity of this historical interpretation and of the image of Jean-Jacques as a latter-day Moses is beside the point. More important is what such interpretations tell us about the young literati who believed in them.

It was because the Revolution of 1911 failed, because constitutional democracy did not make the nation strong, that Sun Yat-sen sent his party to another school, the Bolshevik school, a move that quickly carried it to victory. But as changing and apparently contradictory as Sun's methods were, the basis of his doctrine stayed the same. Why make revolution, he asked in a famous passage. "Because . . . we have neither cohesion nor resistance. We have become scattered grains of sand." That is what allows imperialism to oppress us. Revolution and revolution alone would make it possible to restore China to her rightful place—first.

If China reaches the standard of Japan, she will be equal to ten great powers. At present there are only five great powers—Great Britain, the United States, France, Japan, and Italy—and when Germany and Russia recover [Sun was writing in 1924], there will be only six or seven. If China gets only as far as Japan, she will have the strength of ten powers in her one state, and will then be able to recover her predominant national position.[4]

---

[4] *Three Principles of the People*, p. 146.

It is not so paradoxical after all that Sun Yat-sen, poet and father of Chinese nationalism, should today be venerated in both Taipei and Peking.[5]

The heirs of Sun Yat-sen clashed, however, over patriotic questions and the problem of national resistance to Japanese aggression, which after 1930 became more and more overt. At the decisive hour it was not in fact white imperialism that most seriously threatened China's existence, but the imperialism of her fellow Asians. The "Dwarfs" had all too willingly and aptly assimilated the lessons the Powers had taught them. The Japanese applied the imperialist model to the hilt, and to them fell the dubious honor of precipitating the birth of the Chinese nation.

Let us briefly review the main stages and repercussions of Japanese imperialism in China, without getting into underlying causes:

(1) In January 1915 Japan presented Yuan Shih-k'ai with the Twenty-One Demands, whose ultimate aim was to make China a vassal of Japan. The demands, soon followed by an ultimatum, were presented at a time when the First World War had temporarily eliminated European competition in China.

(2) From 1915 on, there were many manifestations of Japanese expansionism—for example, the designs on Shantung mentioned earlier in connection with the May Fourth Movement. Japan's ambitions were temporarily thwarted by the Washington Conference of 1921–22 but were pressed with renewed vigor from 1928 on, as if in hopes of warding off future more effective resistance from China, which was then in the course of being

[5] At least until the Cultural Revolution, when for the first time some discordant notes marred the usual chorus of homage to "the Father of the Revolution." Among other things, the Red Guards attacked Sun's hitherto sacrosanct widow, the Vice-President of the Chinese People's Republic. The all-encompassing nature of nationalism is aptly symbolized by two contemporaries: the Nationalist Chiang Kai-shek, who was born in 1887, and the Communist Chu Teh, who was born in 1886. The remarks of Sun Yat-sen quoted above can be compared to the excerpts from Chiang's *China's Destiny* in Chapter Five. As for Chu Teh, his autobiography, as related to Agnes Smedley, strongly implies that what made the future head of the Red Army a revolutionary was outraged national pride.

unified under the Nanking government. The rhythm of aggression accelerated continuously, first in Manchuria, then in North
China.

(3) From 1931 on, every year saw a new incident or further
Japanese encroachments on Chinese territory, with the exception
of 1934, which Japan spent digesting its new acquisitions. On
September 18, 1931, the Mukden Incident touched off the invasion of Manchuria, which in early 1932 became the Japanese
puppet state of Manchukuo. In January-March 1932 patriotic
Chinese resistance resulted in an undeclared war in Shanghai.
From 1933 to 1935 the Japanese advanced inexorably from their
base in Manchukuo toward the west (occupying Jehol in March
1933) and the south. In the region south of Manchukuo they
tried to establish a second puppet state, made up of the five
provinces of North China (including Hopei, the province in
which Peking and Tientsin are situated).

While Chinese territory was thus systematically nibbled away,
Chiang Kai-shek temporized. By an ironic quirk of fate, this
intransigent nationalist was compelled to fall back before the
enemy and negotiate instead of fight.[6] His uncharacteristic response was an ineluctable necessity; knowing that China was
not ready to meet Japan head on, he pulled back, avoided open
conflict, and patiently set about putting together a modern army.
His policy was to set about unifying the country against its domestic enemies (this was the period of the Extermination Campaigns against the Kiangsi soviets) while temporarily tolerating
the foreign enemy's assaults on the nation's integrity. The Generalissimo's strategy was summed up in the slogan "Unification
and *then* resistance."

It was precisely this order of priorities that came under mount-
ing fire from an increasingly assertive public opinion. The point
is worth dwelling on, for it involves the essential question of
the relationship between nationalism and the Chinese Revolu-

[6] In 1933 he was forced to accept the establishment of a demilitarized zone between
Peking and the Great Wall, which amounted to de facto recognition of Manchukuo.
By the terms of a 1935 accord, North China became a neutral zone and the Nanking
government undertook to suppress anti-Japanese agitation in the territory under its
control!

tion. The six years between the assault on Manchuria in September 1931 and the outbreak of open warfare in July 1937 were a crucial period in the emergence of a Chinese public opinion and the formation of a Chinese nation. The two developments were simultaneous and related: the public opinion that began asserting itself with a forcefulness unknown even during the May Fourth Movement was an essentially patriotic one. Ten or fifteen years earlier the terms of the debate had been ideological; now they were political. At issue was an immediate and concrete problem—how best to resist Japan.

In the national resistance movement, the intelligentsia played a leading role; and as in the May Fourth Movement, it furnished not only the inspiration behind the movement, but also the largest number and most zealous of the active resistance workers. Businessmen and coolies practiced only one form of resistance, though to be sure a rather effective one—a boycott of Japanese goods.[7] Sometimes merchants participated in the resistance movement only after being threatened by students with the seizure and public burning of Japanese merchandise. As for the peasants, their role can best be described by saying that the agitation did not reach the countryside.[8]

The student movement even came to be identified with the nationalist (i.e. national resistance) movement. In the fall of 1931, for example, some 15,000 high school and university students stormed trains destined for Nanking, held military exercises in the streets of the capital, and staged daily demonstrations to stop negotiations and force the government to declare war on Japan.[9] Four years later, in December 1935, Peking student dem-

[7] Within a few short months in 1931–32, Japanese exports to China were cut in half, falling to their 1908 level.

[8] In the exceptional cases where it did, e.g., in Hopei villages worked by traveling teams of Peking students, it aroused little response; only the local teacher and occasionally his oldest pupils listened sympathetically to the students' anti-Japanese harangues. One could hardly expect peasants to believe that a plague they had never seen could be worse than landlords, drought, locusts, and the land tax.

[9] They roughed up the minister of foreign affairs and forced him to resign, and they sacked the office of the semiofficial Kuomintang paper *Chung-yang jih-pao*. They also presented a petition to Chiang Kai-shek. He at first refused to receive them but finally appeared after they had waited in the rain for 28 hours, having for once been bested in a contest of sheer obstinacy.

onstrations even larger than those of May 1919 played a decisive role in preventing the Japanese from carrying out their plan to detach the five northern provinces from the rest of China. Finally, in May 1936, the National Salvation Association was founded on student initiative; it soon became the core of a powerful patriotic movement that was strongly critical of the government. The prestigious association, with Madame Sun Yat-sen as its honorary head and well-known lawyers, journalists, and professors as its directors, called for an end to civil war and for the united resistance of all Chinese against Japan. Ending the civil war meant essentially calling off the struggle against the Communists and the Red Army. The association explicitly endorsed the notion of a united front, a term first put forth by the Comintern. In this period of popular fronts, the CCP, too, took up the new strategy; after the Long March, it issued an appeal for united resistance against the nation's enemies.[10]

This was the state of affairs at the time of the extraordinary Sian Incident, the key episode in the formation of Chinese nationalism (as well as a turning point in the fate of modern China). On December 12, 1936, Chiang Kai-shek was kidnapped by one of his generals while on a visit to Sian, the capital of Shensi province. It was not unheard of in the 1930's for a Chinese general to rebel against his commandant and take him captive, but this particular incident had a special significance. The general in question, Chang Hsüeh-liang, had been sent to Shensi in pursuit of the Red Army, which was trying to establish another soviet area in northern Shensi. A young warlord, Chang had been divested of his rich provinces in Manchuria by the Japanese invasion a scant three years after succeeding his father, who was murdered by the Japanese for being insufficiently compliant. Chang's troops longed to return to Manchuria. They were not happy about fighting their compatriots, whether or not they

---

[10] The appeal most often cited actually was published during the Long March, in August 1935; but that appeal was only for a "united front from below," which excluded Chiang Kai-shek. It was not until a year later, in the summer of 1936, that the CCP included the Nanking government and Chiang himself as acceptable allies in a "united front from above."

were Communists; in the words of a popular slogan, "Chinese do not fight Chinese." What they really wanted to fight for was the liberation of their homeland.

When at dawn on December 12 Chang Hsüeh-liang took Chiang Kai-shek prisoner, his intent was to force Chiang to reverse his priorities.[11] Of the Eight Demands presented to Chiang, seven echoed the main points of the program the CCP had formulated two weeks earlier, a program that came down to substituting war against the invader for civil war. The resolution of the Sian Incident was as abrupt and bizarre as its beginning: on the thirteenth day of Chiang's captivity, while a new civil war was brewing,[12] he was set free, in part owing to the good offices of Chou En-lai, who journeyed to Sian to plead the cause of the man responsible for thousands of Communist deaths.[18] Chiang's liberation seems to have been granted on the condition that he support the united front and a policy of resisting Japanese aggression.[14] Whatever the tenor of the discussions at Sian, the next few months saw the initiation of a united front after ten years of bloodshed. More important, the new firmness of the Nanking government toward Japanese encroachments soon brought it to the brink of war. Indeed, when war finally broke out in July 1937, it came as the result of an incident much like many others that had preceded it while Chiang was wholly preoccupied with fighting the Communists. In the long run, as Chang Hsüeh-liang had hoped, the Sian Incident not only put

[11] According to Chang, military pressure was the only means of getting an undemocratic regime to accept his point of view: he had repeatedly urged his views on Chiang to no avail.

[12] Nanking government planes attacked Chang's armies thirty miles from Sian; fortunately for Chiang, a snowstorm kept the planes from bombing the city where he was being held.

[18] The CCP's attitude was strongly encouraged, if not actually dictated, by Stalin, who was more concerned with securing the Soviet Union's eastern borders than with advancing the Chinese Revolution. He was convinced that Chiang Kai-shek was the only leader capable of effectively opposing Japanese imperialism in Asia.

[14] Despite the voluminous literature on the Sian Incident, we still do not know exactly what happened during those thirteen crucial days. At present, neither the main actors in the drama in Taipei and Peking nor Stalin's successors in Moscow have any interest in revealing what they know.

an end to civil war (parallel declarations by the CCP and the Kuomintang in September 1937 made the united front official policy), but touched off a war of national resistance.[15]

Chiang Kai-shek emerged from these travails with greater prestige than ever. He became the living symbol of national unity. Was this new stature undeserved because it resulted from a policy that was forced on him against his will? We must at least admit that his policy prior to the Sian Incident was not lacking in courage; he was courting unpopularity and, though himself a nationalist, deliberately alienating the flower and hope of Chinese nationalism.[16] Nor was his policy lacking in coherence; he was more clear-sighted and more realistic than most of his young opponents, who did not appreciate either Japan's real strength or China's weakness. Deserved or not, Chiang's temporary victory over his domestic enemies, who were forced to rally around him in a Sacred Union, was pyrrhic.[17] For the war that thus began, and in beginning made him a national hero, was to be the direct cause of his downfall.

Communism and Nationalism

One place after another in China fell with almost ridiculous ease before the Japanese *Blitzkrieg* (if we may use a term that had not yet been coined). But like Napoleon's army in Russia over a century before, the Japanese Imperial Army never took possession of the land it had conquered. It was swallowed up in the vastness of China, holding nothing but cities and connecting roads and railways. There were only two real campaigns in eight years of war, of which the second was just a continuation of the first. What was left to conquer in 1938, after the first campaign? Everything in China that counted was in Japanese hands: the

---

15 That is, if we consider only the direct cause of the war. It was obvious that sooner or later Japanese military activity in China would lead to open warfare; what the Sian Incident did was speed up the process.

16 To be sure, popularity and the support of public opinion mattered little to him. In his eyes, the flower and hope of Chinese nationalism was a well-equipped army, not a mob of enthusiastic students.

17 [The expression sacred union was first used by Raymond Poincaré in August 1914, in an appeal to Frenchmen of all political persuasions—and particularly the socialists, members of the Second International—to join in opposing German aggression.—Trans.]

great ports, the industrial and commercial centers, and the capital. In theory Japan occupied everything east of the line joining Peking to Canton via Hankow, the richest and most populous part of the country. Between the fall of 1938 and the spring of 1944, when the Japanese army launched another major campaign, the front was more or less stabilized along the Peking-Canton axis.

But the real war went on behind the front. Against an opponent of overwhelming economic and military superiority, China had two great assets. One was her enormous population and its morale; Chinese patriotism, so long considered a joke by skeptical Western residents, had at last under the pressure of extreme and desperate conditions become a force to be reckoned with. The other was the foreign assistance that was bound to come once Japan's imperialist designs finally impinged on countries more powerful than China. China's problem was to hold out until this assistance came; her assets were exploitable only in a protracted war because a short war meant the victory of the stronger. This was perfectly understood by Chiang Kai-shek, who announced his intention of "trading space for time." He did so with his habitual resoluteness, abandoning the important centers of the East and taking refuge in the underdeveloped and inaccessible interior.[18] But he failed to do the one thing that would have given his strategy of local war maximum effectiveness—namely, to conduct guerrilla warfare behind the Japanese lines.[19]

The social implications of guerrilla warfare are obvious. Mobilizing the rural masses would have required transforming the Chinese countryside and limiting the power of large landowners; hence Chiang's aversion to the idea. The same consideration explains why the Communists were the first to urge a strategy of protracted war, and why they were the most active, if not the

[18] His wartime capital, Chungking, was in railroadless Szechwan province; moreover, the fog that shrouded the city for six months of the year made air attacks impossible during that period. The reasons for Chiang's choice were similar to the Communists' reasons for choosing Kiangsi as their soviet base area.

[19] There were in fact some Nationalist, i.e. Kuomintang, guerrilla forces, but in most cases they were formed on local initiative.

only, leaders of guerrilla resistance efforts. Guerrilla activities benefited the Communists even more than the nation as a whole. From their stronghold in Shensi, they gradually infiltrated much of North China, occupying most of Shansi, Hopei, and Shantung behind the Japanese lines. In January 1938 they were among the founders of a local anti-Japanese government, the so-called Border Region Government, that coordinated the activities of the first guerrilla base area.[20] When Japan surrendered in 1945, there were nineteen Communist base areas, most of them in North China. There were 80,000 men in the Red Army in 1937; in 1945 there were 900,000, plus a militia force of 2.2 million men.[21] In 1937 the CCP governed 1.5 million peasants in desolate Shensi; in 1945 there were 90 million peasants under Communist rule, which extended across the whole North China Plain. In 1936 the Communists had their backs to the wall; their position was far more precarious than at the time of the Kiangsi soviets, and at times downright desperate. In 1945 the party had 1.2 million members and was a serious contender for power. So great was the CCP's growth during the war that by 1944 some informed observers were asking themselves if the Communists had not already won the impending civil war.

How did such an extraordinary change come about? In the first place, the CCP played the card of united front and national resistance for all it was worth. At the cost of relatively minor concessions, the party won official status for the first time, and was thus in a position to exploit the new possibilities created by a state of war. It all but abandoned its program of social revolution, including the confiscation of large landholdings (there were in any case fewer large landowners in North China than in Central or South China), and was content instead with strict enforcement of the law limiting land rent. This was enough to

20 The Border Region Government of Hopei, Shansi, and Chahar was set up as a rival to the puppet government installed in Peking a month earlier by the Japanese. At first the Border Region Government had only two Communist members out of nine, but Communist influence spread rapidly throughout the region under its control.

21 These are the official figures, and they are probably inflated. The Kuomintang, whose figures are distorted in the opposite direction, estimated Communist regulars in 1945 at 600,000, and Communist militiamen at 400,000.

win over the tenant farmers without jeopardizing the party's official moderate image. For the peasant majority—the huge class of small owners—the party enacted and enforced a decrease in interest rates, which it fixed at 10 per cent a year, and a reduction in taxes, which it made progressive. That was all—and as many observers noted, it was reform, not revolution.

With social concerns relegated to the background, the accent was on national resistance. The CCP constantly invoked the necessity of "national salvation" (*chiu-kuo*). In *On New Democracy*, published in 1940, Mao unblinkingly presented himself as the faithful follower and rightful successor of Sun Yat-sen. Sun's doctrine, Mao asserted, was correct and well-suited to his time, and lacked only one thing to make it equally applicable to the modern era: a concern with mobilizing the masses. The CCP's mobilization of the peasants, along with its emphasis on national resistance, was the second reason for its growth during the war. Patriotic propaganda was much more successful in winning over the peasants than agrarian revolution had been several years before. The peasantry supported the Border Region Government and actively assisted the Red Army, supplying among other things the best part of its troops.[22]

Why were the Communists so successful? First of all, because the anti-Japanese Border Region Government, which was dominated by the CCP, filled an important void; many Kuomintang

---

[22] The army was renamed the Eighth Route Army (*pa-lu-chün*) after the accord with the Kuomintang. During the civil war, its name was changed again, but it continued to be popularly known as the Eighth Route Army. In order not to confuse the reader, the term Red Army is used whenever the specific context does not require greater precision. In fact, the Eighth Route Army was only the most important and most celebrated of the Communist armies. Of the 86 members of one Eighth Route Army unit fighting in western Hopei in 1940, 70 were poor peasants and none were intellectuals. Only eleven had been to school, but only two of the other 75 were illiterate: 73 had learned to read thanks to the Red Army. Of the 29 who were members of the CCP, 28 had joined since the beginning of the war with Japan—eloquent testimony to the effect of patriotism on party membership. Similar evidence comes from northern Kiangsu in February 1941. Of 197 officers of the New Fourth Army (the most important Communist army outside North China), only 25 had joined the Red Army by 1936; the others had joined since 1937—to fight the Japanese. These examples are taken from Chalmers Johnson, *Peasant Nationalism and Communist Power: The Emergence of Revolutionary China, 1937–1945* (Stanford, Calif.: Stanford University Press, 1962), pp. 103, 155. This important book will be discussed shortly.

officials fled or resigned their government posts at the first sign of danger. Second, because under the new government the peasantry served an apprenticeship in mass-style democracy, including public assemblies and meetings of associations of poor peasants, women, youth, militiamen. Far removed though it may have been from Western-style democracy, this was something altogether new in the peasant world and was in itself revolutionary. Last and most important, because the inhabitants of North China had no choice. The CCP's greatest ally was the Japanese army, whose atrocities left the peasantry in such desperate straits that it had no recourse but to seek the Red Army's protection. The Japanese response to guerrilla warfare, assassination, and sabotage was systematic destruction and the indiscriminate slaughter of peasant villagers. The Japanese army launched "mopping-up" campaigns against "infested areas" (the term has a familiar ring today), guided by the "three-all" policy ("burn all, kill all, loot all" within a given area, so as to make it uninhabitable). Poisonous fumes were pumped into tunnels in which the local population had taken refuge (800 inhabitants of one Hopei village were asphyxiated in this manner one sunny day in the summer of 1942); rapes in which fathers and brothers were forced at bayonet point to participate, and more—the war in Asia awaits its Malaparte.[23] The thing to remember is that the peasant was often safer if he joined a guerrilla detachment: since his life was in constant danger anyway, he was better off if he at least had a weapon. This was all the more true since the North China front was at once nowhere and everywhere; it was not a geographic front like the one between Kuomintang-ruled China to the Southwest and occupied China in the Southeast, but, in Fairbank's words, "the omnipresent social front of popular resistance."

The peasants of North China in wartime took orders from two sets of authorities, one by day, the other by night. On the orders of the Japanese, trenches were filled in by day that had

---

23 [In *Kaputt*, Malaparte gives a vivid and grisly account of his experiences as a war correspondent accompanying the German army in Russia during the Second World War.—Trans.]

been dug the night before on the orders of the guerrillas—another practice familiar to us from the Algerian and Vietnamese wars. The peasants paid two sets of taxes, organized two different sets of village leaders to deal with their daytime and nighttime masters, and suffered reprisals from each side for carrying out the orders of the other. Though the Communists often were intruders in a village and though they sometimes took control by force,[24] they soon came to symbolize the nationalism to which the war they were waging had given birth. Left to themselves, the peasants certainly would not have resisted the Japanese army.[25] They would simply have lain low, in their customary fashion, in the hope of escaping notice. But once the Communists' guerrilla tactics had thrown the Japanese off balance and provoked them into retaliating with a wave of raids and massacres, the villagers came to hate the invaders with all their heart and soul. Hatred, it seems, is the most powerful agent of national self-consciousness.

War and Revolution

The foregoing analysis is much indebted to Chalmers Johnson's bold and intelligent study *Peasant Nationalism and Communist Power: The Emergence of Revolutionary China, 1937–1945*, one of the indispensable books on contemporary China. In fairness to Professor Johnson, be it noted that my presentation of his thesis includes examples and observations with which he might not agree. Since *Peasant Nationalism* goes straight to the central issues of the Chinese Revolution, it seems useful to begin by summarizing and discussing its main conclusions.

In Johnson's view, the Communist revolution succeeded not because of peasant misery but because of the Second World War. The cause of the revolution was not social or economic, but

[24] In relatively peaceful areas (along the Yangtze, for example, where the pro-Japanese Nanking government offered the peasants relative security), the New Fourth Army made little headway and even resorted to destroying the *pao-chia* registers and residence certificates to force peasant villagers to oppose the Japanese.

[25] They probably would have killed a few Japanese here and there, out of the same kind of xenophobia that led to the murder of missionaries in the nineteenth century. But such incidents would have been no more than a petty nuisance to the Japanese.

political. The war, in his judgment, contributed to the Communist triumph in two ways. First, it created peasant nationalism, a mass nationalism that differed fundamentally from the nationalism of the intellectuals so clearly in evidence before the outbreak of war. The nationalism of the intellectuals resembled that of the nineteenth-century European bourgeoisie; peasant nationalism, by contrast, more primitive but in the end decisive, was a nationalism of despair. Second, the war allowed the Communists to present themselves as nationalists and thus to win the peasantry's support as the natural leaders of patriotic resistance to the Japanese. In effect, Johnson concludes, during the war Communism came to be identified with nationalism. It was presented to the peasants as just another variety of nationalism, "a species of nationalist movement," and it was as such that it came to power.

Furthermore, the breaches in the united front, which became more numerous and more serious with every passing year of the war, tended to leave the Communists with a monopoly on patriotic resistance. The two camps were equally responsible for these breaches, but episodes like the New Fourth Army Incident, in which a Communist force of 9,000 men was encircled and destroyed by a Kuomintang division in January 1941, did much to confer on the Reds the halo of martyrs. Japanese anti-Communist propaganda, which tried to drive a wedge in the Chinese national front and justify Japan's invasion as an anti-Bolshevik crusade ("The Communists are our No. 1 enemies"), had the same result.[26] Judiciously exploited by written and verbal propaganda emanating from Yenan, the Communist capital, the Japanese propaganda efforts ended up persuading many peasants that the meaning of this new term "Communist" was simply "patriot."[27] This mistake was the more natural because the identity of names led many peasants to confuse the Kuomintang in Chungking with the collaborationist Kuomintang in Nanking.

For purposes of comparison and generalization, Johnson con-

[26] The collaborationist Nanking government headed by Wang Ching-wei called for an anti-Communist front uniting the Nanking and Chungking governments.

[27] Along with reminders of the contacts taking place between men close to the Chungking government and representatives of Japan.

cludes by pointing to the similarities between the Chinese and Yugoslav experiences in the Second World War. In particular, he shows how Tito paved the way for the triumph of the revolution by coming to represent, as opposed to Drasha Mihailović, the principle of resistance to the Nazis. A "national Communism," inclined to independence from Moscow, became the practice, if not the ideology, of the only two people's democracies whose leaders had come to power without the help of the Russian army.

All this is very stimulating and seems to me for the most part well-founded. In what follows, my purpose is not so much to criticize Johnson's thesis as to qualify and supplement it. Some of his fundamental conclusions seem to me to be irrefutable. There can be no question, first of all, about the decisive importance of the Second World War. It was the war that brought the Chinese peasantry and China to revolution; at the very least, it considerably accelerated the CCP's rise to power. Second, it is clear that economic reasons alone were not enough to mobilize the peasantry. This point is implicit in the conclusion to Chapter Four, which is based on my own research; indeed, I tend to think that before the outbreak of war the peasantry was not in fact ripe for revolution. Finally, on a more general level, the importance of nationalism in the play of forces that led to the Chinese Revolution is beyond dispute.

Now let us return briefly to peasant nationalism and to the influence of the war as such. Johnson's study deals primarily with North China, the China of the Communist guerrilla armies. In the parts of China under Kuomintang control, what was the relationship between the peasantry and the Nationalist army, and how did the peasants regard the war?

Neither question can be answered without reference to how the army treated its recruits and how it behaved toward the peasant population. In fact, if not in theory, conscription affected only the poor and middle peasants; prosperous families either paid for a substitute or bribed the recruiting officer. Kuomintang soldiers were so badly fed that some actually died of starvation. A greater number were lost in epidemics, made the more disastrous by a total lack of hygiene, or died of tuberculosis, which they gave one another by eating from a common plate or bowl in the customary Chinese fashion. Since most soldiers could not read or write and their pitifully low pay put the services of a public scribe beyond their reach, they completely lost touch with their families. "For his family, a conscript's life usually ended on the day he disappeared down the road, shackled to his fellows"[28]—except when he managed to desert before his unit had gone too far. And the army was all too alert to the possibility of desertion: in one case, 200 conscripts were burned to death in a train bombed by the Japanese when their officers decided not to risk opening the train's locked doors.[29]

As for civilians, requisitions and pillaging were so frequent an occurrence that most peasants hated their own army more than the Japanese.[30] In some cases starving Chinese soldiers killed peasants who resisted their efforts to steal grain; in at least one case fleeing soldiers killed peasants for their clothing, with which they hoped to disguise themselves from their Japanese pursuers.[31] In 1938, to slow down the Japanese advance and protect the city of Chengchow, the government opened the dikes on the Yellow River, causing it to return to the course it had followed almost a hundred years before—a "heroic" decision that resulted in the death by drowning or starvation of thousands of peasants in eastern Honan.

One can easily imagine the peasants' reaction to the way the army behaved and carried on the war: they tried to defend themselves and to survive. They mixed sand in the rice requisitioned by the Kuomintang army, sent their idiot and invalid sons to fill their conscription quotas, and emigrated en masse to occupied areas when the Japanese offered good wages for peasant

[28] Graham Peck, *Two Kinds of Time*, p. 226. A good many of the examples and concrete details given below come from this book, which is just as indispensable for this period as Johnson's *Peasant Nationalism* and Edgar Snow's famous *Red Star over China*.

[29] This incident occurred in western Honan in 1941 on the Lunghai railroad, the major rail route from the East to the Northwest.

[30] "Their own" is of course misleading, since they never thought in such terms. Japanese soldiers, Kuomintang soldiers—they were the same plague, something inflicted from outside. And the Japanese army, being better fed, did not steal as much.

[31] This happened in the mountains on the Honan-Shansi border in 1941.

labor on their strategic connecting roads.[32] Sometimes peasants formed bands that attacked isolated Kuomintang soldiers or killed recruiting agents. In Honan province, the indifference, incompetence, grain hoarding, and speculation of government officials greatly aggravated the famine of 1942–43, which according to unverified estimates left two million dead. When the Japanese reinvaded Honan in 1944,[33] they met next to no resistance; as their advance progressed, the peasants attacked, disarmed, and in some cases murdered the Nationalist soldiers.

What did the villagers know about the war's progress? Less than Stendhal's Fabrice at Waterloo. They never knew the invaders were near until they saw the Japanese soldiers' rifles on the horizon. Imperturbably they went about their daily rounds in the midst of danger; death would strike in any case if the planting and harvesting were not done on time. One May evening in 1941 the road running west from the western suburbs of Loyang, the capital of Honan, offered an unusual spectacle. A great crowd of townspeople fleeing the bombed city for the mountains kept having its progress impeded by another great crowd, made up of peaceable, tired peasants who were returning to their villages after harvesting grain all day. Although bombs were falling on Loyang, the city was not deserted; red banners aloft, delegations of old peasants were heading for the city's main temples as fast as their bound feet allowed. They wanted to burn incense in order to bring rain. The townspeople hoped the clouded sky would bring them protection against air raids; the peasants watched it with the same impatience, hoping for rainfall to save their drought-threatened crops.

---

[32] Here is another vignette, one that tells more than any abstract discussion about the peasants' attitude toward conscription, one of those brutal facts that defies being reduced to a statistic. A poor, middle-aged peasant couple of Kunghsien, in Honan province, were dependent for their subsistence on the wages of their only son, who worked in a coal mine. When the couple, who were in their forties, unexpectedly had a second son, the conscription officers informed them that their older son would have to serve in the army, since the law exempted only one son per family. The wife pleaded with them, explaining that they would starve to death if the older boy left. When the local authorities dismissed her pleas, "she went home and beat her baby on the ground until it was dead." Peck, *Two Kinds of Time*, pp. 266–67.

[33] They had occupied it previously at the outbreak of the war.

But all these various grounds for caution in discussing the birth of peasant nationalism refer to the part of China under Kuomintang control, whereas the Johnson analysis refers to the guerrilla bases of North China, where the rural masses were mobilized in the fight against the Japanese. Do the data from the Kuomintang areas amount to a proof by converse of the Johnson thesis? Not exactly. Indeed, the attitude of the Nationalist army and local Kuomintang officials suggests to me that the upsurge of popular support for the Communists, over and above its obvious debt to the party's organizational and mass mobilization techniques, owed less to national than to social considerations; that its explanation lies less in the anti-Japanese activities of the party's cadres and the Red Army's officers and men than in their unprecedented conduct and responsiveness to the people's needs. True, the Communists were on the whole more determined and effective than the Kuomintang against the Japanese; but more important, they were a government and an army of the people. The peasantry had always regarded government as evil, and the military as the quintessence of evil. Now along came a new government, calling itself Communist, which on the whole treated the peasants rather well; even if this government had renounced agrarian revolution and the confiscation of large landholdings, it forced local despots and their men to accept its authority and to change their ways, just as it constrained mothers-in-law to be considerate toward their daughters-in-law, husbands to stop beating their wives, etc. The high-and-mighty district magistrate before whom one prostrated oneself gave way to a "delegate" who brought his camp bed with him and could hardly be distinguished from the local villagers. Above all, the way the Eighth Route Army behaved toward the peasants contradicted their entire previous experience of the military. What strange soldiers these were, who paid for what they bought, cleaned up the rooms they stayed in, mingled socially with the villagers, and were not above lending a hand in the fields![34]

---

[34] "Support our army, the people's army that is really our own" (*yung-hu tsa-men lao-pai-hsing tzu-t'i ti chün-tui*) read the legend on a war poster showing peasants

Why did the Communists succeed in winning over the peasant masses? Because in addition to being authentic patriots they were genuine revolutionaries, men who understood the needs of the people, knew what changes had to be made, and set about making them. It need hardly be said that they were insincere in their dealings with the Kuomintang, subordinating even national resistance to their ultimate aims;[35] but they were always close to the people, the masses that they alone addressed with understanding. Seen in this way, the successive stages and tactical shifts in the CCP's history have an underlying principle of continuity: the Communists' fidelity to their calling and their past.

It was during the Second World War that the Communists won the civil war; this is true—but it is not the whole truth. We must add a further point: it was during the Second World War that the Kuomintang *lost* the civil war. War puts every belligerent power to the test and shows up outmoded regimes for what they are. As Lenin remarked on hearing of the first Japanese victories over Nicholas II's naval squadron in 1905: "Tsushima is the Japanese bourgeoisie's critique of tsarism." In China, the war hastened the collapse of a weak regime. It stripped bare the Kuomintang's ineffectuality and rendered its contradictions more acute; chaos and negligence are the two words that constantly recur in the descriptions of neutral and even sympathetic observers. At the same time the war exposed the weakness of China's military force, and particularly its faction-ridden and incompetent command structure; an American general summed up the situation with the words "We are allied to a corpse." Once again we come back to the conclusions of

welcoming Red Army soldiers, sending recruits, bringing soldiers hot water, caring for the wounded, donating farm animals for food and transportation, etc. From J. K. Fairbank, E. O. Reischauer, and A. M. Craig, *East Asia: The Modern Transformation* (Boston: Houghton Mifflin, 1965), p. 856.

[35] In this connection, one must make distinctions not only of place (North China as opposed to Southwest China) but also of time. During the last two years of the war, when it had become clear that civil war was inevitable and that the United States would defeat Japan, both the Communists and the Kuomintang took care not to risk against the Japanese the crack troops they were counting on to win the postwar battle for China.

the two preceding chapters: the gravity and complexity of China's social problems on the one hand, the inadequacy of the Kuomintang on the other. In short, we come back to the real tensions of Chinese society, tensions that could not be conjured away by the mere advent of a state of war.

Indeed, the war aggravated these tensions in at least two ways. First, it made the regime even more conservative; once the government was installed in the back country and thus cut off from the merchant bourgeoisie of the eastern ports and great cities, its social base consisted almost exclusively of that most conservative of classes, the large landowners. Second, and more important, the war touched off one of the greatest inflations of all time. The roots of this inflation undeniably lay in prewar financial and fiscal practices,[36] but its direct causes were war-related: the loss of major sources of revenue (customs duties were now collected by the Japanese), the need to finance the increased expenditures of wartime with the resources of a few poor provinces in the interior, and the unremitting efforts of the Japanese (who knew their enemy's weak point) to undermine price stability in Kuomintang-ruled China.[37] During the war the inflationary trend never reached the spectacular heights of the postwar years 1945 to 1949.[38] Even so, things were bad enough; to take just one example, businessmen making the most trivial purchases had to be accompanied by coolies carrying enormous sacks of banknotes. No serious steps were taken to correct this sorry state

[36] Before the war there was a large and chronic deficit: more than a fifth of the government's expenditures were financed by loans. Interest on the national debt absorbed one-third of the state's revenues year in and year out. The main problem may have been the government's excessive dependence on customs duties, which alone accounted for 53 per cent of its total revenues (excluding loans). The Kuomintang regime was only partly responsible for this state of affairs, which was inherited from an earlier period: in efficient foreign hands, customs collections brought a better return than other sources of revenue. Moreover, many other sources of income were in the hands of the warlords.

[37] In 1941 the government's income amounted to 15 per cent of its expenditures. But we must also take into account American aid, which was substantial even before Pearl Harbor.

[38] The following figures show the wartime rise in prices in Kuomintang-ruled China, with one *fapi* (a Chinese monetary unit) in June 1937 as the base: 1938, 1.25 fapi; 1939, 2 fapi; 1940, 5 fapi; 1941, 13 fapi; 1942, 40 fapi; 1943, 140 fapi; 1944, 500 fapi. On the postwar inflation, see Chapter Seven.

of affairs, which as in the Weimar Republic hit the white-collar workers particularly hard. Government officials and clerks with fixed salaries saw their income shrink steadily; their very survival came to depend on monthly rice allotments, graft, and odd jobs the tax collector would not hear about. Thus it was some of the most modern elements of Chinese society, people indispensable to the war effort, who suffered most from inflation.

Inflation had the usual consequences—widespread financial speculation and corruption. To be sure, both speculation and corruption were ingrained in certain deep-seated practices of traditional Chinese society; among the many opportunities wartime offered the speculator, inflation was only a secondary consideration. That a 1940 investigation uncovered exorbitant profiteering by Szechwanese grain merchants is hardly surprising,[39] and has no direct relation to the war. The same cannot be said of the traffic in contraband Japanese goods, for which the Nationalist army furnished an important outlet and its high-ranking officers the major middlemen.[40] For members of the ruling class who were close to both the central government and provincial administrators, the American presence created opportunities for all kinds of fruitful deals, few of them honest. Whether the United States Army undertook to build an airstrip or simply to rent a building for offices and personnel, the fabulous sums at the disposal of the Quartermaster Corps were an irresistible invitation to the ingenious swindler. The effects of this particular kind of windfall on the morale of an impoverished country we can readily infer from the present-day example of South Vietnam.

Two other factors further undermined the country's morale: the gradual erosion produced by a protracted war and the feeling that the outcome of the war was no longer in China's hands. After the heroism of the early years (notably in Nanking in 1937 and in Chungking during the air raids of 1939 and 1940), patriotic fervor subsided. In the years following Pearl Harbor, the

[39] The portion of their profit deemed excessive by the investigators (once the "normal" return had been deducted) was in itself more than the price paid to the farmer.
[40] Which made it easy for enemy spies to operate in the guise of black marketeers.

will to resist was replaced by feverish individual efforts to escape the worst consequences of the war, and amidst the collective torment to salvage and if possible promote personal and family interests. The last Japanese campaign, in the spring of 1944, led to apocalyptic scenes that were not so much a matter of the invaders' cruelty, though that was real enough, as a consequence of their opponents' confused scramble for safety, a fierce *sauve-qui-peut* that took the place of Chinese resistance.

These, however, were not the most profound effects of the war. Just as brutal and generally more lasting were certain major changes in urban and rural life that occurred within a very short time. Chungking's response to aerial bombardment has just been mentioned; let us briefly compare this little-known case with the justly celebrated example of London. In the Chinese capital, the panic to be overcome was of an entirely different order. What remedy could a people who prayed for rain imagine against mechanical monsters that spat fire from the sky?[41] How dramatic the story of wartime Chungking is: the sudden elevation of a great rural market town, filled with the stench and the squealing of pigs, the cackling of chickens, the chanting of coolies, and the morning cry of the night soil collector, to the rank of a great Allied capital![42] Except for a rare trip up the Yangtze by steamer, the twentieth century had scarcely made contact with the city by the winter of 1938;[43] in the short time between then and the summer of 1939 its population of 200,000 quintupled. The newcomers assumed they were there only temporarily; they stayed

41 During the first air attack, on May 3, 1939, a dozen fires started by Japanese incendiary bombs swallowed up large slum areas of the city in less than two hours, and thousands of slum-dwellers along with them. The next night, as every Szechwanese can tell you, a lunar eclipse showed the Great Dog of the Heavens preparing to devour the moon. Throughout the night, gongs loud enough to frighten away the giant dog were sounded to help the moon—and to drown out the groans of people wounded the night before. At dawn the next day, Chungking was bombed again. Theodore H. White and Annalee Jacoby, *Thunder Out of China* (New York: William Sloane, 1946), p. 11.

42 The American embassy in Chungking ranked immediately below those in London and Moscow.

43 On the toil of the boat haulers in the gorges of the Yangtze, see Han Suyin, *The Crippled Tree*, pp. 150–57. Chungking became China's capital only seven years after its first telephone was installed and three years after round-the-clock electricity became available.

six years. No one felt at home in this hybrid metropolis (an appropriate symbol of China herself, or rather of a moment in her history when great changes were taking place, when conflicting forces were colliding at every turn)—neither the refugees from the coast, who were disconcerted to find themselves back in medieval China, nor the native residents, who regarded the people "from below the river" as foreigners[44] and blamed them for bringing bombs and rising prices in their wake. Six years was perhaps not long enough to unify a community divided by such incomprehension and animosity. It was long enough, however, to shatter the mental universe of both parties. This spiritual upheaval was duly reflected in the city itself, which swallowed in one gulp the rice fields formerly outside its walls and saw its familiar landmarks altered: a People's Welfare Street ran through the Seven Stars Ravine, a Third Central Street across the Cliff of the Compassionate Buddha.

Even if prewar Chungking was nothing but a great market center that brought clothing and lamp-oil to thousands of villages in exchange for rice, meat, and opium, it was still a city. Yunnan, southwest of Szechwan, was a wholly rural province, where the Chinese farmers who worked the plain lived at several thousand years' remove from their closest neighbors, mountain tribesmen descended from the aboriginal peoples uprooted by the first Han settlers.[45] Into this universe, or rather these distinct universes, the war suddenly brought not only refugees, but highways, airports, a university, and American G.I.'s. The sociologist Fei Hsiao-tung, who did fieldwork in Yunnan in 1942, discovered there "the whole process of cultural development, from primitive headhunters to sophisticated and individualized city-dwellers." In Kunming, the neon-lit capital of Yunnan, students discussed Plato's *Republic* and Einstein's theory of rela-

---

[44] And as such, fair game for exploitation. The newcomers, for their part, acted as if they were in a foreign land; they had nothing but scorn for the native Szechwanese, who did not know what a trolley car was and wore such dirty turbans. The river in question was the Yangtze, which some thousand miles downstream from Chungking flowed into Nanking and Shanghai.

[45] Han means Chinese. Non-Han minorities account for 6 per cent of China's population.

tivity. In the suburbs, munitions plants surrounded the Flying Tigers' bases. Just outside the Valley of Kunming, an observer could watch rituals intended to ward off both air attacks and the evil spirits that spread epidemics. Should a traveler fall in with mountain tribesmen returning from the market to their native villages, he might be the honored guest that night at a "bachelor house," an establishment that Fei (a student of Malinowski) describes as comparable in every way to the similar establishments of the Trobriand Islands. "In a single day," Fei concludes, such a visitor "will have traveled from Polynesia to New York."[46]

The contact between these two worlds could not help but be explosive. With the upheavals and suffering that followed in its wake, the war opened up new possibilities for action and at the same time made such action seem necessary and even urgent to the masses. Like the Algerian fellahin before independence, tens of millions of Chinese sped past several historical stages, thinking the unthinkable and preparing themselves for the most radical changes.[47] Everyone today knows that war has no equal as a catalyst of revolution. Our experience, or that of our parents, encompasses two world wars; in one generation they led to the two greatest revolutions in history. Martin du Gard's Meynestrel was at least consistent when he busied himself to bring about the fertile mass slaughter of the First World War.[48]

The Triumph of Chinese Nationalism

The triumph of Chinese nationalism was born of the extremity of the threat to China. The Japanese invasion not only helped China attain self-conscious nationhood, but also constrained the Allies, as reformed imperialists, to accord China the equal status that until then they had resolutely denied her. In 1943 the Americans and British renounced the extraterritorial privileges that

46 See Fei Hsiao-tung and Chang Chih-i, *Earthbound China*, p. 9.
47 On the Algerian experience, see Pierre Bourdieu and Abdelmalek Sayad, *Le Déracinement: La Crise de l'agriculture traditionelle en Algérie* (Paris: Editions de Minuit, 1964).
48 Roger Martin du Gard, *Summer, 1914* (volume II of *The World of the Thibaults*).

Chinese nationalists had been inveighing against for a century.[49] In the same year Churchill and Roosevelt conferred with their colleague Chiang Kai-shek in Cairo, thus seemingly according equality to a country that for so long had had little more than colonial status in the white world. The end of the war in 1945 brought even more striking recognition: China was officially proclaimed one of the victorious Big Four.

But did Chinese nationalism triumph in 1945 or in 1949? To ask the question this way is to answer it. Despite the official celebrations, 1945 was too obviously someone else's victory, with Hiroshima bringing to a close an air and sea struggle in which China had had little part. The war itself had already shown the illusory character of the diplomatic successes China had been allowed to win. The abolition of extraterritoriality was followed almost immediately by an agreement between Chungking and Washington removing American servicemen from the jurisdiction of Chinese courts. The American presence in Kuomintang-ruled China was far greater than it had ever been in the era of "unequal treaties." And the author of *China's Destiny*, who had attributed all the ills of modern China to imperialism, was reduced to making constant requests for the reinforcement and extension of this detested presence.[50] With the Nationalists,[51] Chinese nationalism came to be recognized, but not to be taken seriously.

The Communists, for their part, after shedding the theoretical internationalism that had hampered their early efforts,[52] could plausibly claim to be more nationalist than the Nationalists, and indeed the only real nationalists. Whatever may have been the hidden thoughts and real feelings of the two parties

[49] Even France returned the French Concession in Shanghai to China—that is, to the pro-Japanese Nanking government, for the Vichy regime bowed to pressure from Tokyo in this matter.

[50] The hostile reactions of the Chinese populace were a clear indication of how unpopular this heaven-sent ally was.

[51] We should not forget that this term designates the Kuomintang (Kuomintang is often translated as Nationalist Party), and that nationalism was the first and most important of Sun Yat-sen's Three Principles.

[52] Especially during the first phase of the CCP's history (1921–27), when many of its influential opponents reproached it with being more Russian than Chinese.

during the war with Japan and the civil war, the evidence is beyond dispute: it was the Chinese Revolution, and only the Chinese Revolution, that brought Chinese nationalism to fruition.[53] Did the Communists exploit nationalism for their own ends? Of course they did. But it was through Communism that nationalism triumphed. True Chinese nationalists, far from reproaching the Communists for their sleight of hand, welcomed their contribution to the nationalist cause. Most of the Chinese émigré intellectuals in France, for example, who come largely from the landowning and literati families that were the ruling class of the old regime and are today "enemies of the people," prefer Peking to Taiwan, the China of today to that of yesterday; the People's Republic is their pride.[54] Not a man or woman among them was not gratified by the nuclear explosions in Sinkiang.[55] For the first time since they were children, China is strong, independent, respected, and feared. Such considerations weigh more heavily in their preference for Peking than the regime's social and ideological orientation.

In actual fact, Chinese Communism is first and foremost the triumphant assertion of Chinese nationalism. It is a nationalism of explosive vitality, as aggressive as it is vigorous, as often ill-considered as profound. And this is as it must be. After all, whether we are dealing with classes or with peoples, how else can we imagine the triumph of the oppressed?

[53] It seems clear that "donning a nationalist guise" did no more violence to the real feelings of many of the Red Army's officers than to those of their commander-in-chief, Chu Teh (see note 5). During the civil war the CCP continued to brandish the nationalist flag, noting among other things that its adversary was being equipped by "American imperialists."

[54] And sometimes, as the disorders of the Cultural Revolution make it necessary to add, their torment. But we can safely predict that they will absorb this setback as they have so many others. (A newly published work seems to confirm the accuracy of this prediction, originally made at the height of the Cultural Revolution: Tsien Tche-hao, *La République Populaire de Chine: Droit constitutionnel et institutions* [Paris: R. Pichon et R. Durand-Auzias, 1970]. See especially pp. 531–79 and 593–607.)

[55] Whereas a Frenchman can in good conscience come out against the nuclear establishment at Pierrelatte, to oppose China's bomb is a luxury no Chinese allows himself.

7. The Red Army Triumphs

The last act was armed confrontation: the Chinese Revolution culminated in both a military conquest and a people's war. Mobilization of the masses, who had first arisen against a foreign invader and then turned on their domestic enemies, was the Communists' trump card; and the end of the Second World War left them in a strong position to play it.

On the basis of the relative size of the opposing armies (the Communist troops were outnumbered four to one) and the arms and equipment at their disposal, the CCP seemed destined for quick defeat. Even the heightened nationalism of the immediate postwar period seemed for a time to serve the government's advantage. It was the government that public opinion credited with the advances China had made on the international scene,[1] and the government to which people naturally looked for leadership in consolidating these gains. The country's newfound status redounded to the glory of the symbolic leader of national resistance; Chiang Kai-shek's prestige was at its zenith. Fifteen years earlier, at least one sector of the public felt Chiang had betrayed the ideals of the revolutionary party that had brought him to power, ideals upheld by more capable and public-spirited members of the party, among them Wang Ching-wei. Now history adjudged Wang the traitor, Chiang the patriot.[2] Yet three and

---

[1] China was one of the official sponsors of the United Nations when the new international organization was launched in San Francisco in 1945, and later became one of the five permanent members of the Security Council.

[2] Wang died in Japan in November 1944.

a half years later, Chiang was a fallen dictator, forced to resign as President of the Chinese Republic and take refuge on Taiwan while the triumphant Red Army paraded through the streets of Peking. What accounts for the revolutionaries' swift and total victory? Was it their strength or the weakness of the regime they replaced, and in a sense the weakness of China herself?

The Negotiating Game

The war against Japan slowed down and overshadowed the civil war, and it did not immediately flare up again when Japan surrendered. At first the negotiating table seemed to be the place where history would be made. But while the negotiations occupied center stage, the many incidents occurring in the wings went unobserved, and revolutionary changes spread unnoticed throughout the countryside.

Glimpses of the coming struggle for power were nonetheless in evidence from the first. Even before Japan had formally surrendered, there was a race between the Communists and the Nationalists for Japanese-held territory and for whatever arms and equipment could be seized from the routed enemy.[3] The first atomic bomb was dropped on Hiroshima on August 6, 1945, the second on Nagasaki on August 9; on August 10 two general orders were issued to Chinese troops:

(1) Generalissimo Chiang Kai-shek to General Chu Teh, commander-in-chief of the Eighth Route Army: "Remain in your positions and do not accept the surrender of any unit whatever of the Japanese army."

(2) General Chu Teh to all anti-Japanese forces in the "Liberated Areas": "Disarm all Japanese and puppet troops immediately; seize and take over cities and communication lines previously held by the Japanese or their Chinese lackeys."

The conflict implicit in these contradictory orders was soon joined, at least on paper. On the day Japan surrendered, Gen-

---

[3] There were approximately 1.9 million Japanese soldiers in China and Manchuria at the end of the war, and some 780,000 Chinese soldiers taking orders from the various collaborationist governments. The collaborationist troops represented not only arms and equipment to be seized, but recruits to be enlisted.

eral Douglas MacArthur, Supreme Commander for the Allied Powers, designated Chiang Kai-shek as the sole authority empowered to accept surrender from the Japanese in China.[4] A Sino-Soviet treaty to the same effect was signed the same day; Moscow, too, regarded the Nationalist government as the only legitimate government of China.

In these circumstances the race for booty and territory went to the Nationalist army. To be sure, the sudden end of the war had caught Chiang Kai-shek with almost all his forces in southwestern China, 600 to 1,500 miles away from the disputed territory in the North and Northeast; but that disadvantage was soon remedied. In September and October 1945 the Americans airlifted Nationalist troops to key points in Japanese-occupied territory in the East and the North, and 50,000 American Marines occupied port areas and airfields on the Nationalists' behalf in Tsingtao, Peking, and Tientsin. Three months after the war ended, the whole of the rich coastal region from Canton to Peking was in Nationalist hands.[5]

The government forces ran into greater difficulties on the other side of the Great Wall, in what had been Manchukuo. There the Japanese had already surrendered to the Soviet Union, which in accord with the Yalta agreements had declared war on Japan on August 8 and had occupied all of Manchuria after a one-week "campaign." If the Russian Red Army gave the Chinese Communists little help, at least it did nothing to impede Lin Piao's guerrillas, who quickly infiltrated the Manchurian countryside from their bases in North China and Chahar.[6] In November 1945 the presence in Manchuria of some 130,000 Communist troops, including a good many former soldiers of the Japanese-trained Manchukuo army, gave the Communists a solid position in the Northeast. They had lost no time where

[4] Also in Formosa and in Indochina north of the 16th parallel.

[5] With the important partial exception of the North China Plain, where the Communists retained control of many villages.

[6] Lin Piao, the youngest of the Communist generals, had graduated from the Whampoa Military Academy while it was under Chiang Kai-shek's direction. A veteran of the Kiangsi period and the anti-Japanese resistance, he was one of the great heroes of the civil war.

American aid did not hopelessly weight the odds against them.

While this division of the enemy army's spoils was proceeding, in the capital city of Chungking apparently good-natured conversations were taking place almost daily between Chiang Kai-shek and Mao Tse-tung. Desultory negotiations had been conducted since well before the war ended, but with the coming of peace they suddenly started up again at a much higher level—Mao himself arrived in Chungking on August 28. The Communists had nothing to lose by going through the motions of negotiating. Moreover, they had no real alternative, since the war-weary Chinese public would have turned against whichever side betrayed any inclination to settle matters by renewed fighting.[7] The Communists accordingly announced their willingness to participate in a "democratic coalition government," a reasonable enough position given their strength in 1945 and their belief (shared with many non-Communists) that the Chungking government represented a single-party dictatorship.[8]

But why were the Kuomintang's leaders so ready to negotiate, when their only goal was to settle accounts with what their official dispatches would soon resume calling the "Communist bandits"? For two reasons. In the first place, like the Communists, the Nationalists had no choice; they could not defy the Chinese public's longing for peace. In the second place, they could not afford to offend their American allies, who had eliminated the Japanese threat to China and had just lent the Nationalist army such prodigious logistical assistance. As for the Americans, with the Cold War dawning they feared that a Nationalist refusal to compromise would drive the Chinese Communists into the arms of Moscow. They were equally fearful of getting involved in another war in Asia; what they wanted above all, in fact, was to "bring the boys home." The American embassy accordingly brought great pressure to bear for a successful outcome to the Chungking talks. The American ambassador, General Patrick J. Hurley, was no diplomat; he bluntly gave both camps to understand that he would not stand for a failure to reach some sort

---

[7] This was especially true of the liberals, the only significant body of public opinion besides the Nationalists and the Communists.

[8] Or more precisely, a dictatorship of the most conservative faction of that party.

of agreement. The Chinese docilely complied, at least on paper. The Mao-Chiang conversations ended with a joint communiqué issued on October 11, 1945; it was a moderate-sounding statement that exuded good will and settled nothing.[9]

When it came to "serious" negotiations, however, the Americans were not content to leave things to the Chinese. On Christmas Eve of 1945 General George C. Marshall, who would shortly give his name to the famous Marshall Plan for Europe, arrived in China at the head of the so-called Marshall Mission. Marshall immediately set about trying to find a way to make the Communists effective members of a coalition government, as they were at the time in France, for example. Though he never wore down Chiang's stubborn opposition on this point, by January 1946 he had at least succeeded in getting a truce proclaimed and establishing two tripartite bodies (composed of Nationalists, Communists, and Americans) for the peaceful settlement of disputes. One of these bodies was set up in Peking, the other in Chungking. The latter body, a Committee of Three (Marshall, Chou En-lai, and a Nationalist general), was to serve as a court of last resort for disputes that could not be settled on the spot.

Despite these initial achievements, the Marshall Mission ended its life in January 1947 in total failure. Its failure was not only total but inevitable. In the first place, the American position was at best ambiguous; though Marshall himself maintained strict neutrality, the United States continued to furnish the Nationalist government with arms and equipment. The Communists, predictably, pointed out the contradiction and denounced the United States for interfering in Chinese affairs. In the second place, the American negotiators were pursuing unattainable and conflicting goals. In trying to force Chiang Kai-shek to adopt reforms that would cut the ground out from under the revolutionaries, they were years too late. The revolution was at hand, and reforms would only have weakened the autocratic power that the Americans were trying desperately to shore up.

More important than the Americans' shortcomings and con-

[9] No mention was made of organizing a coalition government, which Chiang refused to consider, and thorny issues such as political control of the Liberated Areas were carefully skirted.

tradictory aims was the wholly justified mutual distrust of the two Chinese camps. There is no use trying to assign responsibility for local infractions of the accords or for the breakdown of the truce. Civil war was inevitable and both sides knew it, just as they knew they had to act out what Jacques Guillermaz calls "the comedy of peaceful intentions" to satisfy public opinion. Neither side ever really considered granting China's exhausted people a respite; the movement that had been gathering force for a good half-century was not going to come to a halt just when the decks had been cleared for the final showdown. Ten years earlier the Sian Incident had imposed a fragile veneer of unity on a badly riven reality, but the accord of 1937, poorly observed as it was, was sealed in the name of a united front against the nation's common enemy. Against whom could there be a united front in 1946, and to what end? China's number one problem was not imperialist aggression, which for the first time in a hundred years was not an immediate threat,[10] but the absolute opposition between two national political forces with antithetical programs and irreconcilable ambitions. One intended to seize power, the other to retain it; one was determined to promote social revolution in the countryside, the other to prevent it.

Precisely where and when the accord so laboriously worked out by General Marshall was broken hardly matters. It is in any case difficult to pinpoint any one incident as the opening round of the civil war. What we know is that incidents between the two sides became increasingly frequent and increasingly serious in Manchuria in the spring of 1946.[11]

Manchuria was the base from which the Red Army launched its successful offensive. It was also, as we have seen, the only part of China where the Communists succeeded in seizing a substantial part of Japanese-occupied territory and Japanese equipment. Because it was also the Russians' stronghold, some people

---

[10] Later in this chapter we shall come back to the subject of the American presence in China during the civil war and American aid to Chiang.

[11] In April 1946 the Red Army launched a battle for control of the Szeping railway terminal near the Liaoning-Kirin border. This was their first major pitched battle with the Nationalists since the flight from Kiangsi in October 1934.

have been quick to attribute the victory of the Chinese Revolution to Russian intrigue and President Roosevelt's fatal mistakes at Yalta. What exactly did the Russian army's aid amount to?[12] Marshal Malinovsky, the commander of the Soviet occupying army in Manchuria, let the Chinese Communists spread through the countryside and seize whatever Japanese weapons they could find. If he had also turned over to the Chinese Communists the cities of Manchuria with their great industrial potential, the Communists would have overcome one of their major handicaps in the impending civil war.[13]

Instead, Manchuria's industrial plant was systematically dismantled by the Russian army and shipped to the Soviet Union via the Trans-Siberian Railway. By this decision the Chinese Communists lost the entire industrial infrastructure of a region indispensable to the building of a modern China, and of socialism. The factories had been installed by the Japanese and worked for the Japanese army, and in the Russian view these were ample grounds for treating the factories, like the gold stored in Manchurian banks, as war booty.

The cities themselves were simply turned over to the Nationalists—after some delay, for given the Communist strength in the Northeast the government armies were not prepared to occupy them right away. Chiang Kai-shek had accordingly urged Moscow to defer the evacuation of Manchuria, and Stalin had readily granted the request. As it turned out, however, the Russians delayed their departure longer than Chiang wished, and they were careful to evacuate northern Manchuria at a time when the Nationalist army was tied up farther south. The re-

[12] The simplification of the political picture during the last phase of the Chinese Revolution is worth noting. Only two parties were left as credible contenders for power within the country, and only two foreign powers could pretend to affect the outcome—the USSR and the United States. Even Britain was out of the running, as were France and the defeated Axis powers, Germany and Japan, not to mention the lesser powers (Belgium, Italy, etc.) that had once shared in the spoils.

[13] The whole industrial plant of eastern China, it will be recalled, was then in the hands of Chiang Kai-shek. Throughout the Communist-controlled portion of the country, munitions factories and the like were extremely primitive. So was transportation: all the Communists had were pack mules and a few antiquated trucks captured from the Nationalists. It was not merely for strategic reasons that the Red Army's general staff and the ministers of the "People's Government" were sheltered in villages.

sult was that in April and May 1946 the Chinese Communists occupied much of the territory vacated by the 300,000 departing Russian soldiers.

This was practically the full extent of the Russians' aid to their Chinese comrades for the duration of the civil war. Did the Russians fail to assist the Chinese further out of Machiavellian premonitions of future disagreements? Any such argument underestimates the role in human affairs of ignorance and errors in judgment, from which the party faithful and fervent anti-Communists alike assume the Kremlin to be exempt. The struggle against Hitler and the European war had absorbed Russian energies for four years, and for once Stalin was probably sincere when he expressed skepticism about the Chinese Communists' chances of success to various American visitors in 1945.[14] The almost wholly rural basis of the Chinese revolutionaries' experience, the unorthodoxy of their Marxism, their lack of experience in conventional warfare—all these considerations could not help but throw off the strategists in Moscow.[15] In fact, however, the Chinese Revolution was simply taking a different course from the Bolshevik Revolution of 1917.

Civil War

With no basis for agreement in sight, one last truce, signed in Manchuria, expired on June 30, 1946. In July the Communists announced the creation of the People's Liberation Army;[16] the die was cast. On November 19 Chou En-lai, the perennial negotiator, left Chungking for Yenan for the last time.

Confirming the prognostications of most observers and the ratio of visible strength, the Nationalists made striking gains

14 See p. 76.
15 According to an apocryphal story making the rounds in Peking during the civil war, in 1945 Stalin sent Mao a manual on guerrilla warfare based on the Soviet people's resistance to the German invasion. Mao passed the book on to Lin Piao, the Chinese expert on guerrilla warfare, who opined after reading it that "if we had used this book as a manual, we would have been wiped out ten years ago." Cited in C. P. Fitzgerald, *The Birth of Communist China* (New York: Praeger, 1966), p. 100. Fitzgerald (pp. 97–100) analyzes the Soviet attitude with trenchant good sense.
16 The PLA was made up essentially of the Eighth Route Army, the remnants of the New Fourth Army, and the forces recently assembled in Manchuria.

during the first phase of the war (summer 1946–spring 1947), advancing throughout much of Manchuria and North China, the only areas held by the Communists. In March 1947 they brought off a victory of symbolic if not strategic significance by taking Yenan, the Communists' by now legendary capital. The Nationalists' victories, however, were more impressive on the map than on the ground. Their advance was facilitated by the Communists' strategy of avoiding fixed-position warfare, systematically abandoning cities, and concentrating on the destruction of enemy forces rather than the occupation of geographic objectives. The government forces soon extended themselves far beyond their support capacity, scattering garrisons along continent-long communications routes,[17] while behind the "front" the Communists revived the tactic they had used so successfully against the Japanese, spreading through the villages and there consolidating their power.

In mid-1947 the Communists took the initiative in Manchuria, and they never relinquished it. Two offensives directed by Lin Piao, combined with the cutting of the main Manchurian rail routes by saboteurs, pinned down isolated Nationalist garrisons in Changchun, Kirin, and Mukden, forcing the government to airlift large reinforcements to those cities at great expense. The same patient, inexorable isolation and carving up of government forces was then carried out in North China, accompanied by a southward thrust toward the Yangtze.[18] By the end of the year the Communists controlled much of Hopei and virtually all of Shansi province except the capital. In his important report of December 25, 1947, to the Central Committee, Mao exuded confidence: "The revolutionary war of the Chinese people has reached the turning point; . . . a turning point in history."[19]

The decisive battles of the civil war were fought in 1948. By the spring of that year the previous year's massive infiltration of the countryside had begun to pay military dividends. In April

[17] General David G. Barr, the American military adviser, had tried to dissuade Chiang Kai-shek from occupying Manchuria on just these grounds.

[18] By August 1947 there were two Communist armies in action south of the Yellow River, where they posed a direct threat to Central China.

[19] "The Present Situation and Our Tasks," *Selected Works* (Peking), IV, 157.

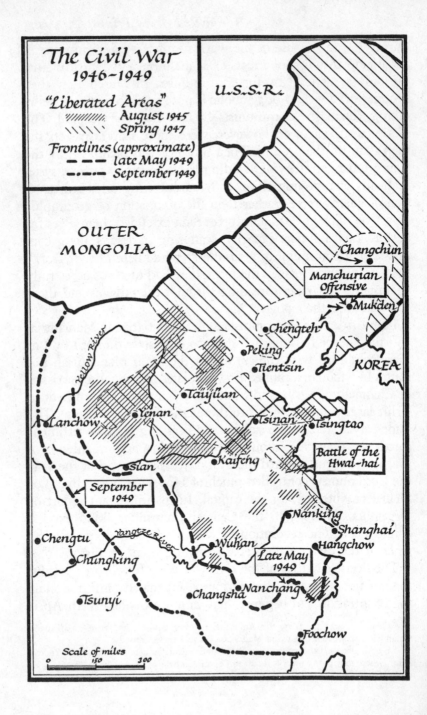

The Civil War
1946~1949

"Liberated Areas"
///////// August 1945
\\\\\\\ Spring 1947
Frontlines (approximate)
— — — late May 1949
—·—·— September 1949

U.S.S.R.

OUTER MONGOLIA

Changchun

Manchurian Offensive

Mukden

Chengteh

Peking

Tientsin

KOREA

Yellow River

Taiyuan

Tsinan

Tsingtao

Lanchow

Yenan

Sian

Kaifeng

Battle of the Hwai-hai

September 1949

Nanking

Shanghai

Chengtu

Yangtze River

Wuhan

Hangchow

Chungking

Late May 1949

Tsunyi

Changsha

Nanchang

Foochow

Scale of miles
0   150   300

the Red Army recaptured Yenan; soon afterward it took the two largest cities in Honan, Loyang and Kaifeng;[20] in September it took Tsinan, the capital of Shantung. The extended full-dress battle for Kaifeng in June showed that the Communists were ready to move to the last stage of their offensive: attacks on the major cities, where the hard-core Nationalist forces were entrenched.[21]

The coup de grace for the Nationalists came with two successive Communist offensives. In September 1948 Lin Piao launched an attack in Manchuria that far surpassed all previous Red Army offensives in scale. In less than two months, all of Manchuria fell to the Communists. The Red Army captured 230,000 rifles and killed or captured some 400,000 men, including crack Nationalist divisions that had been equipped and partially trained by the Americans.[22] Yet even after these staggering losses, the Kuomintang still had a numerical superiority in men and weapons and a monopoly on airplanes and tanks.

It lost both these advantages, and with them its last chance to stave off defeat, in a battle even more gigantic than the Manchurian offensive: the Hwai-hai campaign of November 1948–January 1949, one of the great battles of modern history. Chiang Kai-shek overruled his advisers and personally selected the site of his Waterloo:[23] the barren plain outside the city of Suchow, about a hundred miles northwest of Nanking. Into this battle he threw fifty-one divisions, which the opposing Communist generals, Ch'en I and the "One-eyed Dragon," Liu Po-ch'eng,

[20] In keeping with a practice dating back to the Kiangsi period, the Red Army quit Kaifeng a week later, after seizing mountains of arms and ammunition.

[21] A consequence of this new strategy was that the CCP reestablished contact with urban, proletarian China after two decades of immersion in the countryside. The importance of this reunion should not be overestimated.

[22] Changchun and Mukden, on which the Nationalist troops had fallen back, fell within two weeks (October 17 and 30, 1948).

[23] This is what O. Edmund Clubb calls the final confrontation between two armies and two worlds in his article "Chiang Kai-shek's Waterloo: The Battle of the Hwai-hai," *Pacific Historical Review*, Vol. XXV, No. 4 (November 1956). It was called the battle of the Hwai-hai because it took place in the valley of the Hwai River (where the Nien Rebellion had broken out a century before), and along the eastern section of the Lunghai railroad.

proceeded to carve up and dispose of piece by piece.[24] The destruction of the Nationalist forces was well under way by the time an army of reinforcements was ordered to join what remained of the 460,000 encircled Nationalists. To break through the Communist cordon, the relief army brought up all its heavy equipment, including American trucks and artillery (not to mention officers' wives and families). The Communists promptly immobilized this "slow-footed military Leviathan" by digging three lines of trenches around it.[25] On learning that the Nanking government planned to bomb the encircled army to keep its precious heavy equipment out of enemy hands, the Nationalist commandant, General Tu Yu-ming, surrendered. The date of his surrender, January 10, 1949, marked the end of the Hwaihai campaign, which in two months and five days wiped out the best part of the remaining Nationalist troops, some 550,000 men.[26] Altogether the government lost almost a million men in the four months from September 1948 to January 1949. The Red Army now had gained the only two advantages it hitherto had lacked: numerical and material superiority.

In late 1948 the Generalissimo suddenly rediscovered the value of political means, which once more seemed better suited to coping with Communist bandits than armed conflict. In his New Year's Day message of 1949, Chiang invoked Sun Yat-sen and his own deep faith in Sun's Three Principles in announcing an offer to negotiate with the Communists.[27] On January 8 he asked the Four Powers (the United States, Great Britain, the Soviet Union, and France) to mediate, and met with four refusals. On the fourteenth the Communists made known their terms, which included elimination of the "war criminal" Chiang Kai-shek. A week later, on January 21, the said war criminal resigned as President of the Republic of China and handed over his powers to his Vice-President, General Li Tsung-jen, an advocate of negotiations with the CCP.

24 There were a million men fighting along a front that extended over two hundred miles.

25 The description is Clubb's.

26 Of which number, according to the Communists, 327,000 were taken prisoner.

27 "The Father of our Republic once said, 'The goal of the national reconstruction of the Republic of China is peace.'"

By this time Tientsin had fallen (January 15) and Peking was about to capitulate (January 23). A month later the Red Army was at the Yangtze. In Peking the new Nationalist team tried to reach an agreement with the CCP before the Communist-imposed deadline of April 20. No settlement having been reached by that date, the People's Liberation Army crossed the Yangtze at dawn on April 21; two days later it took Nanking.[28] Shanghai and several major provincial cities fell in May. The losing side was divided by one last conflict, between the "Southwest strategy" of Acting President Li[29] (who recalled using Kwangsi province as a base for an attempt at wresting regional autonomy from the Nanking government in 1929–30) and the strategy of retreating to Taiwan, for which Chiang had already made preparations. Was Chiang's insistence on the move to Taiwan an example of political clairvoyance,[30] or another manifestation of his consistent tendency to preserve his best troops for his own purposes rather than risk losing them? Whatever the answer, his interference in his successor's actions and his unilateral decision to transfer arms and funds to Taiwan were enough to doom the Acting President's strategy before it could be tried.[31] By mid-October the red flag was flying over Canton. The Nationalist government made one last pilgrimage to Chungking, its wartime capital—a brief stopover on the road to exile.

In Peking a rejoicing people acclaimed the founding of the People's Republic of China on October 1, 1949. It was just thirty-eight years since the fall of the Empire, thirty-two since the Russian Revolution.

Military Factors in the Communists' Success

What made the Communists' victory possible? Although purely military considerations were far from negligible, they were decidedly less important than social and political factors.

[28] The Nationalist government fled to Canton. It was accompanied by only one member of the diplomatic corps—the Soviet ambassador.

[29] Li wanted to establish a Nationalist bastion in the hills and mountains of the Southwest and there await the Third World War.

[30] The Southwest certainly could not have been held for long, since the guerrilla war Li Tsung-jen dreamed of lacked the essential ingredient of popular support.

[31] Li made a futile effort to retrieve at least some of the funds and arms Chiang had commandeered.

"The worse-equipped army will defeat the better-equipped army; the countryside will conquer the city; the party that does not receive foreign assistance will triumph over the party that does." Anyone who heard Red Army officers chanting these slogans with apparent conviction in early 1948 would have dismissed them as bluster intended to boost morale. Today they seem almost banal, and certainly less eloquent than the events they anticipated. For the Chinese Revolution ended in the conquest of a country the size of a continent by an army of beggars, and at a pace that dumbfounded military experts.[32] Less than a year passed between the capture of Mukden on October 30, 1948, and the capture of Canton on October 15, 1949—from Manchuria to the tropics in eleven and a half months!

Extraordinary as the victors' performance was, it is less striking than the disintegration of their foe. In an analysis that bore out the Communists' own, General Barr spelled out some of the reasons behind the Kuomintang's collapse. Since his arrival in China, he wrote, the Nationalists had not lost a single battle for lack of ammunition or equipment. "Their military debacles in my opinion can all be attributed to the world's worst leadership and many other morale destroying factors that lead to a complete loss of will to fight."[33]

So many generals might be cited to exemplify the incompetence of the Nationalists' military leadership that one hesitates to single out any one of them for this purpose. It might nonetheless be observed that when General Tu Yu-ming allowed his troops to be encircled during the Hwai-hai campaign, he was simply giving further evidence of the utter incompetence he had repeatedly shown in Manchuria against the Japanese. The Nationalist army was not entirely devoid of able men, but the most intelligent and experienced officers tended also to be the

---

[32] See, for example, *The Communist Conquest of China: A History of the Civil War, 1945–1949* (Cambridge, Mass.: Harvard University Press, 1965), in which General Lionel Chassin repeatedly expresses his admiration for "a feat which is unique in the military history of the world" (p. 258).

[33] Further on, Barr specifies endemic corruption and dishonesty in the armed forces. "Report to the Department of the Army," November 16, 1948, in *China White Paper*, indexed edition (Stanford, Calif.: Stanford University Press, 1967), p. 358.

most independent, and they were therefore kept under wraps, not to say under suspicion.[34] Even more serious than Chiang Kai-shek's distrust of officers of this sort were the rivalries between cliques[35] and the prevailing norm of barefaced favoritism. Not only were the highest posts in the army reserved for graduates of the Whampoa Military Academy, but it was Chiang's policy to withhold his support from any officers who did not owe their career and their power directly to him.

Were domestic political considerations also responsible for the Generalissimo's practice of intervening in the direction of military operations taking place hundreds of miles from his headquarters or his capital?[36] To some extent, certainly, though domestic politics were probably less important in this respect than certain traits of Chiang's character, such as pride and suspiciousness, that had grown more pronounced with the years. Finally, these same considerations—Chiang's domestic political concerns and his personal characteristics—explain his constant recalling and replacing of army and division commanders. The resulting discontinuity in leadership led to great confusion and chronic uncertainty, which crippled whatever initiative the Nationalist military leadership might otherwise have shown.

The Nationalists' strategy did not err on the side of over-

[34] This was notably true of Generals Li Tsung-jen and Pai Ch'ung-hsi.

[35] And between individual commanders, as an example from the Hwai-hai campaign makes clear. Chiang Kai-shek ordered General Ch'iu Ching-ch'uan (twelve divisions) to relieve the neighboring army corps of General Huang Po-t'ao (ten divisions), which was encircled by the Red Army. But Ch'iu was jealous of Huang, who had been decorated by Chiang several years before, and took his time complying with the order. "We must not deprive General Huang of this great opportunity to show he is worthy of his medals," he told his entourage. Ten days later, General Ch'iu had covered eight of the twenty miles that separated him from the 90,000 men of the ten encircled divisions. A few days later, all but 3,000 of the survivors in the trapped divisions surrendered to the Communists. General Huang did indeed take advantage of the opportunity he had been offered—he died of wounds received in battle. Refusal to cooperate was not unknown in the Chinese military tradition, but in actually stirring up and keeping alive rivalries of this sort, Nanking could hardly expect Nationalist generals and high officials to develop a sense of the public interest.

[36] During the Communists' Manchurian offensive in the fall of 1948, Chiang Kai-shek personally directed the Nationalist defense—from Peking. During the Hwai-hai campaign, he supervised all military operations without ever leaving Nanking; it was on his orders (insofar as they were carried out) that divisions took up a position, advanced, or retreated.

aggressiveness. Their most serious strategic error we have already encountered—the systematic occupation of the largest possible expanse of formerly Japanese-occupied territory. To supply garrisons as far from Central China as Changchun or Kirin, thousands of miles of railroad had to be held and defended. As the months went by, the Nationalist troops were spread thin everywhere—everywhere, that is, along the communications routes and in the cities. They lost the habit of fighting and the impulse to fight. At best they thought only of holding on and hoarding provisions and munitions against the day of the expected Communist assault.

If the best the Nationalist army could manage was this purely defensive stance, what was the worst? Desertion, and particularly as the war moved into its final stages, the defection of entire units. It was not unusual for a whole division to go over to the People's Liberation Army, bringing along its supplies and weapons. Some of the defecting officers were among the bravest and least cynical, the ones who could not passively accept what was happening.[37] Others were content to sell cases of ammunition to guerrilla units. As for the troops, they may not have known what they were fighting for, but they knew that their Communist counterparts were not mistreated. Nationalist army practices, by contrast, were well known to the peasantry, the only class in the Nationalist areas subjected to conscription. Some peasants cut off their fingers or had their wives blind them in one eye to escape military service; a larger number fled to Communist-controlled areas. Moreover, most of the Nationalist soldiers came from Central and South China and thus were fighting far from home amidst a "foreign" and hostile population, whereas the Communists, even the regulars, were for the most part Northerners and were defending what they thought of as their homeland, if not indeed their native province.

By the last phase of the war an unbroken series of defeats had further undermined morale. The prevailing feeling was that a Communist victory was unavoidable, that a city being defended

---

[37] Except at the very end, when a considerable number of generals rebelled or surrendered to save their skin.

would fall sooner or later, and that a government which treated its troops so harshly was not worth dying for. It was on these terms that the American consul at Tsingtao explained the unexpectedly rapid fall of Tsinan to the Communists; he added that with the majority of defending forces resolved not to fight, the minority who wanted to hold out did not know which units could be counted on for support.[38] Until mid-1947 the Communists routinely sent a percentage of their prisoners to reeducation camps. In mid-1947 they abandoned the practice because so many Kuomintang soldiers volunteered to serve in the Red Army after attending a single political education session the day they were captured.

The troops' pessimism, not to say despair or disgust, contrasts strangely with the Nationalist leadership's show of imperturbable optimism.[39] On April 9, 1948, the Generalissimo, who had boasted in 1946 that he would eliminate the Communists in three months, reasserted as Holy Writ that a Communist victory was absolutely impossible "even in sixty years"; in fact that victory was less than sixty weeks away. The Generalissimo's blindness is less surprising than it appears at first glance; it was shared by innumerable journalists, politicians, and experts who gave as much weight as he did to the Nationalists' material advantages. The Communist counteroffensive of the summer of 1947, which threatened all of Central China, surprised no one in Nanking and Shanghai; almost no one in those cities believed it was happening. Even eyewitness accounts were shrugged off. When the evidence could no longer be ignored, the Communist general Liu Po-ch'eng was jeered at for having imprudently ventured so far from his rural bases.

Not only did the Nationalists underestimate their opponent, but they were incapable of adapting to the kind of war he was fighting. The Kuomintang strategists, like their French counterparts, can only be described as one war behind. To confront the

[38] *China White Paper*, pp. 319–20.

[39] It would of course be naïve to take literally any public statement intended to revive a waning public confidence. But Chiang Kai-shek, for one, was given to expressing his real convictions in a terse and deliberately exaggerated manner.

Japanese and his domestic enemies, Chiang Kai-shek had slaved to build a modern army. In part he had succeeded; on the eve of the Second World War, his troops were not only the best in China, but a whole generation more modern than any other Chinese army. Most provincial armies still practiced a traditional and hence prestigious, if ineffective, form of warfare: marches and countermarches, elaborate feints and stratagems, few meaningful battles but many proclamations, and ultimately little bloodshed (except among the civilian population). To those acquainted with these vast, unwieldy premodern armies, the Generalissimo's German-equipped and German-organized elite corps appeared to represent the dynamism of the modern world. And yet the instrument to which Chiang gave such painstaking attention was outmoded as soon as it was ready. In part, of course, this was because his Wehrmacht advisers had based the Nationalist army's strategy on their own First World War experience with fixed-position and trench warfare. But Chiang's army was less outdated in relation to tanks, bombers, and Blitzkrieg tactics than in relation to the kind of revolutionary warfare practiced by the People's Liberation Army.

Almost every major area of Nationalist military weakness was an area of Red Army strength. The same generals—Chu Teh, P'eng Teh-huai, Lin Piao, Ch'en I, and Liu Po-ch'eng—remained in command not only throughout the civil war, but from one war to the other, from the Kiangsi period, the Long March, and the National Resistance War of 1937–45 to the final showdown with the Nationalists. The Communists' strategy was at once simple and clever, as bold as it was natural, and aimed, as we have noted, at destroying enemy forces rather than defending cities or expanses of territory.[40] The Red Army was distinguished by its great mobility, or rather its total movability (everything could be rapidly dismantled and moved, leaving the enemy with a denuded area and a meaningless victory), as contrasted with

---

[40] This was the third and most important of the ten military principles publicly spelled out by Mao in 1947 (*Selected Works*, IV, 161–62). The ten principles are themselves simply the best known of numerous formulations of Maoist strategy, most of which can be found, arranged chronologically, in *Selected Military Writings of Mao Tse-tung* (Peking, 1963).

the relative immobility of the Nationalist garrisons. Because of the Communists' overall numerical inferiority they eschewed full-scale or protracted battles, in which losses and gains would balance out, in favor of attacks in overwhelming force on small, isolated enemy units. At the same time, while applying the thousand and one tactics and tricks of the guerrilla trade, the Red Army prepared for conventional warfare—including great battles and sieges of cities—when the time was right. In this new kind of war, it exploited the enemy's weaknesses and internal conflicts, saving its hardest blows for the "central armies" (i.e. those directly under Chiang and the Nanking government) and temporarily sparing the troops under Fu Tso-i and the Kwangsi general Pai Ch'ung-hsi.[41]

Finally, the morale of the Red Army was as different from that of the forces of order as day from night. Conscription, a tragedy in the government-controlled areas, was an honor in the Liberated Areas.[42] The Communists' morale was reinforced by their tactical successes in the thousand skirmishes and small-scale battles of the nameless war that so disconcerted the Nationalists, but no one would attribute the Communists' superior morale solely to military factors. Indeed, I may have exaggerated the victors' military virtues and underrated the extent to which the gradual crumbling of the enemy army facilitated the Communists' rapid and impressive victory. As we shall see, the collapse of the Nationalist army was hastened by the revolutionaries' social policy.

The People's Victory

Guerrilla warfare is not a special form of the art of war, but the continuation of revolutionary struggle by military means. Mao said as much when he asserted that no matter how assid-

---

[41] Fu was the general who delivered Peking to the Communists in January 1949. He was several times a government minister of the People's Republic.

[42] On the one side, the draftees were poor wretches kidnapped by recruiting agents; on the other, they were representatives of the entire village, feted and escorted on their way to the accompaniment of gongs, cymbals, and flutes. A decision to enlist in the PLA, however, was in many cases the culmination of intense social pressure (see note 49).

uously the Nationalists and their American military advisers studied the Communists' combat techniques, they could never hope to apply them successfully, because they depended on popular support, which the Communists' enemies were inherently incapable of winning.[43] Popular support in China went to the Red Army. There is no need to repeat here our earlier discussion of the relations between the Eighth Route Army and the peasantry during the war of 1937–45. We must ask instead what new forms the old struggle took during the civil war.

Did the fact that a war of national resistance had given way to civil war mean that would-be mobilizers of China's population must now stress social rather than national issues? In practice, both kinds of issues were exploited simultaneously. The Japanese invader was more or less supplanted in the popular mind by the American imperialist, whose evil nature Communist soldiers could verify by inspecting the words "Made in U.S.A." on captured Nationalist weapons.[44] If this familiar phrase was missing, as it was on captured bullets of Chinese manufacture, one could still resort to writing the character *mei* (America) on these bullets before distributing them to the soldiers. Many a guerrilla or militiaman, persuaded by such evidence, must have muttered the vengeful couplet

> Chiang Kai-shek has a stubborn heart,
> America is his father and mother . . .[45]

Nationalism was thus far from a spent force. It made little difference if the terms of the appeal to nationalism were on the whole misleading; an argument is not necessarily the less persuasive for being specious.[46]

---

[43] The precise text is in *Selected Works*, IV, 163.

[44] Weapons captured in application of Mao's ninth principle: "Our army's main sources of manpower and matériel are at the front." *Ibid.*, p. 162.

[45] Jack Belden, *China Shakes the World* (New York: Monthly Review Press, 1970), pp. 262–63.

[46] The reader should avoid making hasty comparisons (with Vietnam in the late 1960's, for example); despite shipments of American arms to Chiang, imperialist intervention played only a subsidiary role in this final phase of the Chinese Revolution. Its various manifestations (among them the persistent if unsuccessful efforts of the United Nations Relief and Rehabilitation Administration to supply medicines to Com-

After the hiatus of the united front period, social issues returned to the fore. But now it was no longer a question of exploiting popular issues for propaganda purposes; the order of the day was social war. Social revolution—terrifying, vast, and primitive—exploded throughout rural China. It did not break out everywhere at the same time. Sometimes the first move was made by the large landowners: on returning to a village they had fled seven or eight years before, they had their henchmen murder the peasants who had seized the land in their absence. At other times the peasants took the lead in settling accounts by lynching a village headman who had collaborated with the Japanese or a peasant who had spied on fellow villagers during the war, and perhaps also, for good measure, whoever happened to be collecting the land tax at the time. Sometimes the leaders of the revolution were outdistanced by the masses; sometimes they left the masses far behind. In 1945, the peasants' insistence on immediate distribution of land dismayed the Communists, who were not eager, for example, to alienate an anti-Japanese landlord they had made local headman, or to lose the support of liberals who had not yet chosen sides. At other times, tenant farmers paralyzed by timidity and respect for the landed upper class had to be led by the hand to claim what Communist leaders pronounced to be their due.

Little by little, however, the peasants became bolder, the direction of the revolution became clearer, and the social conflict became more intense. As late as the spring of 1946, there were many areas in which the peasants' only concern was to avoid involvement in the warfare; when the Eighth Route Army left, the villagers stayed behind and welcomed the Nationalists. Soon, however, it became clear that the return of the Kuomintang meant the undoing of social and political advances the peasants had thought they could take for granted, the repeal of reforms relating to interest rates, land tax, and land rent that they had presumed to be part of any postwar government program, and

---

munist areas despite the obstruction of Nationalist officials) were superficial, desultory, ineffective, and ultimately irrelevant. The real conflict in this period was a family affair, an affair of Chinese against Chinese.

worst of all, a return to the traditional social and political order. In addition, there was the threat of a resurgent White Terror, whose new victims would be former militiamen, local peasant leaders, members of the village Women's Association, and the like.

The term Liberated Areas, by contrast, especially from 1947 on, when the CCP instituted an agrarian policy almost as radical as that of the Kiangsi period, became synonymous with the redistribution of land, the indictment of landlords, and the dictatorship of the Poor Peasants Association. During the winter of 1947-48, while many rich peasants were rallying to the side of the large landowners or trailing in the wake of government troops, some of the most wretched of the rural poor—tenant farmers, small proprietors, farm workers—flocked to the Communists. As the true direction of the revolution became clear, the struggle grew pitiless. When the villagers realized that their hour had come, that they had gone too far to turn back, years of accumulated hatred were unleashed. Landlords guilty of exploiting their tenants were paraded from village to village and slowly chopped to bits along the way by mobs armed with pitchforks, shears, pickaxes, and clubs, which then fought over the flesh of men alleged to have gorged themselves on the flesh of the people, and mutilated their remains. Some landowners hastened the destruction of their class by resorting to the kind of counterterrorism used by the Algerian *pieds-noirs* in the spring of 1962. Furious and terrified, feeling their world crumbling beneath them, they took to murdering their more recalcitrant tenant farmers, whose numbers increased daily. Some had whole families of tenants buried alive (*huo-mai*), instructing their men to club back down any head that rose above ground level.

"A poor man has no right to speak," says an old Shansi maxim. When the dikes of silence and submission were swept away by revolution, the village square was inundated by a torrent of speeches and complaints. An avid audience attended, or rather participated in, "Speak Bitterness Meetings," meetings called by the Red Army at which individual peasants took turns recounting their woes and relating them to the general plight of the peasantry. The assembled village was at once the priest hearing confession, the chorus repeating and amplifying the complaint, and the avenger whose resolve was stiffened by this strange and simple ritual.

This public airing of grievances, which aroused or heightened the villagers' class-consciousness, is a good example of the originality of the Red Army, an army different from any that had gone before. Equally original was its use of information, not only about the movement of enemy forces but also, and more often, about conditions in a newly occupied village. The Red Army had a way of knowing the amount of taxes people owed, the names of farmers who had been evicted from their land or victimized by arbitrary treatment, even the names of women who were being ill-treated by their mothers-in-law.[47] Such information was extremely useful in building a militia, a Women's Association, or a Poor Peasants Association, and in arriving at appropriate political and social policies.[48]

The Red Army and the many local guerrilla units were not so much an army as a people in arms—a people, that is, from the numberless villages of the Northeast and the North China Plain. The enlistment rate closely reflected the progress of agrarian revolution; Manchuria, where the redistribution of land was carried out earliest and most thoroughly, furnished the People's Liberation Army with 1.6 million recruits between June 1946 and June 1948.[49] Since the Red Army was an army of peasants, political education in the camps was handled much as it was

[47] The PLA was an enemy of mothers-in-law as well as landowners. A revolution in mores was an integral part of the great "overturning" (*fan-shen*), of which the social revolution was only the most important and dramatic component.

[48] This does not mean, of course, that the directives were necessarily well-conceived, still less that they were always understood and carried out correctly. Excessive egalitarianism, which led village cadres, for example, to confiscate even the land of upper-middle peasants, was common, and came close to turning a portion of the rural working masses from the path of revolution. For an excellent account of the problems caused by these "deviations," and of the new masters' abuses of power and the subsequent attempts at "rectification" (which resolved some difficulties but created others), see William Hinton's gripping book, *Fanshen: A Documentary of Revolution in a Chinese Village* (New York: Monthly Review Press, 1966).

[49] Enlistment was voluntary, but it was just about impossible for a poor peasant family that had been given a plot of land to resist the steady pressure on them to give a son to the "people's army" in return.

in the villages. Even undermanned front-line regiments had in their ranks instructors and students, actors and actresses, and specialists in agrarian reform and rice-growing. A unit of the Eighth Route Army, wrote Jack Belden, an American war correspondent, was also "a school, theater, labor cooperative, and political club."

In a word, to millions of peasants, soldiers and civilians alike, the Red Army brought the immediate promise of a new existence, of liberation from all the evils of the old society. The guarantee that the promise would be made good took the form of memories that the humblest peasant shared with the army, an army that was at once familiar and fabulous: their joint war against locusts, for example, or the production campaigns organized by the Eighth Route Army during the dark days of 1942–43. The hard times that the people and the Eighth Route Army had lived through together, the suffering they had shared as brothers, forged a bond far stronger than ideology. Here lies the explanation for the immediate response over hundreds of miles to the simple gesture of spreading the thumb and index finger to form the character *pa*, meaning eight.

The Mandate Lost?

While the Eighth Army was coming into its own as the successor of the 108 selfless robbers of the *Shui Hu Chuan*,[50] the regime it opposed was expending what credit it had left. It was as if the Mandate of Heaven had been withdrawn from the Kuomintang. The weaknesses and vices that the anti-Japanese war had brought to light were so aggravated by the civil war that one looked in vain for any sign that the regime could or should be preserved. Political, economic, and moral decay spread at an accelerating rate.

One of the first signs of the regime's disintegration was the falling away of outlying territories only tenuously subjected to the gravitational pull of China proper, notably Manchuria and Taiwan. Both newly freed from the grasp of a Japanese im-

---

[50] *Shi Hu Chuan* (Water Margin), one of the most famous novels in Chinese literature, has as its collective heroes 108 robbers dedicated to righting wrongs.

perialism whose benefits they were soon to miss, these two regions had become rich enough amidst the general poverty of China to arouse the greed of an army of carpetbaggers. What embezzlement, favoritism, and blackmail failed to gain was simply plundered outright by émigré administrators, who affected to scorn the Taiwanese as natives, the Manchurians as collaborators.[51] That the contempt was mutual is plain from cartoons of the time,[52] not to mention the various new meanings given by Taiwanese to the term "Chinese behavior," ranging from nepotism to parasitism and debauchery.

Although theft was apparently more systematic and arbitrary rule and oppression more flagrant in Taiwan, it was in Manchuria that the Nationalists' shortsighted policy of colonial exploitation provoked the simplest and most effective response. Whereas the angry populace of Manchuria had found a natural ally in the numerous Communist guerrillas of that region, the Taiwanese had to stage their own revolt, which they did once they had been driven to desperation by another plague imported from the mainland, a cholera epidemic. The bloody suppression of the Taiwanese revolt in March 1947 was much like the French massacre of the Malagasys a few weeks later. In the short run, the bloodbath was successful; two years later the defeated Nationalists made the "pacified" island their refuge. As time goes by, however, one wonders if this island country, whose only apparent raison d'être is to provide a contrast for descriptions of Communist China as heaven or hell, should not be seen as a laboratory demonstration of the reasons for the fall of the Kuomintang.

Be that as it may, events on Taiwan caused anxiety on the mainland, where support for the regime was becoming more and more tenuous. The intelligentsia led the public opposition to Chiang, just as it had ten years earlier. The issue was basically

---

[51] Most Taiwanese, however, were descendants of Chinese who had emigrated from the coastal provinces (notably Fukien, and to a lesser extent Shantung) several centuries earlier.

[52] In one, seen on a wall in Taipei, a dog (Japanese) is fleeing the island and a pig (Chinese) is taking his place. The legend reads, "A dog defends his masters; a pig does nothing but eat and sleep."

unchanged, despite appearances to the contrary (in 1935–36 the intellectuals had sought to force a war policy on Chiang, in 1945–46 a peace policy). Both sides in the dispute were nationalists; where they disagreed was on how to save the country. Among the intellectuals, anti-Japanese demonstrations gave way to anti-American ones. To prevent the breaking up of China by foreigners, the demonstrators demanded, just as they had ten years earlier, that Chiang come to terms with his unacknowledged compatriots, the Communists—those pestiferous rebels who were by now well on the way to becoming the *real* Chinese.[53] This time, however, the government succeeded in dismissing the demand as unacceptable, a triumph that backfired when the regime's critics promptly rallied to the enemy camp. Terror, which at first succeeded in driving protest underground, ended up driving students into the Communist areas.[54] The CCP was strengthened by this influx, which gave new backbone to the peasant masses of the Liberated Areas.

The play of political forces reflected the same trend. At first all that was left was the Kuomintang itself, then just a fraction of the Kuomintang. In the end the government lost control even of this fraction. Many intellectuals, most liberal politicians, and the small parties of the timid Third Force joined in forming the Democratic League; and in November 1946, in imitation of the Communist party, these middle-of-the-roaders began boycotting the National Assembly, which the government had convoked. Most of the league's members had already chosen sides by the time it was officially disbanded and outlawed on October 27, 1947. Three months later in Hong Kong a group of dignitaries and former military provincial governors set up still another new party, the Revolutionary Committee of the Kuomintang, which called for opposition to the regime.[55] Meanwhile,

[53] By extension the demonstrators were also demanding democracy, or at least the basic freedoms without which they could not even express their own kind of nationalism.

[54] Universities were sealed off by police cordons; students were abducted and sometimes killed; liberal journalists were kidnapped and packed off to camps; famous intellectuals (such as Wen I-to) were murdered.

[55] General Li Chi-shen, who played a leading role in suppressing the 1927 Canton Commune, was president of the Party. In October 1949 he became vice-president of

the official Kuomintang was theoretically passing from "democratic tutelage" to the constitutional regime planned by Sun Yat-sen as the last stage on the road to democracy. In April 1948 presidential elections were organized to choose between what political figures remained available.[56] Chiang Kai-shek was re-elected President of the Republic, but he could not keep the National Assembly's "liberal" elements from electing General Li Tsung-jen Vice-President. According to rumors then current in political circles, Chiang had threatened his minister of defense, General Pai Ch'ung-hsi, with drastic reprisals if he supported the candidacy of his friend General Li; but Pai supported Li anyway, and the Generalissimo was powerless to do more than relieve him of his portfolio. Thus did Chiang and the Kuomintang come to the end of the line for a dictatorial regime, the point where the dictator's personal orders cease to be obeyed.

The political deterioration of the regime was most apparent to the intellectuals, who were also the ones to feel the effects of inflation most directly. But it was because inflation affected other social classes as well that it pulled out the last props from under the regime.

After the steadily worsening inflation of the Chungking period, the restoration of peace brought with it a temporary respite and a fall in prices. Products from the coastal provinces suddenly started flowing into the interior; speculators put their stockpiled wares up for sale; victory stirred optimism and confidence. But this optimism soon proved disastrous, for it led to the overvaluation of the *fapi*, the legal currency of Nationalist

---

the Sino-Soviet Friendship League, by which marvelously symbolic act he joined another leader who had lived on into old age, Stalin, over the graves of the young Communist revolutionaries of 1927 whose slaughter they had brought about. General Li filled various honorific posts in the People's Republic for the ten years before his death in 1959. It is only fair to point out, however, that in 1933 Li had been a leader of the Fukien Rebellion, a movement that condemned the government's temporizing policy toward Japan. In both the Fukien Rebellion, which was one of many expressions of an old-line opposition to Nanking that was at least partially motivated by genuine patriotism, and the Revolutionary Committee of the Kuomintang, Li was joined by General Ts'ai T'ing-k'ai. In November 1947, after failing in an attempt to found what he called an "Anti–Chiang Kai-shek Army," Ts'ai went over to the Liberated Areas. Like Li he had an honorific career in the People's Republic, until his death in 1968.

[56] The electoral corps was limited to members of the Assembly, which met in Nanking in March 1948.

China,[57] particularly in relation to the banknotes issued by the Japanese in the eastern provinces. Refugees returning to Nanking and Shanghai after eight years of privation flooded the shops with their overvalued fapi, and the inflationary spiral began anew. The renewal and extension of hostilities between Nationalists and Communists further aggravated the situation (prices rose 67 times between January 1946 and August 1948), in large part because the government was banking on a quick victory and rarely ruled out a proposed military operation because of its cost.[58] To balance the budget thus unbalanced, it simply manufactured banknotes at an increasingly frenetic pace. Inflation meant larger profits, but no steps were taken to eliminate excess profits or transfer profiteers' gains to the state treasury. The anticipation of new price rises discouraged businessmen from saving; instead, they invested their liquid capital in inventory, in precious metals, and finally in foreign exchange. There were no effective exchange controls until the summer of 1948, and in the absence of such controls and of import quotas, capital fled abroad. In mid-August 1948, one dollar in United States currency was worth approximately twelve million fapi.[59]

On August 19, 1948, the government made a drastic and futile effort to break this vicious cycle. It replaced the fapi with the gold *yuan* note (three million fapi to one yuan), which it sought to support by imposing various long-overdue controls on currency, imports, and prices, and by hunting down speculators. In Shanghai General Chiang Ching-kuo (Chiang Kai-shek's oldest son and heir apparent) was given dictatorial powers over the economy, which he used unsparingly. He declared war on illegally amassed fortunes, and others as well.[60] Armed Shanghai police searched the back rooms of shops, forcing the immediate

57 That is to say, of all of China in 1935, when the fapi was created, of the Kuomintang-ruled areas of China during the war, and again of all China, except the Liberated Areas, from 1945 to 1948.

58 The minister of national defense disclosed that the two-month airlift to Changchun, which was blockaded by the PLA, had by itself exhausted the entire military budget for the second half of 1948.

59 In South China at this time a match cost 200 fapi, a grain of rice 15.

60 A great show was made of the execution of one trafficker in illegal commerce, as in Saigon in the spring of 1966.

sale of whatever goods they found there, and the exchange ot gold, silver, and foreign currency for yuan. The only flaw in this vigorous policy was that yuan were soon issued as freely as the fapi they replaced.[61] In November the central bank began selling gold again, and a month later the yuan collapsed.[62]

The inflation inevitably resulted in a large-scale redistribution of income.[63] But tragic as the social consequences of the inflation may have been to many, the political consequences were crucial. It was the urban middle class that suffered most from the rise in prices, not the masses. In fact galloping inflation enabled more than one peasant family to wipe out in record time the debts of a generation—until it became the general practice to peg land rent and debt payments to the price of grain. Agricultural laborers and urban workers generally suffered more than small peasant proprietors, but those who lost the most ground were people on salary, notably government officials and the military. In the last phase of the inflation, coolies paid by the day and rickshaw drivers paid by the journey fared better than university professors and skilled government officials, who were paid by the month and often late—or those officials, at least, who were unwilling or unable to supplement their salary by illicit means. Corruption accordingly proved irresistible to many government officials, whose real earnings were a tenth of what they had been before the war, and to many army officers as well, some of whom fed their families by selling rice intended for their troops. Such developments, along with the desertion of large numbers of officers and men for purely economic reasons, were an important factor in the regime's collapse.

[61] Not precisely the only flaw, since this belated effort could never have succeeded without a larger measure of public trust and cooperation than the regime could by this time command. We should not forget that this reform did not take effect until mid-September, the time of the great Nationalist defeat in Manchuria.

[62] During the month of November, the Shanghai price index rose from 100 to 1,153; for the eight months from August 1948 to April 1949, it rose from 100 to 13,574,000.

[63] On this important question, see Chou Shun-hsin, *The Chinese Inflation*, pp. 236–58; Chang Kia-Ngau, *The Inflationary Spiral: The Experience in China, 1939–1950* (Cambridge, Mass.: MIT Press, 1958), pp. 59–66; and Arthur N. Young, *China's Wartime Finance and Inflation, 1937–1945* (Cambridge, Mass.: Harvard University Press, 1965), pp. 317–27. Chang and Young, unlike Chou, do not discuss the postwar redistribution of income.

Until the summer of 1948 one class at least had been spared the ravages of inflation: those, of old wealth or new, who lived off profits as opposed to wages. Indeed speculators, and to a much lesser extent merchants and manufacturers, had been the beneficiaries of the inflation. But the terrorist tactics of the fall of 1948[64] and the collapse of the gold yuan, into which all their liquid assets had been forcibly converted, dealt this class a stunning blow. The disarray of capitalists before the specter of financial ruin sometimes took farcical forms. One large paper mill in Kwangtung bought 800 cases of banknotes and pulped them to make new paper. While we await the day promised by Lenin when mankind uses gold to build public urinals, let us hail this conversion of 2,000 gold yuan into raw material. Sometimes, of course, despair took more tragic forms, among them suicide. On the whole, however, China's embryonic capitalism, which had never been allowed to reach maturity, chose life, even at the price of the unlovely status of "national capitalism" in Communist China. When the One-eyed Dragon's troops were advancing through Central China, they came upon convoys of textiles sent by Shanghai mill owners, who suddenly made known their eager desire to clothe the Red Army. Out at sea, meanwhile, a long procession of vessels bore witness to the exodus of Chinese capitalism from its homeland: flotillas of junks carrying cargoes of gas and petroleum, spare parts, and chemical products north to Communist-controlled ports.

While the regime was destroying its own foundations, its subjects were overcome not by sadness at its destruction, but by disgust at its corruption, to which inflation had given new impetus, at its incompetence, and above all at its systematic lying.[65] The regime seemed to think it could conjure away the

---

[64] In Shanghai's overcrowded prisons, several well-known textile manufacturers and important bankers shared accommodations with a horde of petty thieves (guilty of such crimes as plundering rice stockpiles) and a smattering of profiteers.

[65] The arrest by the younger Chiang of the younger Tu, son of the king of the Shanghai underworld, is an example of a characteristic unthinking offhandedness, and even more, of the irony of fate. History had brought the two fathers together for the first time two decades earlier, and Chiang Kai-shek owed his rise to power in part

pit being dug beneath its feet—the pit it was digging itself—by denying its existence. We need only mention the official Central Press Agency's reports to the Chinese people on the Hwai-hai campaign[66] and the bald-faced search for scapegoats after each setback.[67] No one believed the authorities, no one knew what was happening.[68] Mistrust of the government and the weary cynicism its actions engendered were so extensive that the most malign motives were read into every move it made. The monetary reform, for example, was regarded as simple premeditated theft.[69]

The conviction that the Communists could hardly be worse gradually took hold even among the bourgeoisie. The Communists were awaited hopefully or fearfully, with resignation or relief, but they were awaited; at least the uncertainty would be ended, the war would be over, the absurd daily torment would stop. "This can't go on" and "Any change will be for the better" —these judgments were on everyone's lips, said A. Doak Barnett in a perceptive report written in December 1948 after an investi-

---

to the services of Tu Yüeh-sheng's gang. After the tragedy of 1927, the farce of 1948: two decades after Chiang's massacre of Shanghai's Communist party and trade union members, Tu's son was pointlessly jailed just as the sons of the disinherited activists of April 1927 were returning to claim their patrimony.

[66] "The Nationalists have brought off a great victory," the agency announced on November 16, 1948. "Liu Po-ch'eng barely managed to escape with his life. . . . The bandits are in retreat on all fronts." A few days later, when the Communist armies' vise was tightening around the government forces, the agency made another announcement: "Because of Nationalist pressure the Reds have been unable to flee the battlefield; like animals caught in a trap, they have been forced to fight for their lives." "A battle of annihilation," was the agency's description of the Hwai-hai campaign on December 1, an unwittingly accurate description which proves that willful blindness sometimes verges on prophecy.

[67] Chiang Kai-shek publicly labeled the disturbances in Taiwan "the work of Formosan Communists deliberately left behind by the Japanese to incite disorder." Generally speaking, anyone who displeased or criticized the government was considered a Communist.

[68] In Changsha, a provincial capital in South China, a group of professors and other educated persons pressed an American traveler recently returned from the North for news; Mukden had fallen nine days earlier, and no one in the group had heard anything about it.

[69] Government officials for their part attributed the failure of the monetary reform to President Truman, who had refused to recognize the new Chinese currency, and to Russian agents, who were alleged to be behind the widespread growth of blac' markets in China's cities.

gation of five provinces in South and Central China.[70] People were already imputing to the Communists the virtues it was hoped they would have. There was the expectation, then, of Armageddon, but also the hope of an absolutely new beginning. Nationalist China ended in chaos and apocalypse.

[70] *China on the Eve*, p. 97. The material in notes 68 and 69 is drawn from the same report (p. 98).

Conclusion

Graham Peck has observed that "in a society like China's, revolution can be a fundamental and entirely natural fact of life, as hard to slow up as a pregnancy." However overdrawn, the comparison is stimulating.[1] At a certain point in time, revolution and destruction were the natural thing—natural, that is, if we grant China and the Chinese the right to survive.

But if a pregnancy cannot be slowed up, a midwife can at least help bring it to term. Which leads us to ask, what role did the revolutionaries actually play in the birth of the Chinese Revolution?

Did they in fact play an active role? In one view, the Chinese Communists simply stepped into a vacuum: Nationalist China ended in such chaos, the argument runs, that any organized opposition could have seized power in 1949—and the Communist movement was the only organized opposition on the scene. In several places in this book I myself have tried to assess the extent of the Nationalists' contribution to the Communists' triumph. In the closing days of the conflict it seemed as if the Chinese ruling classes simply stepped aside.

As a description of the climax to a bitter and protracted struggle for enormous stakes, this may sound paradoxical; but in fact it is a sensible and superficially accurate description of the last phase of the Chinese Revolution. It is a description, however,

[1] Peck, *Two Kinds of Time*, p. 189. The defect in Peck's formulation is its suggestion that revolution in such a country is as inevitable as the workings of nature, rather than to some extent the work of people and ideas.

not an explanation. It ignores the real questions: why did such a power vacuum exist, and why was the CCP the only cohesive force available to fill it? What, in other words, were the underlying causes of the Chinese Revolution, and how did the Communists exploit them?

Still, the mere fact that we can ask whether the Communists played any positive role in the triumph of the revolution points up the contrast between the relative ease with which the Communists took power and the heavy burden they inherited. All the country's problems had come to a head at once, and the difficulties that made the old regime so vulnerable continued to plague the new one. The striking thing about the struggle for power after 1911 is the material weakness of the contending parties, a weakness that reflected the condition of China. Revolution succeeded in such "backward" countries as Tsarist Russia and Imperial and Nationalist China because it was there that the ruling classes were weakest and contradictions of all sorts most acute; but it is in just such countries that a successful revolution has the greatest difficulty fulfilling its promise. Indeed it is only after power is won that the real difficulties begin. Mao was not exaggerating when he observed in July 1949, "What we have accomplished, victory in a revolutionary war, is only the first step in a long march of 10,000 *li*."[2]

The Formula and Its Limits

In the complex tragedy described in these pages, which elements were crucial, and which of these, if any, was the catalyst? To put the question in its most succinct form, what was the Chinese "formula" for revolution?

Every line of scholarly inquiry tends to generate its futile arguments, its tertiary or even meaningless questions. This is particularly true of the study of a contemporary revolution, which cannot be purely scholarly. Here we must appraise not only the explanations offered by scholars (who of course have their own

[2] Similarly, if somewhat later in the day, Fidel Castro declared, "The most difficult thing is not the capture of Moncada, but to carry the Revolution through after victory." K. S. Karol, *Guerrillas in Action: The Course of the Cuban Revolution* (New York: Hill and Wang, 1970), p. 340.

passions and prejudices) but the assertions and recriminations of interested parties. The triumph of the Chinese revolutionaries is attributed by a Hu Shih to Soviet intrigues and Stalin's "grand strategy,"[3] by an Anthony Kubek to the State Department's incompetence and treachery.[4] Others, more plausibly but still superficially, explain the Nationalists' collapse by their moral failings (corruption and nepotism) or political errors (the stifling of dissent). Still others view the Communists' success as essentially a matter of military conquest or financial collapse (the results of prolonged inflation and its myriad consequences); though still nearer the truth, even these explanations at best capture only the proximate causes of the revolution.

Most interpretations of this sort—whether they denounce the Nationalist regime as corrupt and undemocratic, see it as the innocent victim of a Stalinist plot, or excuse it on the ground that Japanese aggression gave Chiang Kai-shek too little time to carry out his projected reforms—focus on the weaknesses or misfortunes of the Kuomintang. Understandably the diagnosis is made of the ailing patient, the defeated regime. But such a diagnosis is too limited. Although it is true that the Nationalist regime had become profoundly corrupt, reactionary, and above all hopelessly out of step with the times, the Kuomintang's shortcomings do not explain everything, not even the most important things. The roots of the trouble lay deeper.

What kind of crisis was it that had been keeping the country in unprecedented turmoil for more than a century? The Chinese Communists implicitly answered this question long ago, when they summed up their revolution as "anti-feudal and anti-imperialist." Ignoring for a moment the misuse of the term feudal, this seems to me a satisfactory definition of the essential conflict—a struggle against the foreign enemy and against the old China. In the revolutionaries' formula, the representatives of "feudalism" (i.e., the beneficiaries, agents, and supporters of the old regime) were the *ti-chu* or large landowners, the bureau-

[3] Hu Shih, "China in Stalin's Grand Strategy," *Foreign Affairs*, Vol. XXIX, No. 1 (October 1950); cited in Pichon P. Y. Loh, *The Kuomintang Debacle of 1949* (Boston: Heath, 1965), pp. 52ff.
[4] *How the Far East Was Lost* (Chicago: Regnery, 1963).

crats or government officials, and the warlords.[5] If we take the *ti-chu* as the symbolic representative of this unholy trinity, it follows that we must give top priority to two problems, the social (or peasant) problem and the national problem.

Among the many currents contributing to revolution I have accordingly stressed these two. Have we still to choose between them? On the one hand, poverty and injustice by themselves did not suffice to make the peasantry a revolutionary force; it took invasion and war to mobilize the masses and bring the party of revolution to power. On the other hand, I find a certain thinness in the thesis that the Chinese Revolution was entirely the work of imperialism and nationalism. Undoubtedly it was the national problem, not the social problem, that acted as a catalyst; the Chinese Communists' historic opportunity was created by an imperialist war. Whatever the limitations of Lenin's "fundamental law of revolution," it held true in China as it did in Russia. "Revolution is impossible," he wrote in *Left-Wing Communism, an Infantile Disorder*, "without a national crisis affecting both the exploited and the exploiters."[6] But as I have tried to show in my discussion of Chalmers Johnson's thesis, at the very heart of the decisive "national" stage of the revolution lay the social problem.

Even together, the related ills of imperialism and "feudalism" are not enough to make a revolution. The intolerable can go on being tolerated for decades before it gives rise to the organized deluge that is a revolution. No matter what the objective conditions, history records scarcely a case of spontaneous revolution, of revolution caused exclusively by mass revulsion at a situation that "can't go on." In China as elsewhere, the general staff of the revolution made its own effective contribution to disorder, channeling and heightening the natural effect of what Mao calls "antagonistic contradictions." To the revolution's "objective"

[5] By "anti-feudal revolution" the Communists meant simply agrarian revolution, a variant of bourgeois-democratic revolution. I am giving the notion of feudalism a broader meaning here, only to revert almost immediately to Communist usage.

[6] Earlier in the same passage he observed, "Only when the 'lower classes' do not want the old way, and when the 'upper classes' cannot carry on in the old way—only then can revolution triumph." *Left-Wing Communism, an Infantile Disorder* (New York: International Publishers, 1934), p. 65.

causes, then, let us add a subjective cause: the instruments of revolution. Agonizing as the national and social problems were, there would have been no revolution but for the existence of an organized revolutionary movement armed with a doctrine, long-term objectives, and a clear political strategy susceptible to common-sense adjustments in times of crisis.

Perhaps the most important thing about this revolutionary movement is not that it was armed with a doctrine and a strategy, but that it was armed. The army, the second instrument of the Chinese Revolution, ended up being almost more important than the first—the party that forged it. But must one distinguish between them? The Red Army (along with its extension, the peasant militias) was much more than the military instrument with which a revolutionary regime seized power; it provided the setting for the first broad contact of the party and the people and for their ultimate merger, which brought them both a tenfold increase in strength.

Apart from the party, the elements in the Chinese formula— if one may use such a term in connection with a phenomenon as complex as life itself—that I have chosen to emphasize are imperialism, the peasantry, and the army. Let us consider these elements separately in an effort to achieve as precise an understanding as possible of their role—an understanding, it may be hoped, that will make us properly hesitant to generalize about the "Chinese formula."

Imperialism, to take first things first. It was Marx who lauded as "the greatest and in truth the only *social* revolution Asia has ever known" the changes in rural Bengal brought about by the presence of the imperialist British bourgeoisie. In the present natural and probably therapeutic stage of unqualified denunciation of imperialist misdeeds, the Chinese might understandably be reluctant to concede the force of Marx's argument, banal though it may seem to us.[7] But we, who were so quick only

[7] Which does not mean, however, that the Chinese have abandoned the classic Marxist-Leninist view of imperialism as the "instrument of history." This is a contradiction that Chinese nationalism cannot overcome until the imperialist threat to China's existence recedes further into the past.

yesterday to accept the imperialist myths, why should we today surrender to the myth of imperialism? Wallowing in guilt today is the intellectual equivalent of basking in righteousness yesterday. Let us examine the new myths more closely than we did the old. Let us study the impact of economic imperialism on rural handicrafts, for example, before pronouncing it an unmitigated evil. Let us not focus so hard on the "responsibility" of the imperialists that we ignore that of the Chinese ruling class.[8] Let us acknowledge the relationship between the reactionary and chauvinistic nationalism of *China's Destiny* and the nationalism of the People's Republic; rather than deride Chiang and exalt those who are fulfilling some of his dearest wishes, let us recognize that the revolution inherited from Chiang the xenophobia that he himself had inherited from earlier regimes.[9] Let us give proper weight to internal factors, notably population growth, that were undermining traditional Chinese society *before* the imperialists came on the scene. And finally, let us not overlook the iniquitous reality underlying the "marvelous" stability of traditional Chinese society.

So far as the peasants are concerned, the fundamental distinction made earlier between the peasant problem and the peasant movement must be borne in mind. The peasant problem naturally was the first to attract our attention among the causes of

---

[8] The word responsibility reminds us how inappropriate praise and blame are in this context, for material and cultural conditions made China's rulers what they were. This does not mean we cannot evaluate their political and economic behavior. Politically, they were either unwilling or unable to build a modern China. Economically, just as "exploitation" may be of men or of nature, so speculation can have productive side effects. Although China's corrupt administrators and war profiteers, for example, were quick to use newly learned Western techniques to consolidate and extend their gains, most of them never outgrew the traditional view of profits as something to get their hands on rather than something to be created. The result was an even more unequal distribution of China's wealth, which they regarded as fixed and which their actions helped to keep that way.

[9] Among other things inherited by the Communists were the authoritarian and inhumane practices of the Empire and the Kuomintang, and the universities established in China by American Protestant missionaries, which are denounced by present-day Chinese historians as manifestations of cultural imperialism. To cite only such examples as these or to give them undue weight would be malicious misrepresentation. But that does not mean they should never be mentioned.

the Chinese Revolution; its importance can hardly be exaggerated. But what of the role and attitude of the peasantry as a class?

That the participation of the peasantry was essential to the revolution's success is a truism we need hardly dwell on at this point. The little we know, however, of the mentality of those who proved Marx wrong by practicing what he preached hardly justifies substituting an idealized peasantry for a defaulting urban proletariat as Marx's revolutionary vanguard. One can easily understand the reasons behind such a substitution, just as one can understand why Utopian Communists transfer their loyalties from a Soviet Union that has betrayed their expectations to a seemingly pure and uncompromising China. But there is little objective justification for such idealism. Indeed, the setting of the greatest peasant revolution of all time substantiates as much as it belies Marx's famous description of peasant conservatism:

We must not forget that these idyllic village communities [in India, though Marx was discussing the overall prospects for revolution in Asia], inoffensive though they may appear, had always been the solid foundation of Oriental despotism, that they restrained the human mind within the smallest possible compass, making it the unresisting tool of superstition, enslaving it beneath traditional rules, depriving it of all grandeur and historical energies. We must not forget the barbarian egotism which, concentrating on some miserable patch of land, had quietly witnessed the ruin of empires, the perpetration of unspeakable cruelties, the massacre of the population of large towns, with no other consideration bestowed upon them than on natural events, itself the helpless prey of any aggressor who deigned to notice it at all.[10]

What bothers us about this trenchant passage is not its severity or its failure to foresee the revolutionary capacities of the peasantry, but the absence—the deliberate withholding—of sympathy. True, Marx could never have been so wholeheartedly committed to revolution if he had been capable of sympathizing

[10] From "The British Rule in India," New York *Daily Tribune*, June 25, 1853, as reproduced in Shlomo Avineri, ed., *Karl Marx on Colonialism and Modernization* (New York: Doubleday, 1968), pp. 88–89.

with those he perceived as obstacles to the liberation of mankind. Such sympathy is the luxury of the noble-minded; it is incompatible with commitment. But it would have been just as unthinkable for the Chinese peasant to forswear the "barbarian egotism" Marx denounced. To a peasant, selflessness is an absurd concept, like heroism; only a well-fed intellectual can dream up such nonsense. For the Chinese peasant, survival was the ultimate heroism. Attaining sixty or seventy years of age was a sign of unusual merit; eighty-year-olds deserved veneration.

As the classic case of peasant revolution, the Chinese example prompts two observations. On the one hand, wartime upheavals and the efforts of the Chinese Communist Party resulted in a rapid and decisive transformation in the class-consciousness of the peasantry. On the other hand, the distance between Communist perceptions of the peasants' class interest and the peasants' own view was manifest in the kind of bargaining that went on in the early stages of the great social revolution of 1946–49. "The landlord would say: 'You protect me now [while the Red Army is here] and I'll protect you when the Kuomintang comes.' Or the tenant might say: 'You give me your land and I'll give it back when the Kuomintang comes.' "[11] Such petty deals were to social war what the warlords' palavers were to war itself.

Finally, the army. Not only during the civil war, but from the time of its creation in 1927, the Red Army was the mainstay of the CCP. It was no accident that the revolutions of 1911 and 1926–27, particularly the latter, involved military men and military concerns. But as the revolution came down to a matter of military conquest, the proportion of pure military men among its leadership diminished rather than increased. The Revolution of 1911 took place after a number of career officers in the New Army took up revolutionary politics. The combined general staff of the Northern Expedition in 1926–27 included both

[11] Belden, *China Shakes the World*, p. 191. There are many equally striking examples in William Hinton's *Fanshen*.

authentic revolutionaries and professional military men; but it also included leaders in whom the modern-minded nationalist revolutionary and the warrior were inextricably mixed. The victors of 1949 were for the most part professional revolutionaries turned soldier to serve the cause.

In this sense, great as the differences are between the Russian and Chinese revolutions (so great that their historians, including myself, sometimes end up using the same word to describe utterly different phenomena), the manner of the Chinese Communists' rise to power was no distortion of Leninism. It can even be argued that in circumstances particularly propitious for military action, they simply followed Leninism to its logical, i.e. military, extreme. The point is neatly made by Camus, who instinctively dubbed Lenin's indispensable corps of professional revolutionaries the revolution's "professional army."[12]

Marxism as a Tool

Like Lenin, then, the Chinese "Bolsheviks" were essentially preoccupied with strategy. This is the clue to the relationship between Marxist doctrine and the two "Marxist" revolutions: they did not corroborate Marxism, they simply used it. Indeed, it was the Chinese Revolution that made final the long-impending divorce between Marxism as a guide to action and Marxism as a sacred doctrine. Just as the social impact of Christianity was a practical argument for conversion, not ontological proof of its validity, so also what the "Marxist" revolutions prove is simply the effectiveness of Marxism, and particularly of Marxism-Leninism, in the real world.[13] The day has come when a new instrument, better adapted to new tasks, is needed, but the old

[12] In *The Rebel: An Essay on Man in Revolt* (New York: Knopf, 1956), p. 228.

[13] Marxism provides an allegedly coherent concept of the world that enables its followers to shrug off "unresolvable" enigmas; a systematic and universally applicable interpretation of historical facts of interest to men of action; rigorous Leninist principles of organization; and a will to revolution. The last—a determination to change the unacceptable—is perhaps the most important. Most converts to Marxism have embraced it not as a body of truth, but as a "protest in act." Prophets, whether true or false, arise when a situation has become intolerable, when apathy and resignation are no longer acceptable and indignant action is the only right response. In the first half of the twentieth century, there were others (missionaries in rural areas, for example)

one served long, and for a time well. "Marx's theory is all-powerful because it is true." This sophistry of Lenin's does not require refutation; we need simply set against it Mao's resolutely pragmatic advice to his party to "master Marxist theory and apply it, master it for the very purpose of applying it."[14]

---

who passionately wanted to change China, and their ideas were in some ways more perceptive than the Communists'. But unlike the Communists, the others were reluctant to soil their hands and fearful of the upheavals that any fundamental change would provoke.

[14] "Rectify the Party's Style in Work," *Selected Works*, IV, 31.

Suggested Readings

Suggested Readings

The original, French edition of this book included a bibliography deliberately if arbitrarily limited to fifty works in Western languages. In order to keep within the same limits for the present edition, I have added only about a dozen of the many books published since 1966 (the cutoff date for the French bibliography) and have eliminated the same number from my original list (notably French works intended for readers with no knowledge of English).

The motive behind these self-imposed restrictions was a desire to serve the general reader. The specialist or advanced student will learn nothing from this bibliography, which with but a few exceptions contains only well-known works, and which does not make even the classic concession to scholarly convention of systematically mentioning the most recent works on the assumption that they will lead the reader to the older and sometimes more important ones. If my selection can be justified at all, it is by the conviction that reading should be undertaken in an orderly fashion. I have not tried to list the fifty best books (such a list would include a number of works omitted here, including some to which I am greatly indebted), but the fifty with which it seems to me sensible to start. In important areas on which little work has been done, such as the social causes of the revolution (Chapter Four) and the Nationalist regime (Chapter Five), I have even included some less than wholly satisfactory works, and consequently have had to leave out some excellent original works that modify or supplement a standard interpretation in more thoroughly explored fields, such as intellectual history. Even on its own terms the selection is inevitably a subjective one, as it would be no matter which specialist on contemporary China had compiled it.

General Works, Revolution of 1911, Warlordism

The two basic texts are

John K. Fairbank. *The United States and China.* 3d ed. Cambridge, Mass.: Harvard University Press, 1971. Also paperback.
J. K. Fairbank, A. M. Craig, and E. O. Reischauer. *East Asia: The Modern Transformation.* Boston: Houghton Mifflin, 1965.

These may be supplemented by the following work, which is an objective presentation of a massive number of facts:

O. Edmund Clubb. *Twentieth Century China.* New York: Columbia University Press, 1964. Also paperback.

As a relief from textbooks the reader might welcome a novelistic narrative:

Han Suyin. *The Crippled Tree.* New York: Putnam, 1965.

This autobiographical volume is no model of objectivity (though it is much less tendentious than the author's later writings), but one can begin here and correct the details later.

Obviously I have had to omit works dealing with the late Ch'ing (Fairbank et al., *East Asia*, pp. 889–90, lists the major ones that appeared before 1965). Nonetheless, the following important multi-author work cannot go unmentioned:

Mary Clabaugh Wright, ed. *China in Revolution: The First Phase, 1900–1913.* New Haven, Conn.: Yale University Press, 1968.

The phenomenon of warlordism has been studied through the career of a leading warlord:

James E. Sheridan. *Chinese Warlord: The Career of Feng Yü-hsiang.* Stanford, Calif.: Stanford University Press, 1966. Also paperback.

In writing about another warlord, as well known as Feng but more closely tied to a particular province, Donald Gillin has produced the first of the many regional histories needed for a real understanding of modern China:

Donald G. Gillin. *Warlord: Yen Hsi-shan in Shansi Province, 1911–1949.* Princeton, N.J.: Princeton University Press, 1967.

Intellectual Origins, The May Fourth Movement

The standard work, on which much of Chapter Two is based, remains

Chow Tse-tsung. *The May Fourth Movement: Intellectual Revolution in Modern China.* Cambridge, Mass.: Harvard University Press, 1960. Paperback: Stanford.

Among the many works on intellectual history, the two most stimulating are certainly

Benjamin Schwartz. *In Search of Wealth and Power: Yen Fu and the West.* Cambridge, Mass.: Harvard University Press, 1964.
Joseph R. Levenson. *Confucian China and Its Modern Fate: The Problem of Intellectual Continuity.* Berkeley: University of California Press, 1958. Also paperback.

The most convenient introduction to the Chinese novel is

C. T. Hsia. *A History of Modern Chinese Fiction, 1917–1957.* New Haven, Conn.: Yale University Press, 1961.

Finally, two standard anthologies are extremely useful:

Ssu-yü Teng and John K. Fairbank, eds. *China's Response to the West: A Documentary Survey, 1839–1923.* Cambridge, Mass.: Harvard University Press, 1964. Paperback: Atheneum.
Wm. Theodore de Bary, ed. *Sources of Chinese Tradition,* Vol. II. New York: Columbia University Press, 1964. Also paperback.

The Chinese Communist Party and Marxism

Two general histories are

Robert C. North. *Moscow and Chinese Communists.* Rev. ed. Stanford, Calif.: Stanford University Press, 1963. Also paperback.
Jacques Guillermaz. *Histoire du parti communiste chinois (1921–1949).* Paris: Payot, 1968.

The first is no longer as useful as it once was; the second gives a more balanced presentation of the different stages in the CCP's development.

Two collections of documents, published some time ago, are still a useful complement to the aforementioned surveys:

Conrad Brandt, Benjamin Schwartz, and John K. Fairbank. *A Documentary*

> *History of Chinese Communism.* Cambridge, Mass.: Harvard University Press, 1952. Paperback: Atheneum.
>
> C. Martin Wilbur and Julie Lien-ying How. *Documents on Communism, Nationalism, and Soviet Advisers in China, 1918–1927.* New York: Columbia University Press, 1956.

The first, the standard work in the field, covers the entire history of the CCP, whereas the second is limited to what I have called the party's "orthodox stage." The introductions to the seven chapters of the Wilbur-How collection are enormously valuable, and together amount to a history of the events of the period.

On the early phase of CCP history and especially the revolution of 1926–27, it is worthwhile, and very exciting, to read

> Harold R. Isaacs. *The Tragedy of the Chinese Revolution.* 2d rev. ed. Stanford, Calif.: Stanford University Press, 1961. Also paperback.

On the period of the rural revolutionary base areas, one again turns first to a work written some time ago:

> Benjamin I. Schwartz. *Chinese Communism and the Rise of Mao.* Cambridge, Mass.: Harvard University Press, 1951. Paperback: Atheneum.

More recent studies have naturally filled in and modified specific points of the story told in this groundbreaking work, but one always returns to it for its insightful presentation of the broader picture.

The two most reliable biographies of Mao are

> Jerome Ch'en. *Mao and the Chinese Revolution.* London: Oxford University Press, 1967. Also paperback.
>
> Stuart R. Schram. *Mao Tse-tung.* New York: Simon and Schuster, 1967. Paperback: Penguin.

The second author has published an intellectual biography of Mao, together with a selection of Mao's writings:

> Stuart R. Schram. *The Political Thought of Mao Tse-tung.* Rev. ed. New York: Praeger, 1969. Also paperback.

It is advisable to read Schram's *Political Thought* before plunging into

> Mao Tse-tung. *Selected Works.* 4 vols. Peking: Foreign Languages Press, 1961–65.

Social Causes of the Chinese Revolution

Only a small fraction of the next book is concerned with contemporary China, but given the importance both of the subject and of the author's work (despite some valid criticism by demographers), the book must be included even in such an abbreviated reading list as this one:

Ho Ping-ti. *Studies on the Population of China, 1368–1953*. Cambridge, Mass.: Harvard University Press, 1959.

On rural society, the place to start is with a book written almost forty years ago:

R. H. Tawney, *Land and Labour in China*. London: Allen & Unwin, 1932. Paperback: Beacon.

In addition to this brief and penetrating synthesis, Tawney also wrote an introduction to a collection of monographs and articles translated from the Chinese:

Institute of Pacific Relations, comp. *Agrarian China*. Chicago: University of Chicago Press, 1939.

Almost all the contributors to this volume emphasize the social causes of peasant misery and the harmful consequences of imperialism. They also espouse, some more explicitly than others, what Ramon Myers (cited below) calls the "distribution theory." This is true of the two following authors as well, particularly the first:

Ch'en Han-seng. *Landlord and Peasant in China: A Study of the Agrarian Crisis in South China*. New York: International Publishers, 1936.
Fei Hsiao-tung. *Peasant Life in China*. London: Routledge, 1939.

Fei and Ch'en differ substantially on many points, a fact apparent to anyone who has read the other important works written in whole or in part by these two men (there is an incomplete list in Myers). But fundamentally they can both be classed as adherents of the "distribution theory," as contrasted with the two following authors, who consider the theory unduly systematic and ultimately mistaken:

John L. Buck. *Land Utilization in China*. 3 vols. Shanghai: Commercial Press, 1937.

This remains the indispensable reference work in its field, one of the chief sources of our knowledge of contemporary agriculture. The non-specialist need consult only the first volume.

Ramon H. Myers. *The Chinese Peasant Economy: Agricultural Development in Hopei and Shantung, 1890–1940*. Cambridge, Mass.: Harvard University Press. 1970.

On the basis of Japanese inquiries during the Second World War, Myers confirms Buck's findings. The debate is not over, but Myers's book raises a number of pertinent questions.

Although the following rather unsatisfactory book does not live up to the promise of its title, it contains invaluable materials for the study of the social causes of the Chinese Revolution:

Yung-teh Chow. *Social Mobility in China: Status Careers Among the Gentry in a Chinese Community.* New York: Atherton Press, 1966.

The condition of the working class and the beginnings of the labor movement are studied in

Jean Chesneaux. *The Chinese Labor Movement, 1919–1927.* Stanford, Calif.: Stanford University Press, 1968.

Reform or Revolution?

There is still no good biography of Chiang Kai-shek (just some works of hagiography) and no good general work on the "Nanking decade." For an exposition of Chiang's ideas together with critical commentary, see

Chiang Kai-shek. *China's Destiny and Chinese Economic Theory.* Translated and edited by Philip Jaffe. New York: Roy Publishers, 1947.

Political life and institutions under the Nationalist regime are described and analyzed by

Ch'ien Tuan-sheng. *The Government and Politics of China.* Cambridge, Mass.: Harvard University Press, 1950. Paperback: Stanford.

In studying rural and ideological reform, James Thomson illuminates two of the regime's basic problems—its relations with the two pillars of Chinese society, the peasants and the intellectuals:

James C. Thomson, Jr. *While China Faced West: American Reformers in Nationalist China, 1928–1937.* Cambridge, Mass.: Harvard University Press, 1969.

On economic development, one might start with

Alexander Eckstein. "The Economic Heritage." *In* Alexander Eckstein, Walter Galenson, and Ta-Chung Liu, eds. *Economic Trends in Communist China.* Chicago: Aldine, 1968.
Hou Chi-ming. *Foreign Investment and Economic Development in China, 1840–1937.* Cambridge, Mass.: Harvard University Press, 1965.
John K. Chang. *Industrial Development in Pre-Communist China.* Chicago: Aldine, 1969.

Second World War, Nationalism, and Revolution

We must begin with the classic account:

Edgar Snow. *Red Star Over China.* New York: Random House, 1938. Paperback: Grove Press, 1961. Rev. and enlarged ed.: Grove Press, 1968.

Published on the eve of the Sino-Japanese War, Snow's reportage sheds as much light on the Yenan period as it does on the preceding years. As early as 1937 Snow realized that his heroes would be making history. Along with *Red Star Over China* one might read two other great, if less famous, eyewitness accounts. Like Snow's book and other works recommended here (for example, Isaacs's *Tragedy of the Chinese Revolution*), they are worth reading not for their irreproachable objectivity, but for their acute grasp of what was important in the events they described:

Theodore H. White and Annalee Jacoby. *Thunder Out of China.* New York: William Sloane, 1946. Paperback: Apollo.
Graham Peck. *Two Kinds of Time.* Boston: Houghton Mifflin, 1950. Rev. ed. (comprising the first half of the original), 1967. Also paperback.

I am as indebted to Peck's underappreciated masterpiece as I am to the classic works of, say, John Fairbank and Chow Tse-tsung, and to

Chalmers A. Johnson. *Peasant Nationalism and Communist Power: The Emergence of Revolutionary China, 1937–1945.* Stanford, Calif.: Stanford University Press, 1962. Also paperback.

On inflation, the book to begin with is

Chou Shun-hsin. *The Chinese Inflation, 1937–1949.* New York: Columbia University Press, 1963.

Civil War and Agrarian Revolution

For reasons similar to those that led me to recommend the books by Peck and White and Jacoby, I will begin by recommending two great works of reportage:

Jack Belden. *China Shakes the World.* New York: Harper, 1949; reissue, Monthly Review Press, 1970.
William Hinton. *Fanshen: A Documentary of Revolution in a Chinese Village.* New York: Monthly Review Press, 1966. Paperback: Vintage.

Although I have drawn on the second much less than the first (Hinton's work had not yet been published at the time I was writing the

French edition of this book), it is actually the more important of the two. In contrast to Belden and Hinton, most writers on the period have emphasized political history and even diplomatic history, particularly Sino-American relations. One such work is

Herbert Feis. *The China Tangle: The American Effort in China from Pearl Harbor to the Marshall Mission*. Princeton, N.J.: Princeton University Press, 1953. Paperback: Atheneum.

As the title indicates, this work is more concerned with the second half of the war than with the postwar years. The next period, the civil war period properly speaking, has been described many times, beginning as early as August 1949 with

The China White Paper. Indexed edition. Stanford, Calif.: Stanford University Press, 1967. (Originally issued by the Department of State as *United States Relations with China, with Special Reference to the Period 1944–1949*.) Also paperback.

Despite the celebrated irony with which Mao greeted the publication of the *White Paper* (see p. 7 of the Introduction to the Stanford edition), it contains a number of remarkably lucid analyses, which are by no means limited to diplomatic history. It is an indispensable source for the postwar period, as is

A. Doak Barnett. *China on the Eve of Communist Takeover*. New York: Praeger, 1963. Also paperback.

Bibliographies, Reference Works, Journals

A very general bibliography, which will direct the reader to most of the others, is

Charles O. Hucker. *China: A Critical Bibliography*. Tucson: University of Arizona Press, 1962.

A second reference work, and an extremely valuable one, is

Howard L. Boorman and Richard C. Howard, eds. *Biographical Dictionary of Republican China*. 4 vols. New York: Columbia University Press, 1967–71.

Finally, the two most important journals are *The Journal of Asian Studies* (called *The Far Eastern Quarterly* from 1941 to 1956) and *The China Quarterly*.

Index